AN ORI

Arundhati Roy is the author of *The God of Small Things*,
which won the Booker Prize in 1997. Her first volume of
non-fiction writing, *The Algebra of Infinite Justice*, was
published by Penguin India in 2001. She lives in New Delhi.

By the author

The God of Small Things

The Algebra of Infinite Justice

In Which Annie Gives It Those Ones (Screenplay)

an ordinary person's guide to empire

arundhati roy

PENGUIN BOOKS

PENGUIN BOOKS
Published by the Penguin Group
Penguin Books India Pvt. Ltd, 11 Community Centre, Panchsheel Park,
New Delhi 110 017, India
Penguin Group (USA) Inc., 375 Hudson Street, New York, New York
10014, USA
Penguin Group (Canada), 90 Eglinton Avenue East, Suite 700, Toronto,
Ontario, M4P 2Y3, Canada (a division of Pearson Penguin Canada Inc.)
Penguin Books Ltd, 80 Strand, London WC2R 0RL, England
Penguin Ireland, 25 St Stephen's Green, Dublin 2, Ireland (a division of
Penguin Books Ltd)
Penguin Group (Australia), 250 Camberwell Road, Camberwell, Victoria
3124, Australia (a division of Pearson Australia Group Pty Ltd)
Penguin Group (NZ), cnr Airborne and Rosedale Roads, Albany, Auckland
1310, New Zealand (a division of Pearson New Zealand Ltd)
Penguin Group (South Africa) (Pty) Ltd, 24 Sturdee Avenue, Rosebank,
Johannesburg 2196, South Africa

Penguin Books Ltd, Registered Offices: 80 Strand, London WC2R 0RL,
England

First published in Viking by Penguin Books India 2005
Published in Penguin Books 2006
Copyright © Arundhati Roy 2005

Publisher's Note (pages 405-06) is an extension of the copyright page

ISBN 13: 9-780-14400-160-6 ISBN 10: 0-14400-160-8

For sale in the Indian Subcontinent only

Typeset in Bembo by Mantra Vitual Services
Printed at Thomson Press, New Delhi

To those who believe in resistance, who live between hope and impatience and have learned the perils of being reasonable.

To those who understand enough to be afraid and yet retain their fury.

contents

ahimsa

While the rest of us are mesmerized by talk of war and terrorism and wars against terror, in the state of Madhya Pradesh in central India, a little liferaft has set sail into the wind. On a pavement in Bhopal, in an area called Tin Shed, a small group of people has embarked on a journey of faith and hope. There's nothing new in what they're doing. What's new is the climate which they're doing it in.

Today is the twenty-ninth day of the indefinite hunger strike by four activists of the Narmada Bachao Andolan (NBA), the Save the Narmada Movement.[1] They have fasted two days longer than Gandhi did on any of his fasts during the freedom struggle. Their demands are more modest than his ever were. They are protesting against the Madhya Pradesh government's forcible eviction of more than 1000 Adivasi families to make way for the Maan Dam. All they're asking is that the government of Madhya Pradesh implement its own policy of providing land to those being displaced.

There's no controversy here. The dam has been built. The displaced people must be resettled before the reservoir fills up in the monsoon and submerges their villages. The four activists on fast are Vinod Patwa, who was one of the 114,000 people displaced in 1990 by the Bargi Dam (which now, twelve years later, irrigates less land than it submerged); Mangat Verma, who will be displaced by the Maheshwar Dam if it is ever completed; Chittaroopa Palit, who has worked with the NBA for almost fifteen years; and twenty-two-year-old Ram Kunwar, the youngest and frailest of the activists. Hers is the first village that will be submerged when the waters rise in the Maan reservoir. In the weeks since she began her fast, Ram Kunwar has lost twenty pounds—almost one-fourth of her original body weight.

Unlike the other large dams such as the Sardar Sarovar, Maheshwar, and Indira Sagar, where the resettlement of hundreds of thousands of displaced people is simply not possible (except on paper, in court documents), in the case of Maan the total number of displaced people is about 6000. People have even identified land that is available and could be bought and allotted to them by the government. And yet the government refuses.

Instead it's busy distributing paltry cash compensation, which is illegal and violates its own policy. It says quite openly that if it were to give in to the demands of the Maan 'oustees' (that is, if it implemented its own policy), it would set a precedent for the hundreds of thousands of people, most of them Dalits and Adivasis, who are slated to be submerged (without rehabilitation) by the twenty-nine other Big Dams planned in the Narmada valley. And the state government's commitment to these projects remains absolute, regardless of the social and environmental costs.

As Vinod, Mangat, Chittaroopa, and Ram Kunwar gradually weaken, as their systems close down and the risk of irreversible organ failure and sudden death sets in, no government official has bothered to even pay them a visit.

Let me tell you a secret—it's not all unwavering resolve and steely determination on the burning pavement under the pitiless sun at Tin Shed. The jokes about slimming and weight loss are becoming a little poignant now. There are tears of anger and frustration. There is trepidation and real fear. But underneath all that, there's pure grit.

What will happen to them? Will they just go down in the ledgers as 'the price of progress'? That phrase cleverly frames the whole argument as one between those who are pro-development versus those who are anti-development—and suggests the inevitability of the choice you have to make: pro-development, what else? It slyly suggests that movements like the NBA are antiquated and absurdly anti-electricity or anti-irrigation. This of course is nonsense.

The NBA believes that Big Dams are obsolete. It believes there are more democratic, more local, more economically viable and environmentally sustainable ways of generating electricity and managing water systems. It is demanding *more* modernity, not less. It is demanding *more* democracy, not less.

Any government's condemnation of terrorism is only credible if it shows itself to be responsive to persistent, reasonable, closely argued, non-violent dissent. And yet, what's happening is just the opposite.

In Madhya Pradesh, the police and administration

entered Adivasi villages with bulldozers. They sealed handpumps, demolished school buildings, and clear-felled trees in order to force people from their homes. They *sealed* handpumps. The world over, non-violent resistance movements are being crushed and broken. If we do not respect and honour them, by default we privilege those who turn to violent means.

When governments and the media lavish all their time, attention, funds, research, space, sophistication, and seriousness on war talk and terrorism, then the message that goes out is disturbing and dangerous: If you seek to air and redress a public grievance, violence is more effective than non-violence. Unfortunately, if peaceful change is not given a chance, then violent change becomes inevitable. That violence will be (and already is) random, ugly, and unpredictable. What's happening in Kashmir, the northeastern states of India, and Andhra Pradesh is all part of this process.

Right now the NBA is not just fighting Big Dams. It's fighting for the survival of India's greatest gift to the world: non-violent resistance. You could call it the Ahimsa Bachao Andolan or the Save Non-violence Movement.

Over the years our government has shown nothing but contempt for the people of the Narmada valley. Contempt for their argument. Contempt for their movement.

In the twenty-first century the connection between religious fundamentalism, nuclear nationalism, and the pauperization of whole populations because of corporate globalization is becoming impossible to ignore. While the Madhya Pradesh government has categorically said it has no land for the rehabilitation of displaced people, reports say that it is preparing the ground (pardon the pun) to make huge tracts of land available for corporate agriculture. This in turn will set off another cycle of displacement and impoverishment.

Can we prevail on Digvijay Singh—the secular, 'green' chief minister of Madhya Pradesh—to substitute some of his public relations with a *real* change in policy? If he did, he would go down in history as a man of vision and true political courage.

If the Congress Party wishes to be taken seriously as an alternative to the destructive right-wing religious fundamentalists who have brought us to the threshold of ruin, it will have to do more than condemn communalism and participate in empty nationalist rhetoric. It will have to do some real work and some real listening to the people it claims to represent.

As for the rest of us, concerned citizens, peace activists, and the like—it's not enough to sing songs about giving peace a chance. Doing everything we can to support movements like the NBA is *how* we give peace a chance. *This* is the real war against terror.

Go to Bhopal. Just ask for Tin Shed.[3]

June 2002

come september

Writers imagine that they cull stories from the world. I'm beginning to believe that vanity makes them think so. That it's actually the other way around. Stories cull writers from the world. Stories reveal themselves to us. The public narrative, the private narrative—they colonize us. They commission us. They insist on being told. Fiction and non-fiction are only different techniques of storytelling. For reasons I do not fully understand, fiction dances out of me. Non-fiction is wrenched out by the aching, broken world I wake up to every morning.

The theme of much of what I write, fiction as well as non-fiction, is the relationship between power and powerlessness and the endless, circular conflict they're engaged in. John Berger, that most wonderful writer, once wrote, 'Never again will a single story be told as though it's the only one.'[1]

There can never be a single story. There are only ways of seeing. So when I tell a story, I tell it not as an ideologue who wants to pit one absolutist ideology against another, but as a storyteller who wants to share her way of seeing. Though it might appear otherwise, my writing is not really about nations and histories, it's about power. About the paranoia and ruthlessness of power. About the physics of power. I believe that the accumulation of vast unfettered power by a state or a country, a corporation or an institution—or even an individual, a spouse, friend, or sibling—regardless of ideology, results in excesses such as the ones I will recount here.

Living as I do, as millions of us do, in the shadow of the nuclear holocaust that the governments of India and Pakistan keep promising their brainwashed citizenry, and in the global neighbourhood of the War against Terror (what President Bush rather biblically calls 'the task that does not end'), I find myself thinking a great deal about the relationship between citizens and the state.

In India, those of us who have expressed views on nuclear bombs, Big Dams, corporate globalization, and the rising threat of communal

Hindu fascism—views that are at variance with the Indian government's—are branded 'anti-national'. While this accusation does not fill me with indignation, it's not an accurate description of what I do or how I think. An anti-national is a person who is against her own nation and, by inference, is pro some other one. But it isn't necessary to be anti-national to be deeply suspicious of all nationalism, to be anti-national*ism*. Nationalism of one kind or another was the cause of most of the genocides of the twentieth century. Flags are bits of coloured cloth that governments use first to shrink-wrap people's minds and then as ceremonial shrouds to bury the dead. When independent, thinking people (and here I do not include the corporate media) begin to rally under flags, when writers, painters, musicians, film makers suspend their judgement and blindly yoke their art to the service of the nation, it's time for all of us to sit up and worry. In India we saw it happen soon after the nuclear tests in 1998 and during the Kargil War against Pakistan in 1999. In the US we saw it during the Gulf War and we see it now, during the War against Terror. That blizzard of made-in-China American flags.[2]

Recently, those who have criticized the actions of the US government (myself included) have been called 'anti-American.' Anti-Americanism is in the process of being consecrated into an ideology.

The term 'anti-American' is usually used by the American establishment to discredit and—not falsely, but shall we say inaccurately—define its critics. Once someone is branded anti-American, the chances are that he or she will be judged before they're heard and the argument will be lost in the welter of bruised national pride.

What does the term 'anti-American' *mean?* Does it mean you're anti-jazz? Or that you're opposed to free speech? That you don't delight in Toni Morrison or John Updike? That you have a quarrel with giant sequoias? Does it mean you don't admire the hundreds of thousands of American citizens who marched against nuclear weapons, or the thousands of war resisters who forced their government to withdraw from Vietnam? Does it mean that you hate all Americans?

This sly conflation of America's culture, music, literature, the breathtaking physical beauty of the land, the ordinary pleasures of ordinary people, with criticism of the US government's foreign policy (about which, thanks to America's 'free press', sadly, most Americans know very little) is a deliberate and extremely effective strategy. It's like a retreating army taking cover in a heavily populated city, hoping that the prospect of hitting civilian targets will deter enemy fire.

There are many Americans who would be mortified to be associated with their government's policies. The most scholarly, scathing, incisive, hilarious critiques of the hypocrisy and the contradictions in US government policy come from American citizens. When the rest of the world wants to know what the US government is up to, we turn to Noam Chomsky, Edward Said, Howard Zinn, Ed Herman, Amy Goodman, Michael Albert, Chalmers Johnson, William Blum, and Anthony Arnove to tell us what's really going on.

Similarly, in India, not hundreds, but millions of us would be ashamed and offended if we were in any way implicated with the present Indian government's fascist policies which, apart from the perpetration of state terrorism in the valley of Kashmir (in the name of fighting terrorism), have also turned a blind eye to the recent state-

supervised pogrom against Muslims in Gujarat.[3]
It would be absurd to think that those who
criticize the Indian government are 'anti-
Indian'—although the government itself never
hesitates to take that line. It is dangerous to cede
to the Indian government or the American
government or *anyone* for that matter, the right
to define what 'India' or 'America' is, or ought to
be.

To call someone anti-American, indeed, to *be* anti-
American, (or for that matter anti-Indian, or anti-
Timbuktuan) is not just racist, it's a failure of the
imagination. An inability to see the world in terms
other than those that the establishment has set
out for you: If you're not a Bushie, you're a
Taliban. If you don't love us, you hate us. If you're
not Good, you're Evil. If you're not with us,
you're with the terrorists.

Last year, like many others, I too made the
mistake of scoffing at this post–September 11
rhetoric, dismissing it as foolish and arrogant. I've
realized that it's not foolish at all. It's actually a
canny recruitment drive for a misconceived,
dangerous war. Every day I'm taken aback at how
many people believe that opposing the war in
Afghanistan amounts to supporting terrorism, or

voting for the Taliban. Now that the initial aim of the war—capturing Osama bin Laden (dead or alive)—seems to have run into bad weather, the goalposts have been moved.[4] It's being made out that the whole point of the war was to topple the Taliban regime and liberate Afghan women from their burqas. We're being asked to believe that the US marines are actually on a feminist mission. (If so, will their next stop be America's military ally Saudi Arabia?) Think of it this way: In India there are some pretty reprehensible social practices, against 'untouchables,' against Christians and Muslims, against women. Pakistan and Bangladesh have even worse ways of dealing with minority communities and women. Should they be bombed? Should Delhi, Islamabad, and Dhaka be destroyed? Is it possible to bomb bigotry out of India? Can we bomb our way to a feminist paradise? Is that how women won the vote in the United States? Or how slavery was abolished? Can we win redress for the genocide of the millions of Native Americans by bombing Santa Fe?

None of us need anniversaries to remind us of what we cannot forget. So it is no more than coincidence that I happen to be here, on American soil, in September—this month of dreadful anniversaries. Uppermost on everybody's mind of course, particularly here in America, is the horror of what has come to be known as '9/11'. Three thousand civilians lost their lives in that lethal terrorist strike.[5] The grief is still deep. The rage still sharp. The tears have not dried. And a strange, deadly war is raging around the world. Yet, each person who has lost a loved one surely knows secretly, deeply, that no war, no act of revenge, no daisy-cutters dropped on someone else's loved ones or someone else's children will blunt the edges of their pain or bring their own loved ones back. War cannot avenge those who have died. War is only a brutal desecration of their memory.

To fuel yet another war—this time against Iraq—by cynically manipulating people's grief, by packaging it for TV specials sponsored by corporations selling detergent or running shoes, is to cheapen and devalue grief, to drain it of meaning. What we are seeing now is a vulgar display of the *business* of grief, the commerce of grief, the pillaging of even the most private human feelings for political purpose. It is a terrible, violent thing for a state to do to its people.

It's not a clever enough subject to speak of from

a public platform, but what I would really love to talk to you about is loss. Loss and losing. Grief, failure, brokenness, numbness, uncertainty, fear, the death of feeling, the death of dreaming. The absolute, relentless, endless, habitual unfairness of the world. What does loss mean to individuals? What does it mean to whole cultures, whole peoples who have learned to live with it as a constant companion?

Since it is September 11 that we're talking about, perhaps it's in the fitness of things that we remember what that date means, not only to those who lost their loved ones in America last year, but to those in other parts of the world to whom that date has long held significance. This historical dredging is not offered as an accusation or a provocation. But just to share the grief of history. To thin the mist a little. To say to the citizens of America, in the gentlest, most human way: Welcome to the World.

Twenty-nine years ago, in Chile, on 11 September 1973, General Pinochet overthrew the democratically elected government of Salvador Allende in a CIA-backed coup. 'I don't see why we need to stand by and watch a country go Communist due to the irresponsibility of its own people,' said Henry Kissinger, Nobel Peace Laureate, then President Nixon's National Security Adviser.[6]

After the coup President Allende was found dead inside the presidential palace. Whether he was killed or whether he killed himself, we'll never know. In the regime of terror that ensued, thousands of people were killed. Many more simply 'disappeared'. Firing squads conducted public executions. Concentration camps and torture chambers were opened across the country. The dead were buried in mine shafts and unmarked graves. For more than sixteen years the people of Chile lived in dread of the midnight knock, of routine disappearances, of sudden arrest and torture.[7]

In 2000, following the 1998 arrest of General Pinochet in Britain, thousands of secret documents were declassified by the US government.[8] They contain unequivocal evidence of the CIA's involvement in the coup as well as the fact that the US government had detailed information about the situation in Chile during General Pinochet's reign. Yet Kissinger assured the general of his support: 'In the United States, as you know, we are sympathetic with what you are trying to do,' he said. 'We wish your government well.'[9]

Those of us who have only ever known life in a democracy, however flawed, would find it hard to imagine what living in a dictatorship and enduring the absolute loss of freedom really means. It isn't just those whom Pinochet murdered, but the lives he stole from the living that must be accounted for too.

Sadly, Chile was not the only country in South America to be singled out for the US government's attentions. Guatemala, Costa Rica, Ecuador, Brazil, Peru, the Dominican Republic, Bolivia, Nicaragua, Honduras, Panama, El Salvador, Peru, Mexico, and Colombia—they've all been the playground for covert—and overt—operations by the CIA.[10] Hundreds of thousands of Latin Americans have been killed, tortured, or have simply disappeared under the despotic regimes and tin-pot dictators, drug runners, and arms dealers that were propped up in their countries. (Many of them learned their craft in the infamous US government–funded School of Americas in Fort Benning, Georgia, which has produced 60,000 graduates.[11]) If this were not humiliation enough, the people of South America have had to bear the cross of being branded as a people who are incapable of democracy—as if coups and massacres are somehow encrypted in their genes.

This list does not of course include countries in Africa or Asia that suffered US military interventions—Somalia, Vietnam, Korea, Indonesia, Laos, and Cambodia.[12] For how many Septembers for decades together have millions of Asian people been bombed, burned, and slaughtered? How many Septembers have gone by since August 1945, when hundreds of thousands of ordinary Japanese people were obliterated by the nuclear strikes in Hiroshima and Nagasaki? For how many Septembers have the thousands who had the misfortune of surviving those strikes endured the living hell that was visited on them, their unborn children, their children's children, on the earth, the sky, the wind, the water, and all the creatures that swim and walk and crawl and fly? Not far from here, in Albuquerque, is the National Atomic Museum, where Fat Man and Little Boy (the affectionate nicknames for the bombs that were dropped on Hiroshima and Nagasaki) were available as souvenir earrings. Funky young people wore them. A massacre dangling in each ear. But I am straying from my theme. It's September that we're talking about, not August.

September 11 has a tragic resonance in the Middle East too. On 11 September 1922, ignoring Arab outrage, the British government proclaimed a mandate in Palestine, a follow-up to the 1917 Balfour Declaration, which imperial Britain issued, with its army massed outside the gates of the city of Gaza.[13] The Balfour Declaration promised European Zionists 'a national home for Jewish people'. (At the time, the empire on which the sun never set was free to snatch and bequeath national homes like the school bully distributes marbles.) Two years after the declaration, Lord Arthur James Balfour, the British foreign secretary said:

> [I]n Palestine we do not propose even to go through the form of consulting the wishes of the present inhabitants of the country . . . Zionism, be it right or wrong, good or bad, is rooted in age-long tradition, in present needs, in future hopes, of far profounder import than the desires and prejudices of the 700,000

Arabs who now inhabit that ancient land.[14]

How carelessly imperial power decreed whose needs were profound and whose were not. How carelessly it vivisected ancient civilizations. Palestine and Kashmir are imperial Britain's festering, blood-drenched gifts to the modern world. Both are fault lines in the raging international conflicts of today.

In 1937 Winston Churchill said of the Palestinians:

> I do not agree that the dog in a manger has the final right to the manger, even though he may have lain there for a very long time. I do not admit that right. I do not admit, for instance, that a great wrong has been done to the Red Indians of America, or the black people of Australia. I do not admit that a wrong has been done to these people by the fact that a stronger race, a higher grade race, a more worldly-wise race, to put it that way, has come in and taken their place.[15]

That set the trend for the Israeli state's attitude toward Palestinians. In 1969, Israeli prime minister Golda Meir said, 'Palestinians do not exist.' Her successor, prime minister Levi Eshkol said, 'Where are Palestinians? When I came here [to Palestine] there were 250,000 non-Jews, mainly Arabs and Bedouins. It was desert, more than underdeveloped. Nothing.' Prime minister Menachem Begin called Palestinians 'two-legged beasts'. Prime minister Yitzhak Shamir called them '"grasshoppers" who could be crushed'.[16] This is the language of heads of state, not the words of ordinary people. In 1947, the UN formally partitioned Palestine and allotted 55 per cent of Palestine's land to the Zionists. Within a year they had captured more than 76 per cent.[17] On 14 May 1948, the State of Israel was declared. Minutes after the declaration, the United States recognized Israel. The West Bank was annexed by Jordan. The Gaza Strip came under the military control of Egypt.[18] Formally, Palestine ceased to exist except in the minds and hearts of the hundreds of thousands of Palestinian people who became refugees.

In the summer of 1967, Israel occupied the West Bank and the Gaza Strip. Settlers were offered state subsidies and development aid to move into the occupied territories. Almost every day more Palestinian families are forced off their lands and driven into refugee camps. Palestinians who continue to live in Israel do not have the same rights as Israelis and live as second-class citizens in their former homeland.[19]

Over the decades there have been uprisings, wars, *intifadas*. Thousands have lost their lives.[20] Accords and treaties have been signed. Ceasefires declared and violated. But the bloodshed doesn't end. Palestine still remains illegally occupied. Its people live in inhuman conditions, in virtual Bantustans, where they are subjected to collective punishments and twenty-four-hour curfews, where they are humiliated and brutalized on a daily basis. They never know when their homes will be demolished, when their children will be shot, when their precious trees will be cut, when their roads will be closed, when they will be allowed to walk down to the market to buy food and medicine. And when they will not. They live with no semblance of dignity. With not much hope in sight. They have no control over their lands, their security, their movement, their communication, their water supply. So when accords are signed and words like 'autonomy' and even 'statehood' are bandied about, it's always worth asking: What sort of autonomy? What sort of state? What sort of rights will its citizens have?

Young Palestinians who cannot contain their anger turn themselves into human bombs and haunt Israel's streets and public places, blowing themselves up, killing ordinary people, injecting terror into daily life, and eventually hardening both societies' suspicion and mutual hatred of each other. Each bombing invites merciless reprisals and even more hardship on Palestinian people. But then suicide bombing is an act of individual despair, not a revolutionary tactic. Although Palestinian attacks strike terror into Israeli civilians, they provide the perfect cover for the Israeli government's daily incursions into Palestinian territory, the perfect excuse for old-fashioned, nineteenth-century colonialism, dressed up as a new-fashioned, twenty-first-century war.

Israel's staunchest political and military ally is and always has been the US government. The US government has blocked, along with Israel, almost every UN resolution that sought a peaceful, equitable solution to the conflict.[21] It has supported almost every war that Israel has fought. When Israel attacks Palestine, it is American missiles that smash through Palestinian homes. And every year Israel receives several billion dollars from the United States. In addition to more than $3 billion annually in official Foreign Military Financing, the US government supplies Israel with economic assistance, loans, technology transfers, and arms sales.[22]

What lessons should we draw from this tragic conflict? Is it really impossible for Jewish people who suffered so cruelly themselves—more cruelly perhaps than any other people in history— to understand the vulnerability and the yearning of those whom they have displaced? Does extreme suffering always kindle cruelty? What hope does this leave the human race with? What will happen to the Palestinian people in the event of a victory? When a nation without a state eventually proclaims a state, what kind of state will it be? What horrors will be perpetrated under its flag? Is it a separate state that we should be fighting for, or the rights to a life of liberty and dignity for everyone regardless of their ethnicity or religion?

Palestine was once a secular bulwark in the

Middle East. But now the weak, undemocratic, by all accounts corrupt, but avowedly non-sectarian Palestine Liberation Organization (PLO) is losing ground to Hamas, which espouses an overtly sectarian ideology and fights in the name of Islam. To quote from its manifesto: 'We will be its soldiers and the firewood of its fire, which will burn the enemies.'[23]

The world is called upon to condemn suicide bombers. But can we ignore the long road they have journeyed on before they arrived at this destination? From 11 September 1922 to 11 September 2002—eighty years is a long, long time to have been waging war. Is there some advice the world can give the people of Palestine? Some scrap of hope we can hold out? Should they just settle for the crumbs that are thrown their way and behave like the grasshoppers or two-legged beasts they've been described as? Should they just take Golda Meir's suggestion and make a real effort to not exist?

In another part of the Middle East, 11 September strikes a more recent chord. It was on 11 September 1990 that George W. Bush Sr, then President of the United States, made a speech to a joint session of Congress announcing his government's decision to go to war against Iraq.[24]

The US government says that Saddam Hussein is a war criminal, a cruel military despot who has committed genocide against his own people. That's a fairly accurate description of the man. In 1988 he razed hundreds of villages in northern Iraq and used chemical weapons and machine-guns to kill thousands of Kurdish people. Today we know that, that same year, the US government provided him with $500 million in subsidies to buy American agricultural products. The next year, after he had successfully completed his genocidal campaign, the US government doubled its subsidy to one billion dollars.[25] It also provided him with high quality germ seed for anthrax, as well as helicopters and dual-use material that could be used to manufacture chemical and biological weapons.[26]

So it turns out that while Saddam Hussein was carrying out his worst atrocities, the US and the UK governments were his close allies. Even today, the government of Turkey, which has one of the most appalling human rights records in the world, is one of US government's closest allies. The fact that the Turkish government has oppressed and murdered Kurdish people for years has not prevented the US government from plying Turkey with weapons and development aid.[27] Clearly it was not concern for the Kurdish people that provoked President Bush's speech to Congress.

What changed? In August 1990, Saddam Hussein invaded Kuwait. His sin was not so much that he had committed an act of war, but that he acted independently, without orders from his masters. This display of independence was enough to upset the power equation in the Gulf. So it was decided that Saddam Hussein be exterminated, like a pet that has outlived its owner's affection.

The first Allied attack on Iraq took place in January 1991. The world watched the prime-time war as it was played out on TV. (In India those days, you had to go to a five-star hotel lobby to watch CNN.) Tens of thousands of people were killed in a month of devastating bombing.[28] What many do not know is that the war did not end then. The initial fury simmered down into the longest sustained air attack on a country since the Vietnam War. Over the last decade, American and British forces have fired thousands of missiles and bombs on Iraq. Iraq's fields and farmlands have been shelled with 300 tonnes of depleted uranium.[29] In their bombing sorties, the Allies targeted and destroyed water treatment plants, aware of the fact that they could not be repaired without foreign assistance.[30] In southern Iraq, there has been a fourfold increase in cancer among children. In the decade of economic sanctions that followed the war, Iraqi civilians have been denied food, medicine, hospital equipment, ambulances, clean water—the basic essentials.[31]

About half a million Iraqi children have died as a result of the sanctions. Of them, Madeleine Albright, then US Ambassador to the United Nations, famously said, 'I think this is a very hard choice, but the price—we think the price is worth it.'[32] 'Moral equivalence' was the term that was used to denounce those who criticized the war on Afghanistan. Madeleine Albright cannot be accused of moral equivalence. What she said was just straightforward algebra.

A decade of bombing has not managed to dislodge Saddam Hussein, the 'Beast of Baghdad'. Now, almost twelve years on, President George Bush Jr has ratcheted up the rhetoric once again. He's proposing an all-out war whose goal is nothing short of a 'regime change'. The *New York Times* says that the Bush administration is 'following a meticulously planned strategy to persuade the public, the Congress and the allies of the need to confront the threat of Saddam Hussein'. Andrew Card, the White House Chief of Staff, described how the administration was stepping up its war plans for the fall: 'From a marketing point of view,' he said, 'you don't introduce new products in August.'[33] This time the catchphrase for Washington's 'new product' is not the plight of Kuwaiti people but the assertion that Iraq has weapons of mass destruction. Forget 'the feckless moralizing of "peace" lobbies,' wrote Richard Perle, chairman of the Defence Policy Board, the United States will 'act alone if necessary' and use a 'pre-emptive strike' if it determines it's in US interests.[34]

Weapons inspectors have conflicting reports about the status of Iraq's 'weapons of mass destruction', and many have said clearly that its arsenal has been dismantled and that it does not have the capacity to build one.[35] However, there is no confusion over the extent and range of America's arsenal of nuclear and chemical weapons. Would the US government welcome weapons inspectors? Would the UK? Or Israel?

What if Iraq *does* have a nuclear weapon, does that justify a pre-emptive US strike? The United States has the largest arsenal of nuclear weapons in the world. It's the only country in the world to have actually used them on civilian populations. If the United States is justified in launching a pre-emptive attack on Iraq, why then, any nuclear power is justified in carrying out a pre-emptive attack on any other. India could attack Pakistan, or the other way around. If the US government develops a distaste for the Indian prime minister, can it just 'take him out' with a pre-emptive strike?

Recently the United States played an important part in forcing India and Pakistan back from the brink of war. Is it so hard for it to take its own advice? Who is guilty of feckless moralizing? Of preaching peace while it wages war? The United States, which George Bush calls 'a peaceful nation', has been at war with one country or another every year for the last fifty years.[36]

Wars are never fought for altruistic reasons. They're usually fought for hegemony, for business. And then of course, there's the business of war. Protecting its control of the world's oil is fundamental to US foreign policy. The US government's recent military interventions in the Balkans and Central Asia have to do with oil. Hamid Karzai, the puppet President of Afghanistan installed by the United States, is said to be a former employee of Unocal, the American-based oil company.[37] The US government's paranoid patrolling of the Middle East is because it has two-thirds of the world's oil reserves.[38] Oil keeps America's engines purring sweetly. Oil keeps the free market rolling. Whoever controls the world's oil controls the world's markets.

And how do you control the oil? Nobody puts it more elegantly than the *New York Times*'s columnist Thomas Friedman. In an article called 'Craziness Pays', he says 'the US has to make clear to Iraq and US allies that . . . America will use force, without negotiation, hesitation, or UN approval'.[39] His advice was well taken. In the wars against Iraq and Afghanistan, as well as in the almost daily humiliation the US government heaps on the UN. In his book on globalization, *The Lexus and the Olive Tree,* Friedman says, 'The hidden hand of the market will never work without a hidden fist. McDonald's cannot flourish without McDonnell Douglas . . . And the hidden fist that keeps the world safe for Silicon Valley's technologies to flourish is called the US Army, Air Force, Navy, and Marine Corps.'[40]

Perhaps this was written in a moment of vulnerability, but it's certainly the most succinct, accurate description of the project of corporate globalization that I have read.

After September 11, 2001, and the War against Terror, the hidden hand and fist have had their cover blown, and we have a clear view now of America's other weapon—the free market—bearing down on the developing world, with a clenched unsmiling smile. The Task That Does Not End is America's perfect war, the perfect vehicle for the endless expansion of American imperialism. In Urdu, the word for profit is *fayda*. *Al Qaida* means The Word, The Word of God, The Law. So, in India some of us call the War against Terror, *Al Qaida* versus *Al Fayda*—The Word versus The Profit (no pun intended). For the moment it looks as though *Al Fayda* will carry the day. But then you never know . . .

In the last ten years of unbridled corporate globalization, the world's total income has increased by an average of 2.5 per cent a year.

And yet the numbers of the poor in the world has increased by one hundred million. Of the top 100 biggest economies, fifty-one are corporations, not countries. The top 1 per cent of the world has the same combined income as the bottom 57 per cent and the disparity is growing.[41] Now, under the spreading canopy of the War against Terror, this process is being hustled along. The men in suits are in an unseemly hurry. While bombs rain down on us, and cruise missiles skid across the skies, while nuclear weapons are stockpiled to make the world a safer place, contracts are being signed, patents are being registered, oil pipelines are being laid, natural resources are being plundered, water is being privatized, and democracies are being undermined.

In a country like India, the 'structural adjustment' end of the corporate globalization project is ripping through people's lives. 'Development' projects, massive privatization, and labour 'reforms' are pushing people off their lands and out of their jobs, resulting in a kind of barbaric dispossession that has few parallels in history. Across the world as the free market brazenly protects Western markets and forces developing countries to lift their trade barriers, the poor are getting poorer and the rich richer. Civil unrest has begun to erupt in the global village. In countries like Argentina, Brazil, Mexico, Bolivia, and India, the resistance movements against corporate globalization are growing. To contain them, governments are tightening their control. Protesters are being labelled 'terrorists' and then being dealt with as such. But civil unrest does not only mean marches and demonstrations and protests against globalization. Unfortunately, it also means a desperate downward spiral into crime and chaos and all kinds of despair and disillusionment which, as we know from history (and from what we see unspooling before our eyes), gradually becomes a fertile breeding ground for terrible things—cultural nationalism, religious bigotry, fascism, and of course terrorism.

All these march arm in arm with corporate globalization.

There is a notion gaining credence that the free market breaks down national barriers, and that corporate globalization's ultimate destination is a hippie paradise where the heart is the only passport and we all live together happily inside a John Lennon song (*Imagine there's no country…*).[42]

This is a canard.

What the free market undermines is not just national sovereignty, but *democracy*. As the disparity between the rich and poor grows, the hidden fist has its work cut out for it. Multinational corporations on the prowl for sweetheart deals that yield enormous profits cannot push through those deals and administer those projects in developing countries without the active connivance of state machinery—the police, the courts, sometimes even the army. Today corporate globalization needs an international confederation of loyal, corrupt, authoritarian governments in poorer countries to push through unpopular reforms and quell the mutinies. It needs a press that pretends to be free. It needs courts that pretend to dispense justice. It needs nuclear bombs, standing armies, sterner immigration laws, and watchful coastal patrols to make sure that it's only money, goods, patents, and services that are globalized—not the free movement of people, not a respect for human rights, not international treaties on racial discrimination, or chemical and nuclear weapons, or greenhouse gas emissions, climate change, or, god forbid, justice.[43] It's as though even a *gesture* toward international accountability would wreck the whole enterprise.

Close to one year after the War against Terror was officially flagged off in the ruins of Afghanistan, freedoms are being curtailed in country after country in the name of protecting freedom, civil liberties are being suspended in the name of protecting democracy.[44] All kinds of dissent are being defined as 'terrorism'. All kinds of laws are being passed to deal with it. Osama bin Laden seems to have vanished into thin air. Mullah Omar is said to have made his escape on a motorbike.[45] (They could have sent Tintin after him.) The Taliban may have disappeared but their spirit, and their system of summary justice, is surfacing in the unlikeliest of places. In India, in Pakistan, in Nigeria, in America, in all the Central Asian republics run by all manner of despots, and of course in Afghanistan under the US-backed Northern Alliance.[46]

Meanwhile down at the mall there's a mid-season sale. Everything's discounted—oceans, rivers, oil, gene pools, fig wasps, flowers, childhoods, aluminium factories, phone companies, wisdom, wilderness, civil rights, ecosystems, air—all 4.6 billion years of evolution. It's packed, sealed, tagged, valued, and available off the rack (no returns). As for justice—I'm told it's on offer too. You can get the best that money can buy.

Donald Rumsfeld said that his mission in the War against Terror was to persuade the world that Americans must be allowed to continue their way of life.[47] When the maddened king stamps his foot, slaves tremble in their quarters. So, standing here today, it's hard for me to say this, but The American Way of Life is simply not sustainable. Because it doesn't acknowledge that there is a world beyond America.

Fortunately power has a shelf life. When the time comes, maybe this mighty empire will, like others before it, overreach itself and implode from within. It looks as though structural cracks have already appeared. As the War against Terror casts its net wider and wider, America's corporate heart is haemorrhaging. For all the endless empty chatter about democracy, today the world is run by three of the most secretive institutions in the world: the International Monetary Fund, the World Bank, and the World Trade Organization, all three of which, in turn, are dominated by the United States. Their decisions are made in secret. The people who head them are appointed behind closed doors. Nobody really knows anything about them, their politics, their beliefs, their intentions. Nobody elected them. Nobody said they could make decisions on our behalf. A world run by a handful of greedy bankers and CEOs whom nobody elected can't possibly last.

Soviet-style communism failed, not because it was intrinsically evil, but because it was flawed. It allowed too few people to usurp too much power. Twenty-first century market capitalism, American-style, will fail for the same reasons. Both are edifices constructed by human intelligence, undone by human nature.

The time has come, the Walrus said. Perhaps things will get worse and then better. Perhaps there's a small god up in heaven readying herself for us. Another world is not only possible, she's on her way. Maybe many of us won't be here to greet her, but on a quiet day, if I listen very carefully, I can hear her breathing.

September 2002

the loneliness of noam chomsky

the loneliness of noam chomsky

*I will never apologize for the United States of America—
I don't care what the facts are.*

—President George Bush Sr[1]

Sitting in my home in New Delhi, watching an American TV news channel promote itself ('We report. You decide'), I imagine Noam Chomsky's amused, chipped-tooth smile.

Everybody knows that authoritarian regimes, regardless of their ideology, use the mass media for propaganda. But what about democratically elected regimes in the 'free world'?

Today, thanks to Noam Chomsky and his fellow media analysts, it is almost axiomatic for thousands, possibly millions, of us that public opinion in 'free market' democracies is manufactured just like any other mass market product—soap, switches, or sliced bread.[2] We know that while, legally and constitutionally, speech may be free, the space in which that freedom can be exercised has been snatched from us and auctioned to the highest bidders. Neoliberal capitalism isn't just about the accumulation of capital (for some). It's also about the accumulation of power (for some), the accumulation of freedom (for some). Conversely, for the rest of the world, the people who are excluded from neoliberalism's governing body, it's about the *erosion* of capital, the *erosion* of power, the *erosion* of freedom. In the 'free' market, free speech has become a commodity like everything else—justice, human rights, drinking water, clean air. It's available only to those who can afford it. And naturally, those who can afford it use free speech to manufacture the kind of product, confect the kind of public opinion, that best suits their purpose. (News they can use.) Exactly how they do this has been the subject of much of Noam Chomsky's political writing.

Prime Minister Silvio Berlusconi, for instance, has a controlling interest in major Italian newspapers, magazines, television channels, and publishing houses. '[T]he prime minister in effect controls about 90 per cent of Italian TV viewership,' reports the *Financial Times*.[3]

What price free speech? Free speech for *whom?* Admittedly, Berlusconi is an extreme example. In other democracies—the United States in particular—media barons, powerful corporate lobbies, and government officials are imbricated in a more elaborate but less obvious manner. (George Bush Jr's connections to the oil lobby, to the arms industry, and to Enron, and Enron's infiltration of US government institutions and the mass media—all this is public knowledge now.)

After the September 11, 2001 terrorist strikes in New York and Washington, the mainstream media's blatant performance as the US government's mouthpiece, its display of vengeful patriotism, its willingness to publish Pentagon press handouts as news, and its explicit censorship of dissenting opinion became the butt of some pretty black humour in the rest of the world.

Then the New York Stock Exchange crashed, bankrupt airline companies appealed to the government for financial bailouts, and there was talk of circumventing patent laws in order to manufacture generic drugs to fight the anthrax scare (*much* more important and urgent of course than the production of generics to fight AIDS in Africa).[4]

Suddenly, it began to seem as though the twin myths of Free Speech and the Free Market might come crashing down alongside the Twin Towers of the World Trade Centre.

But of course that never happened. The myths live on.

There is however, a brighter side to the amount of energy and money that the establishment pours into the business of 'managing' public opinion. It suggests a very real *fear* of public opinion. It suggests a persistent and valid worry that if people were to discover (and fully comprehend) the real nature of things that are done in their name, they might *act* upon that knowledge. Powerful people know that ordinary people are not always reflexively ruthless and selfish. (When ordinary people weigh costs and benefits, something like an uneasy conscience could easily tip the scales.) For this reason, they must be guarded against reality, reared in a controlled climate, in an altered reality, like broiler chickens or pigs in a pen.

Those of us who have managed to escape this fate and are scratching about in the backyard, no longer believe everything we read in the papers and watch on TV. We put our ears to the ground and look for other ways of making sense of the world. We search for the untold story, the mentioned-in-passing military coup, the unreported genocide, the civil war in an African country written up in a one-column-inch story next to a full-page advertisement for lace underwear.

We don't always remember, and many don't even know, that this way of thinking, this easy acuity, this instinctive mistrust of the mass media, would at best be a political hunch and at worst a loose accusation, if it were not for the relentless and unswerving media analysis of one of the world's greatest minds. And this is only *one* of the ways in which Noam Chomsky has radically altered our understanding of the society in which we live. Or should I say, our understanding of the elaborate rules of the lunatic asylum in which we are all voluntary inmates?

Speaking about the September 11 attacks in New York and Washington, President George W. Bush called the enemies of the United States 'enemies of freedom'. 'Americans are asking why do they hate us?' he said. 'They hate our freedoms, our freedom of religion, our freedom of speech, our freedom to vote and assemble and disagree with each other.'[5]

If people in the United States want a real answer to that question (as opposed to the ones in the *Idiot's Guide to Anti-Americanism,* that is: 'Because they're jealous of us', 'Because they hate freedom,' 'Because they're losers', 'Because we're good and they're evil'), I'd say, read Chomsky. Read Chomsky on US military interventions in Indochina, Latin America, Iraq, Bosnia, the former Yugoslavia, Afghanistan, and the Middle East. If ordinary people in the United States read Chomsky, perhaps their questions would be framed a little differently. Perhaps it would be: 'Why don't they hate us more than they do?' or 'Isn't it surprising that September 11 didn't happen earlier?'

Unfortunately, in these nationalistic times, words like 'us' and 'them' are used loosely. The line between citizens and the state is being deliberately and successfully blurred, not just by governments, but also by terrorists. The underlying logic of terrorist attacks, as well as 'retaliatory' wars against governments that 'support terrorism', is the same: both punish citizens for the actions of their governments.

If I were asked to choose *one* of Noam Chomsky's major contributions to the world, it would be the fact that he has unmasked the ugly, manipulative, ruthless universe that exists behind that beautiful, sunny word 'freedom'. He has done this rationally and empirically. The mass of evidence he has marshalled to construct his case is formidable. Terrifying, actually. The starting premise of Chomsky's method is not ideological, but it *is* intensely political. He embarks on his course of inquiry with an anarchist's instinctive mistrust of power. He takes us on a tour of the bog of the US establishment, and leads us through the dizzying maze of corridors that connects the government, big business, and the business of managing public opinion.

Chomsky shows us how phrases like 'free speech', the 'free market', and the 'free world' have little, if anything, to do with freedom. He shows us that, among the myriad freedoms claimed by the US government are the freedom to murder, annihilate, and dominate other people. The freedom to finance and sponsor despots and dictators across the world. The freedom to train, arm, and shelter terrorists. The freedom to topple democratically elected governments. The freedom to amass and use weapons of mass destruction—chemical, biological, and nuclear. The freedom to go to war against any country whose government it disagrees with. And, most terrible of all, the freedom to commit these crimes against humanity in the name of 'justice', in the name of 'righteousness', in the name of 'freedom'.

Attorney General John Ashcroft has declared that US freedoms are 'not the grant of any government or document, but . . . our endowment from God'.[6] So, basically, we're confronted with a country armed with a mandate from heaven. Perhaps this explains why the US government refuses to judge itself by the same moral standards by which it judges others. (Any attempt to do this is shouted down as 'moral equivalence'.) Its technique is to position itself as the well-intentioned giant whose good deeds are confounded in strange countries by their scheming natives, whose markets it's trying to free, whose societies it's trying to modernize, whose women it's trying to liberate, whose souls it's trying to save.

Perhaps this belief in its own divinity also explains why the US government has conferred upon itself the right and freedom to murder and exterminate people 'for their own good'.

When he announced the US air strikes against Afghanistan, President Bush Jr said, 'We're a peaceful nation.'[7] He went on to say, 'This is the calling of the United States of America, the most free nation in the world, a nation built on fundamental values, that rejects hate, rejects violence, rejects murderers, rejects evil. And we will not tire.'[8]

The US empire rests on a grisly foundation: the massacre of millions of indigenous people, the stealing of their lands, and following this, the kidnapping and enslavement of millions of black people from Africa to work on that land. Thousands died on the seas while they were being shipped like caged cattle between continents.[9]

'Stolen from Africa, brought to America'—Bob Marley's 'Buffalo Soldier' contains a whole universe of unspeakable sadness.[10] It tells of the loss of dignity, the loss of wilderness, the loss of freedom, the shattered pride of a people. Genocide and slavery provide the social and economic underpinning of the nation whose fundamental values reject hate, murderers, and evil.

Here is Chomsky, writing in the essay 'The Manufacture of Consent', on the founding of the United States of America:

> During the Thanksgiving holiday a few weeks ago, I took a walk with some friends and family in a national park. We came across a gravestone, which had on it the following inscription: 'Here lies an Indian woman, a Wampanoag, whose family and tribe gave of themselves and their land that this great nation might be born and grow.'
>
> Of course, it is not quite accurate to say that the indigenous population gave of themselves and their land for that noble purpose. Rather, they were slaughtered, decimated, and dispersed in the course of one of the greatest exercises in genocide in human history . . . which we celebrate each October when we honor Columbus—a notable mass murderer himself—on Columbus Day.
>
> Hundreds of American citizens, well-meaning and decent people, troop by

that gravestone regularly and read it, apparently without reaction; except, perhaps, a feeling of satisfaction that at last we are giving some due recognition to the sacrifices of the native peoples ... They might react differently if they were to visit Auschwitz or Dachau and find a gravestone reading: 'Here lies a woman, a Jew, whose family and people gave of themselves and their possessions that this great nation might grow and prosper.'[11]

How has the United States survived its terrible past and emerged smelling so sweet? Not by owning up to it, not by making reparations, not by apologizing to black Americans or native Americans, and certainly not by changing its ways (it *exports* its cruelties now). Like most other countries, the United States has rewritten its history. But what sets the United States apart from other countries, and puts it way ahead in the race, is that it has enlisted the services of the most powerful, most successful publicity firm in the world: Hollywood.

In the best-selling version of popular myth as

history, US 'goodness' peaked during World War II (*aka* America's War against Fascism). Lost in the din of trumpet sound and angel song is the fact that when fascism was in full stride in Europe, the US government actually looked away. When Hitler was carrying out his genocidal pogrom against Jews, US officials refused entry to Jewish refugees fleeing Germany. The United States entered the war only *after* the Japanese bombed Pearl Harbour. Drowned out by the noisy hosannas is its most barbaric act, in fact the single most savage act the world has ever witnessed: the dropping of the atomic bomb on civilian populations in Hiroshima and Nagasaki. The war was nearly over. The hundreds of thousands of Japanese people who were killed, the countless others who were crippled by cancers for generations to come, were not a threat to world peace. They were *civilians*. Just as the victims of the World Trade Centre and Pentagon bombings were civilians. Just as the hundreds of thousands of people who died in Iraq because of the US-led sanctions were civilians. The bombing of Hiroshima and Nagasaki was a cold, calculated experiment carried out to demonstrate America's power. At the time, President Truman described it as 'the greatest thing in history'.[12]

World War II, we're told, was a 'war for peace'. The atomic bomb was a 'weapon of peace'. We're invited to believe that nuclear deterrence prevented World War III. (That was before President George Bush Jr came up with the 'preemptive strike doctrine'.[13]) *Was* there an outbreak of peace after World War II? Certainly there was (relative) peace in Europe and America—but does that count as world peace? Not unless savage, proxy wars fought in lands where the coloured races live (chinks, niggers, dinks, wogs, gooks) don't count as wars at all.

Since World War II, the United States has been at war with or has attacked, among other countries, Korea, Guatemala, Cuba, Laos, Vietnam, Cambodia, Grenada, Libya, El Salvador, Nicaragua, Panama, Iraq, Somalia, Sudan, Yugoslavia, and Afghanistan. This list should also include the US government's covert operations in Africa, Asia, and Latin America, the coups it has engineered, and the dictators it has armed and supported. It should include Israel's US-backed war on Lebanon, in which thousands were killed. It should include the key role America has played in the conflict in the Middle East, in which thousands have died fighting Israel's illegal occupation of Palestinian territory. It should include America's role in the civil war in Afghanistan in the 1980s, in which more than one million people were killed.[14] It should include the embargos and sanctions that have led directly and indirectly to the death of hundreds of thousands of people, most visibly in Iraq.[15] Put it all together, and it sounds very much as though there has been a World War III, and that the US government was (or is) one of its chief protagonists.

Most of the essays in Chomsky's *For Reasons of State* are about US aggression in South Vietnam, North Vietnam, Laos, and Cambodia. It was a war that lasted more than twelve years. Fifty-eight thousand Americans and approximately two million Vietnamese, Cambodians, and Laotians lost their lives.[16] The United States deployed half a million ground troops, dropped more than six million tons of bombs.[17] And yet, though you wouldn't believe it if you watched most Hollywood movies, America lost the war.

The war began in South Vietnam and then spread to North Vietnam, Laos, and Cambodia. After putting in place a client regime in Saigon, the US government invited itself in to fight a communist insurgency—Vietcong guerillas who had infiltrated rural regions of South Vietnam where villagers were sheltering them. This was exactly the model that Russia replicated when, in 1979, it invited itself into Afghanistan. Nobody in the 'free world' is in any doubt about the fact that Russia invaded Afghanistan. After glasnost, even a Soviet foreign minister called the Soviet invasion of Afghanistan 'illegal and immoral'.[18] But there has been no such introspection in the United States. In 1984, in a stunning revelation, Chomsky wrote:

> For the past twenty-two years, I have been searching to find some reference in mainstream journalism or scholarship to an American invasion of South Vietnam in 1962 (or ever), or an American attack against South Vietnam, or American aggression in Indochina— without success. There is no such event in history. Rather, there is an American *defense* of South Vietnam against terrorists supported from the outside (namely from Vietnam).[19]

There is no such event in history!

In 1962, the US Air Force began to bomb rural South Vietnam, where 80 per cent of the population lived. The bombing lasted for more than a decade. Thousands of people were killed. The idea was to bomb on a scale colossal enough to induce panic migration from villages into cities, where people could be held in refugee camps. Samuel Huntington referred to this as a process of 'urbanization'.[20] (I learned about urbanization when I was in architecture school in India. Somehow I don't remember aerial bombing being part of the syllabus.) Huntington—famous today for his essay 'The Clash of Civilizations?'— was at the time Chairman of the Council on Vietnamese Studies of the Southeast Asia Development Advisory Group. Chomsky quotes him describing the Vietcong as 'a powerful force which cannot be dislodged from its constituency so long as the constituency continues to exist'.[21] Huntington went on to advise 'direct application of mechanical and conventional power'—in other words, to crush a people's war, eliminate the people.[22] (Or, perhaps, to update the thesis—in order to prevent a clash of civilizations, annihilate a civilization.)

Here's one observer from the time on the limitations of America's mechanical power: 'The problem is that American machines are not equal to the task of killing communist soldiers except as part of a scorched-earth policy that destroys everything else as well.'[23] That problem has been solved now. Not with less destructive bombs, but with more imaginative language. There's a more elegant way of saying 'that destroys everything else as well'. The phrase is 'collateral damage'.

And here's a firsthand account of what America's 'machines' (Huntington called them 'modernizing instruments' and staff officers in the Pentagon called them 'bomb-o-grams') can do.[24] This is T.D. Allman flying over the Plain of Jars in Laos:

> Even if the war in Laos ended tomorrow, the restoration of its ecological balance might take several years. The reconstruction of the Plain's totally destroyed towns and villages might take just as long. Even if this was done, the Plain might long prove perilous to

human habitation because of the hundreds of thousands of unexploded bombs, mines and booby traps.

A recent flight around the Plain of Jars revealed what less than three years of intensive American bombing can do to a rural area, even after its civilian population has been evacuated. In large areas, the primary tropical colour— bright green—has been replaced by an abstract pattern of black, and bright metallic colours. Much of the remaining foliage is stunted, dulled by defoliants.

Today, black is the dominant colour of the northern and eastern reaches of the Plain. Napalm is dropped regularly to burn off the grass and undergrowth that cover the Plains and fill its many narrow ravines. The fires seem to burn constantly, creating rectangles of black. During the flight, plumes of smoke could be seen rising from freshly bombed areas.

The main routes, coming into the Plain from communist-held territory, are bombed mercilessly, apparently on a non-stop basis. There, and along the rim of the Plain, the dominant colour is yellow. All vegetation has been destroyed. The craters are countless ... [T]he area has been bombed so repeatedly that the land resembles the pocked, churned desert in storm-hit areas of the North African desert.

Further to the southeast, Xieng Khouangville—once the most populous town in communist Laos—lies empty, destroyed. To the north of the Plain, the little resort of Khang Khay also has been destroyed.

Around the landing field at the base of King Kong, the main colours are yellow (from upturned soil) and black (from napalm), relieved by patches of bright red and blue: parachutes used to drop supplies.

[T]he last local inhabitants were being carted into air transports. Abandoned vegetable gardens that would never be harvested grew near abandoned houses with plates still on the tables and calendars on the walls.[25]

(Never counted in the 'costs' of war are the dead birds, the charred animals, the murdered fish, incinerated insects, poisoned water sources, destroyed vegetation. Rarely mentioned is the arrogance of the human race toward other living things with which it shares this planet. All these are forgotten in the fight for markets and ideologies. This arrogance will probably be the ultimate undoing of the human species.)

The centrepiece of *For Reasons of State* is an essay called 'The Mentality of the Backroom Boys', in which Chomsky offers an extraordinarily supple, exhaustive analysis of the Pentagon Papers, which he says 'provide documentary evidence of a conspiracy to use force in international affairs in violation of law'.[26] Here, too, Chomsky makes note of the fact that while the bombing of North Vietnam is discussed at some length in the Pentagon Papers, the invasion of South Vietnam barely merits a mention.[27]

The Pentagon Papers are mesmerizing, not as documentation of the history of the US war in Indochina, but as insight into the minds of the men who planned and executed it. It's fascinating to be privy to the ideas that were being tossed around, the suggestions that were made, the proposals that were put forward. In a section called 'The Asian Mind—the American Mind', Chomsky examines the discussion of the mentality of the enemy that 'stoically accept[s] the destruction of wealth and the loss of lives', whereas 'We want life, happiness, wealth, power', and, for us, 'death and suffering are irrational choices when alternatives exist'.[28] So, we learn that the Asian poor, presumably because they cannot comprehend the meaning of happiness, wealth, and power, invite America to carry this 'strategic logic to its conclusion, which is genocide'. But, then 'we' baulk because 'genocide is a terrible burden to bear'.[29] (Eventually, of course, 'we' went ahead and committed genocide any way, and then pretended that it never really happened.)

Of course, the Pentagon Papers contain some moderate proposals, as well.

> Strikes at population targets (per se) are likely not only to create a counterproductive wave of revulsion abroad and at home, but greatly to increase the risk of enlarging the war with China and the Soviet Union.

Destruction of locks and dams, however—if handled right—might . . . offer promise. It should be studied. Such destruction does not kill or drown people. By shallow-flooding the rice, it leads after time to widespread starvation (more than a million?) unless food is provided—which we could offer to do 'at the conference table'.[30]

Layer by layer, Chomsky strips down the process of decision-making by US government officials, to reveal at its core the pitiless heart of the American war machine, completely insulated from the realities of war, blinded by ideology, and willing to annihilate millions of human beings, civilians, soldiers, women, children, villages, whole cities, whole ecosystems—with scientifically honed methods of brutality. Here's an American pilot talking about the joys of napalm:

We sure are pleased with those backroom boys at Dow. The original product wasn't so hot—if the gooks were quick they could scrape it off. So the boys started adding polystyrene—now it sticks like shit to a blanket. But then if the gooks jumped under water it stopped burning, so they started adding Willie Peter [white phosphorous] so's to make it burn better. It'll even burn under water now. And just one drop is enough, it'll keep on burning right down to the bone so they die anyway from phosphorous poisoning.[31]

So the lucky gooks were annihilated for their own good. Better Dead than Red. Thanks to the seductive charms of Hollywood and the irresistible appeal of America's mass media, all these years later, the world views the war as an *American* story. Indochina provided the lush, tropical backdrop against which the United States played out its fantasies of violence, tested its latest technology, furthered its ideology, examined its conscience, agonised over its moral dilemmas, and dealt with its guilt (or pretended to). The Vietnamese, the Cambodians, and Laotians were only script props. Nameless, faceless, slit-eyed humanoids. They were just the people who died. Gooks.

The only real lesson the US government learned from its invasion of Indochina is how to go to war without committing American troops and risking American lives. So now we have wars waged with long-range cruise missiles, Black Hawks, 'bunker busters'. Wars in which the 'Allies' lose more journalists than soldiers.

As a child growing up in the state of Kerala, in South India—where the first democratically elected Communist government in the world came to power in 1959, the year I was born—I worried terribly about being a gook. Kerala was only a few thousand miles west of Vietnam. We had jungles and rivers and rice fields, and communists, too. I kept imagining my mother, my brother, and myself being blown out of the bushes by a grenade, or mowed down, like the gooks in the movies, by an American marine with muscled arms and chewing gum and a loud background score. In my dreams, I was the burning girl in the famous photograph taken on the road from Trang Bang.

As someone who grew up on the cusp of both

American and Soviet propaganda (which more or less neutralized each other), when I first read Noam Chomsky, it occurred to me that his marshalling of evidence, the volume of it, the relentlessness of it, was a little—how shall I put it?—insane. Even a quarter of the evidence he had compiled would have been enough to convince me. I used to wonder why he needed to do so much *work*. But now I understand that the magnitude and intensity of Chomsky's work is a barometer of the magnitude, scope, and relentlessness of the propaganda machine that he's up against. He's like the wood-borer who lives inside the third rack of my bookshelf. Day and night, I hear his jaws crunching through the wood, grinding it to a fine dust. It's as though he disagrees with the literature and wants to destroy the very structure on which it rests. I call him Chompsky.

Being an American working in America, writing to convince Americans of his point of view must really be like having to tunnel through hard wood. Chomsky is one of a small band of individuals fighting a whole industry. And that makes him not only brilliant, but heroic.

Some years ago, in a poignant interview with

James Peck, Chomsky spoke about his memory of the day Hiroshima was bombed. He was sixteen years old:

> I remember that I literally couldn't talk to anybody. There was nobody. I just walked off by myself. I was at a summer camp at the time, and I walked off into the woods and stayed alone for a couple of hours when I heard about it. I could never talk to anyone about it and never understood anyone's reaction. I felt completely isolated.[32]

That isolation produced one of the greatest, most radical public thinkers of our time. When the sun sets on the American empire, as it will, as it must, Noam Chomsky's work will survive. It will point a cool, incriminating finger at a merciless, Machiavellian empire as cruel, self-righteous, and hypocritical as the ones it has replaced. (The only difference is that it is armed with technology that can visit the kind of devastation on the world that history has never known and the human race cannot begin to imagine.)

As a could've been gook, and who knows, perhaps a potential gook, hardly a day goes by when I don't find myself thinking—for one reason or another—'Chomsky Zindabad'.

January 2003

confronting empire

I've been asked to speak about 'How to confront Empire?' It's a huge question, and I have no easy answers.

When we speak of confronting Empire, we need to identify what Empire means. Does it mean the US government (and its European satellites), the World Bank, the International Monetary Fund (IMF), the World Trade Organization (WTO), and multinational corporations? Or is it something more than that?

In many countries, Empire has sprouted other subsidiary heads, some dangerous by-products— nationalism, religious bigotry, fascism and, of course, terrorism. All these march arm in arm with the project of corporate globalization.

Let me illustrate what I mean. India—the world's biggest democracy—is currently at the forefront of the corporate globalization project. Its 'market' of one billion people is being pried open by the

WTO. Corporatization and privatization are being welcomed by the government and the Indian elite.

It is not a coincidence that the prime minister, the home minister, the disinvestment minister—the men who signed the deal with Enron in India, the men who are selling the country's infrastructure to corporate multinationals, the men who want to privatize water, electricity, oil, coal, steel, health, education, and telecommunication—are all members or admirers of the Rashtriya Swayamsevak Sangh (RSS), a right wing, ultra-nationalist Hindu guild which has openly admired Hitler and his methods.

The dismantling of democracy is proceeding with the speed and efficiency of a Structural Adjustment Programme. While the project of corporate globalization rips through people's lives in India, massive privatization and labour 'reforms' are pushing people off their land and out of their jobs. Hundreds of impoverished farmers are committing suicide by consuming pesticide.[1] Reports of starvation deaths are coming in from all over the country.[2]

While the elite journeys to its imaginary destination somewhere near the top of the world, the dispossessed are spiralling downwards into crime and chaos. This climate of frustration and national disillusionment is the perfect breeding ground, history tells us, for fascism.

The two arms of the Indian government have evolved the perfect pincer action. While one arm is busy selling India off in chunks, the other, to divert attention, is orchestrating a howling, baying chorus of Hindu nationalism and religious fascism. It is conducting nuclear tests, rewriting history books, burning churches, and demolishing mosques. Censorship, surveillance, the suspension of civil liberties and human rights, the questioning of who is an Indian citizen and who is not, particularly with regard to religious minorities, are all becoming common practice now.

Last March, in the state of Gujarat, 2000 Muslims were butchered in a state-sponsored pogrom. Muslim women were specially targeted. They were stripped, and gang-raped, before being burned alive. Arsonists burned and looted shops, homes, textiles mills, and mosques.[3] More than a 150,000 Muslims have been driven from their homes. The economic base of the Muslim community has been devastated.

While Gujarat burned, the Indian prime minister was on MTV promoting his new poems. In December 2002, the government that orchestrated the killing was voted back into office with a comfortable majority.[4] Nobody has been punished for the genocide. Narendra Modi, architect of the pogrom, proud member of the RSS, has embarked on his second term as the chief minister of Gujarat. If he were Saddam Hussein, of course each atrocity would have been on CNN. But since he's not—and since the Indian 'market' is open to global investors—the massacre is not even an embarrassing inconvenience. There are more than one hundred million Muslims in India. A time bomb is ticking in our ancient land.

All this is to say that it is a myth that the free market breaks down national barriers. The free market does not threaten national sovereignty, it undermines democracy. As the disparity between the rich and the poor grows, the fight to corner resources is intensifying. To push through their 'sweetheart deals', to corporatize the crops we grow, the water we drink, the air we breathe, and the dreams we dream, corporate globalization needs an international confederation of loyal, corrupt, authoritarian governments in poorer countries to push through unpopular reforms and quell the mutinies. Corporate globalization—or shall we call it by its name? Imperialism—needs a press that pretends to be free. It needs courts that pretend to dispense justice.

Meanwhile, the countries of the North harden their borders and stockpile weapons of mass destruction. After all they have to make sure that it's only money, goods, patents, and services that are globalized. Not the free movement of people. Not a respect for human rights. Not international treaties on racial discrimination or chemical and nuclear weapons or greenhouse gas emissions or climate change or—God forbid—justice.

So this—*all* this—is Empire. This loyal confederation, this obscene accumulation of power, this greatly increased distance between those who make the decisions and those who have to suffer them.

Our fight, our goal, our vision of another world must be to eliminate that distance. So how do we resist Empire?

The good news is that we're not doing too badly. There have been major victories. Here in Latin

America you have had so many—in Bolivia, you have Cochabamba.[5] In Peru, there was the uprising in Arequipa.[6] In Venezuela, President Hugo Chavez is holding on, despite the US government's best efforts.[7] And the world's gaze is on the people of Argentina, who are trying to refashion a country from the ashes of the havoc wrought by the IMF.[8]

In India the movement against corporate globalization is gathering momentum and is poised to become the only real political force to counter religious fascism.

As for corporate globalization's glittering ambassadors—Enron, Bechtel, WorldCom, Arthur Andersen— where were they last year, and where are they now?

And of course here in Brazil we must ask: who was the President last year, and who is it now?

Still, many of us have dark moments of hopelessness and despair. We know that under the spreading canopy of the War against Terrorism, the men in suits are hard at work.

While bombs rain down on us and cruise missiles skid across the skies, we know that contracts are being signed, patents are being registered, oil pipelines are being laid, natural resources are being plundered, water is being privatized, and George Bush is planning to go to war against Iraq.

If we look at this conflict as a straightforward eyeball to eyeball confrontation between Empire and those of us who are resisting it, it might seem that we are losing.

But there is another way of looking at it. We, all of us gathered here, have, each in our own way, laid siege to Empire.

We may not have stopped it in its tracks—yet— but we have stripped it down. We have made it drop its mask. We have forced it into the open. It now stands before us on the world's stage in all its brutish, iniquitous nakedness.

Empire may well go to war, but it's out in the open now—too ugly to behold its own reflection. Too ugly even to rally its own people. It won't be long before the majority of American people become our allies.

In Washington, a quarter of a million people marched against the war on Iraq.[9] Each month, the protest is gathering momentum. Before 11 September 2001 America had a secret history. Secret especially from its own people. But now

America's secrets are history, and its history is public knowledge. It's street talk.

Today, we know that every argument that is being used to escalate the war against Iraq is a lie. The most ludicrous of them being the US government's deep commitment to bring democracy to Iraq.

Killing people to save them from dictatorship or ideological corruption is, of course, an old US government sport. Here in Latin America, you know that better than most.

Nobody doubts that Saddam Hussein is a ruthless dictator, a murderer (whose worst excesses were supported by the governments of the United States and Great Britain). There's no doubt that Iraqis would be better off without him.

But, then, the whole world would be better off without a certain Mr Bush. In fact, he is far more dangerous than Saddam Hussein.

So, should we bomb Bush out of the White House?

It's more than clear that Bush is determined to go to war against Iraq, *regardless* of the facts—and regardless of international public opinion.

In its recruitment drive for allies, the United

States is prepared to *invent* facts. The charade with weapons inspectors is the US government's offensive, insulting concession to some twisted form of international etiquette. It's like leaving the 'doggie door' open for last minute 'allies' or maybe the United Nations to crawl through. But for all intents and purposes, the new war against Iraq has begun.

What can we do?

We can hone our memory, we can learn from our history. We can continue to build public opinion until it becomes a deafening roar.

We can turn the war on Iraq into a fishbowl of the US government's excesses.

We can expose George Bush and Tony Blair—and their allies—for the cowardly baby killers, water poisoners, and pusillanimous long-distance bombers that they are. We can reinvent civil disobedience in a million different ways. In other words, we can come up with a million ways of becoming a collective pain in the ass.

When George Bush says 'You're either with us, or you are with the terrorists,' we can say 'No thank you.' We can let him know that the people of the world do not need to choose between a

Malevolent Mickey Mouse and the Mad Mullahs.

Our strategy should be not only to confront Empire, but to lay siege to it. To deprive it of oxygen. To shame it. To mock it. With our art, our music, our literature, our stubbornness, our joy, our brilliance, our sheer relentlessness—and our ability to tell our own stories. Stories that are different from the ones we're being brainwashed to believe.

The corporate revolution will collapse if we refuse to buy what they are selling—their ideas, their version of history, their wars, their weapons, their notion of inevitability.

Remember this: We be many and they be few. They need us more than we need them.

February 2003

peace is war

The Collateral Damage of Breaking News

There's been a delicious debate in the Indian press of late. A prominent English daily announced that it would sell space on page three (its gossip section) to anyone who was willing to pay to be featured. The inference is that the rest of the news in the paper is in some way unsponsored, unsullied, 'pure news'. The announcement provoked a series of responses—most of them outraged—that the proud tradition of impartial journalism could sink to such depths. Personally, I was delighted. For a major, mainstream newspaper to introduce the *notion* of 'paid for' news is a giant step forward in the project of educating a largely credulous public about how the mass media operates. Once the idea of 'paid for' news has been mooted, once it's been ushered through the portals of popular imagination, it won't be hard for people to work out that if gossip columns in newspapers can be auctioned, why not the rest of the column space? After all, in this age of the 'market' when everything's up for sale what's special about news? Sponsored News— what a delectable idea! 'This report is brought to you by . . .' There could be a state-regulated sliding scale for rates (headlines, page one, page two, sports section, and so on). Or on second thought we could leave that to be regulated by the 'free market'—as it is now. Why change a winning formula?

The debate about whether mass-circulation newspapers and commercial TV channels are finely plotted ideological conspiracies or apolitical, benign anarchies that bumble along as best they can, is an old one and needs no elaboration. After the September 11 attack on the World Trade Centre, the US mainstream media's blatant performance as the government's mouthpiece was the butt of some pretty black humour in the rest of the world. It brought the myth of the Free Press in America crashing down. But before we gloat, the Indian mass media behaved no differently during the Pokhran nuclear tests and the Kargil War. There was no bumbling and very little was benign in the shameful coverage of the 13 December attack on the Indian Parliament and the trial of S.A.R. Geelani, who was sentenced to death after having been the subject of a media trial fuelled by a campaign of nationalist hysteria and outright lies. On a more everyday basis: Would anybody who depends on the Indian mass media for information know that 80,000 people have been killed in Kashmir since 1989, most of them Muslims, most of them by Indian security forces?[1] Most Indians would be outraged if it were suggested to them that the killings and 'disappearances' in the Kashmir valley put India on a par with any banana republic.

Modern democracies have been around for long enough for neoliberal capitalists to learn how to subvert them. They have mastered the technique of infiltrating the instruments of democracy—the 'independent' judiciary, the 'free' press, the parliament—and moulding them to their purpose. The project of corporate globalization has cracked the code. Free elections, a free press, and an independent judiciary mean little when the free market has reduced them to commodities available on sale to the highest bidder.

To control a democracy, it is becoming more and

more vital to control the media. The principal media outlets in America are owned by six major companies.[2] The six largest cable companies have 80 per cent of cable television subscribers.[3] Even Internet websites are being colonized by giant media corporations.[4]

It's a mistake to think that the corporate media supports the neoliberal project. It *is* the neoliberal project. It is the nexus, the confluence, the convergence, the union, the chosen medium of those who have power and money. As the project of corporate globalization increases the disparity between the rich and the poor, as the world grows more and more restive, corporations on the prowl for sweetheart deals need repressive governments to quell the mutinies in the servants' quarters. And governments, of course, need corporations. This mutual dependence spawns a sort of corporate nationalism if you can imagine such a thing. It has become the unwavering anthem of the mass media.

One of our main tasks is to expose the complex mess of cables that connect power to money to the supposedly 'neutral' free press.

In the last couple of years, New Media has embarked on just such an enterprise. It has descended on Old Media like an annoying swarm of bees buzzing around an old buffalo, going where it goes, stopping where it stops, commenting on and critiquing its every move. New Media has managed not to transform, but to create the possibility of transforming conventional mass media from the sophisticated propaganda machine into a vast CD-ROM. Picture it: The old buffalo is the text, the bees are the hyperlinks that deconstruct it. Click a bee, get the inside story.

Basically, for the lucky few who have access to the Internet, the mass media has been contextualized and shown up for what it really is—an elaborate boardroom bulletin that reports and analyses the concerns of powerful people. For the bees it's a phenomenal achievement. For the buffalo, obviously, it's not much fun.

For the bees it's a significant victory, but by no means a conquest. Because it's still the annoyed buffalo stumbling across the plains, lurching from crisis to crisis, from war to war, who sets the pace. It's still the buffalo that decides which particular crisis will be the main course on the menu and what's for dessert. So here we are today, the buffalo and the bees—on the verge of a war that could redraw the political map of the world and alter the course of history. As the United States gears up to attack Iraq, the US government's lies are being amplified, its reheated doctrine of pre-emptive strike talked up, its war machine deployed. There is still no sign of Iraq's so-called arsenal of weapons of mass destruction.

Even before the next phase of the war—the American occupation of Iraq—has begun (the war itself is thirteen years old), thanks to the busy bees the extent and scale, the speed and strength of the mobilization against the war have been unprecedented in history. On 15 February 2003, in an extraordinary display of public morality, millions of people took to the streets in hundreds of cities across the world, to protest against the invasion of Iraq.[5] If the US government and its allies choose to ignore this and continue with their plans to invade and occupy Iraq, it could bring about a serious predicament in the modern world's understanding of democracy.

But then again, maybe we'll get used to it. Governments have learned to wait out crises— because they know that crises by definition must be short-lived. They know that a crisis-driven media simply cannot afford to hang about in the same place for too long. It must be off for its next appointment with the next crisis. Like business houses need a cash turnover, the media needs a crisis turnover. Whole countries become old news. They cease to exist. And the darkness becomes deeper than it was before the light was shone on them. We saw that in Afghanistan when the Soviets withdrew. We are being given a repeat performance now.

And eventually, when the buffalo stumbles away, the bees go, too.

Crisis reportage in the twenty-first century has evolved into an independent discipline—almost a science. The money, the technology, and the orchestrated mass hysteria that goes into crisis reporting have a curious effect. It isolates the crisis, unmoors it from the particularities of the history, the geography, and the culture that produced it. Eventually it floats free like a hot-air balloon, carrying its cargo of international gadflies—specialists, analysts, foreign correspondents, and crisis photographers with their enormous telephoto lenses.

Somewhere mid-journey and without prior notice, the gadflies auto-eject and parachute down to the site of the next crisis, leaving the crestfallen, abandoned balloon drifting aimlessly in the sky, pathetically masquerading as a current event, hoping it will at least make history.

There are few things sadder than a consumed, spent crisis. (For field research, look up Kabul, Afghanistan, AD 2002 and Gujarat, India, AD 2003.)

Crisis reportage has left us with a double-edged legacy. While governments hone the art of crisis management (the art of waiting out a crisis), resistance movements are increasingly being ensnared in a sort of vortex of crisis production. They have to find ways of precipitating crises, of manufacturing them in easily consumable, spectator-friendly formats. We have entered the era of crisis as a consumer item, crisis as spectacle, as theatre. It's not new, but it's evolving, morphing, taking on new aspects. Flying planes into buildings is its most modern, most extreme form.

The disturbing thing nowadays is that Crisis as Spectacle has cut loose from its origins in genuine, long-term civil disobedience and is gradually becoming an instrument of resistance that is more symbolic than real. Also, it has begun to stray into other territory. Right now, it's blurring the lines that separate resistance movements from campaigns by political parties. I'm thinking here of L.K. Advani's Rath Yatra, which eventually led to the demolition of the Babri Masjid, and of the *kar seva* campaign for the construction of the Ram Temple at Ayodhya, which is brought to a boil by the Sangh Parivar each time elections come around.[6]

Both resistance movements and political election campaigns are in search of spectacle—though, of course, the kind of spectacle they choose differs vastly.

On the occasions when symbolic political theatre shades into action that actually breaks the law, then it is the response of the State which usually provides the clarity to differentiate between a campaign by a political party and an action by a people's resistance movement. For instance, the police never opened fire on the rampaging mob that demolished the Babri Masjid, or those who participated in the mass murder of Sikhs led by the Congress Party in Delhi in 1984, or the Shiv Sena led massacre of Muslims in Bombay in 1993, or the Bajrang Dal led genocide against Muslims in Gujarat in 2002.[7] Neither the police, nor the courts, nor the government has taken serious action against anybody who participated in this violence.

Yet recently the police have repeatedly opened fire on unarmed people, including women and children, who have protested against the violation of their rights to life and livelihood by the government's 'development projects'.[8]

In this era of crisis reportage, if you don't have a crisis to call your own, you're not in the news. And if you're not in the news, you don't exist. It's as though the virtual world constructed in the media has become more real than the real world.

Every self-respecting people's movement, every 'issue', needs to have its own hot-air balloon in the sky advertising its brand and purpose. For this reason, starvation deaths are more effective advertisements for drought and skewed food distribution, than cases of severe malnutrition— which don't quite make the cut. Standing in the rising water of a reservoir for days on end watching your home and belongings float away to protest against a Big Dam used to be an effective strategy, but isn't any more. People resisting dams are expected to either conjure new tricks or give up the struggle. In the despair created by the Indian Supreme Court's appalling judgement on the Sardar Sarovar Dam, senior activists of the Narmada Bachao Andolan (NBA) began once again to talk of *jal samarpan*—drowning themselves in the rising waters.[9] They were mocked for not really meaning what they said.

Crisis as a blood sport.

The Indian State and the mass media have shown themselves to be benignly tolerant of the phenomenon of Resistance as a Symbolic Spectacle. (It actually helps them to hold down the country's reputation as the world's biggest democracy). But whenever civil resistance has shown the slightest signs of metamorphosing from symbolic acts (dharnas, demonstrations, hunger strikes) into anything remotely resembling genuine civil disobedience— blockading villages, occupying forest land—the State has cracked down mercilessly.

In April 2001 the police opened fire on a peaceful meeting of the Adivasi Mukti Sangathan in Mehndi Kheda, Madhya Pradesh. On 2 February 2001, police fired on a peaceful protest of Munda Adivasis in Jharkhand, who were part of the protest against the Koel Karo hydroelectric, killing eight people and wounding twelve.[10] On 7 April 2000, the Gujarat police attacked a peaceful demonstration by the Kinara Bachao Sangharsh Samiti (the Save the Coast Action Committee) against the consortium of NATELCO and UNOCAL who were trying to do a survey for a proposed private port. Lieutenant Colonel Pratap Save, one of the main activists, was beaten to death.[11] In Orissa, three Adivasis were killed for protesting a bauxite mining project in December 2000.[12] In Chilika, police fired on fisherfolk demanding the restoration of their fishing rights. Four people were killed.[13]

The instances of repression go on and on— Jambudweep, Kashipur, Maikanj. The most recent, of course, is the incident in Muthanga in Wyanad, Kerala. In February 2003, 4000 displaced Adivasis, including women and children, occupied a small part of a wildlife sanctuary, demanding that they be given the land the government had promised them the previous year. The deadline had come and gone and there had been no sign that the government had any intention of keeping its word. As the tension built up over the days, the Kerala police surrounded the protestors and opened fire, killing one person and severely injuring several others.[14]

Interestingly, when it comes to the poor and, in particular, Dalit and Adivasi communities, they get killed for encroaching on forest land

(Muthanga), as well as when they're trying to protect forest land from dams, mining operations and steel plants (Koel Karo, Nagarnar).[15]

In almost every instance of police firing, the State's strategy is to say the firing was provoked by an act of violence. Those who have been fired upon are immediately called militant (PWG, MCC, ISI, LTTE) agents.[16] In Muthanga, the police and the government claimed that the Adivasis had staged an armed insurrection and attempted to set up a parallel government. The speaker of the Kerala assembly said that they should have been 'suppressed or shot'.[17]

At the scene of the firing, the police had put together an 'ammunition display'. It consisted of some stones, a couple of sickles and axes, bows and arrows, and a few kitchen knives. One of the major weapons used in the uprising was a polythene bag full of bees.[18] (Imagine the young man collecting bees in the forest to protect himself and his little family against the Kerala police. What a delightful parallel government his would be!)

According to the State, when victims refuse to be victims, they become terrorists and are dealt with as such. They're either killed or arrested under POTA (Prevention of Terrorism Act). In states like Orissa, Bihar, and Jharkhand, which are rich in mineral resources and, therefore, vulnerable to ruthless corporations on the hunt, hundreds of villagers, including minors, have been arrested under POTA and are being held in jail without trial. Some states have special police battalions for 'anti-development' activity. This is quite apart from the other use that POTA is being put to—terrorizing Muslims, particularly in states like Jammu and Kashmir and Gujarat. The space for genuine non-violent civil disobedience is atrophying. In the era of corporate globalization, poverty is a crime, and protesting against further impoverishment is terrorism. In the era of the War on Terror, poverty is being slyly conflated with terrorism.

Calling anyone who protests against the violation of their human and constitutional rights a terrorist can end up becoming a self-fulfilling accusation. When every avenue of non-violent dissent is closed down, should we really be surprised that the forests are filling up with extremists, insurgents, and militants? Large tracts of the country are already more or less beyond the control of the Indian state—Kashmir, the North East, parts of

Madhya Pradesh, Chhattisgarh, and Jharkhand.

It is utterly urgent for resistance movements and those of us who support them to reclaim the space for civil disobedience. To do this we will have to liberate ourselves from being manipulated, perverted, and headed off in the wrong direction by the desire to feed the media's endless appetite for theatre. Because that saps energy and imagination.

There are signs that the battle has been joined. At a massive rally on 27 February 2003, the Nimad Malwa Kisan Mazdoor Sangathan (Nimad Malwa Farmers and Workers' Organization), in its protest against the privatization of power, declared that farmers and agricultural workers would not pay their electricity bills.[19] The Madhya Pradesh government has not yet responded. It'll be interesting to see what happens.

We have to find a way of forcing the real issues back into the news. For example, the real issue in the Narmada valley is not whether people will drown themselves or not. The NBA's strategies, its successes and failures are an issue, but a separate issue from the problem of Big Dams.

The real issue is that the privatization of essential

infrastructure is essentially undemocratic. The real issue is the towering mass of incriminating evidence against Big Dams. The real issue is the fact that over the last fifty years in India alone Big Dams have displaced more than thirty-three million people.[20] The real issue is the fact that Big Dams are obsolete. They're ecologically destructive, economically unviable, and politically undemocratic. The real issue is the fact that the Supreme Court of India ordered the construction of the Sardar Sarovar Dam to proceed even though it is aware that it violates the fundamental rights to life and livelihood of the citizens of India.[21]

Unfortunately, the mass media, through a combination of ignorance and design, has framed the whole argument as one between those who are pro-development and those who are anti-development; it slyly suggests that the NBA is anti-electricity and anti-irrigation. And, of course, anti-Gujarat. This is complete nonsense. The NBA believes that Big Dams are obsolete. They're not just bad for displaced people, they're bad for Gujarat, too. They're too expensive, the water will not go where it's supposed to, and eventually the area that is supposed to 'benefit' will pay a heavy price.[22] Like what is happening in the command area of India's favourite dam—the Bhakra Nangal. The NBA believes that there are more local, more democratic, ecologically sustainable, economically viable ways of generating electricity and managing water systems. It is demanding more modernity, not less. More democracy, not less.

After the Supreme Court delivered what is generally considered to be a knockout blow to the most spectacular resistance movement in India, the vultures are back, circling over the kill. The World Bank's new *Water Resources Sector Strategy* clarifies that the World Bank will return to its policy of funding Big Dams.[23] Meanwhile the Indian government, directed by the venerable Supreme Court, has trundled out an ancient, hairbrained, Stalinist scheme of linking India's rivers. The order was given based on no real information or research—just on the whim of an ageing judge.[24] The river-linking project makes Big Dams look like enlightenment itself. It will become to the development debate what the Ram Mandir in Ayodhya is to the communal debate—a venal campaign gimmick that can be rolled out just before every election. It is destructive even if it is never realized. It will be used to block every other more local, more effective, more democratic irrigation project. It will be used to siphon off enormous sums of public money.

Linking India's rivers would lead to massive social upheavals and ecological devastation. Any modern ecologist who hears about this plan bursts out laughing. Yet leading papers and journals like *Indian Express* and *India Today* carry laudatory pieces full of absurd information.

Coming back to the tyranny of crisis reportage: One way to cut loose is to understand that for most people in the world, peace is war—a daily battle against hunger, thirst, and the violation of their dignity. Wars are often the end result of a flawed peace, a putative peace. And it is the flaws, the systemic flaws in what is normally *considered* to be 'peace', that we ought to be writing about. We have to—at least some of us have to—become peace correspondents instead of war correspondents. We have to lose our terror of the mundane. We have to use our skills and imagination and our art, to re-create the rhythms of the endless crisis of normality, and in doing so, expose the policies and processes that make ordinary things—food, water, shelter, and dignity—such a distant dream for ordinary people.

Most important of all, we have to turn our skills toward understanding and exposing the instruments of the State. In India, for instance, the institution that is least scrutinized and least accountable takes every major political, cultural, and executive decision today. The Indian Supreme Court is one of the most powerful courts in the world. It decides whether dams should be built or not, whether slums should be cleared, whether industry should be removed from urban areas. It takes decisions on issues like privatization and disinvestment. On the content of school textbooks. It micro-manages our lives. Its orders affect the lives of millions of people. Whether you agree with the Supreme Court's decisions—all of them, some of them, none of them—or not, as an institution the Supreme Court has to be accountable. In a democracy, you have checks and balances, not hierarchies. And yet, because of the Contempt of Court law, we cannot criticize the Supreme Court or call it to account. How can you have an undemocratic institution in a democratic society? It will automatically become a floor trap that accumulates authority, that confers supreme powers on itself. And that's exactly what has happened. We live in a judicial dictatorship. And we don't seem to have even begun to realize it.

The only way to make democracy real is to begin a process of constant questioning, permanent provocation, and continuous public conversation between citizens and the State. That conversation is quite different from the conversation between political parties. (Representing the views of rival political parties is what the mass media thinks of as 'balanced' reporting.) Patrolling the borders of our liberty is the only way we can guard against the snatching away of our freedoms. All over the world today, freedoms are being curbed in the name of protecting freedom. Once freedoms are surrendered by civil society, they cannot be retrieved without a struggle. It is so much easier to relinquish them than to recover them.

It is important to remember that our freedoms, such as they are, were never given to us by any government, they have been wrested by us. If we do not use them, if we do not test them from time to time, they atrophy. If we do not guard them constantly, they will be taken away from us. If we do not demand more and more, we will be left with less and less.

Understanding these things and then using them as tools to interrogate what we consider 'normalcy' is a way of subverting the tyranny of crisis reportage.

Finally, there's another worrying kind of collateral damage caused by crisis reportage. Crisis reportage flips history over, turns it belly-up. It tells stories back to front. So we begin with the news of a crisis, and end (if we're lucky) with an account of the events that led to it. For example, we enter the history of Afghanistan through the debris of the World Trade Centre in New York, the history of Iraq through Operation Desert Storm. We enter the story of the Adivasi struggle for justice in Kerala through the news of police firing on those who dared to 'encroach' on a wildlife sanctuary. So crisis reportage forces us to view a complex evolving historical process through the distorting prism of a single current event.

Crises polarize people. They hustle us into making uninformed choices: 'You're either with us or with the terrorists.' 'You're either pro "efficient" private sector or "inefficient" public sector.' 'If you're not pro-Bush, you're pro-Saddam Hussein.' 'If you're not good, you're evil.'

These are spurious choices. They're not the only ones available to us. But in a crisis, we become like goalkeepers in a penalty shootout of a soccer match. We imagine that we have to commit ourselves to one side or another. We have nothing to go on but instinct and social conditioning. And once we're committed, it's hard to realign oneself. In this process, those who ought to be natural allies become enemies.

For example, when the police fired on the Adivasis who 'encroached' on the wildlife sanctuary in Muthanga, Kerala, environmentalists did not come to their defence because they were outraged that the Adivasis had dared to encroach on a wildlife sanctuary. In actual fact the 'sanctuary' was a eucalyptus plantation.[25] Years ago, old-growth forest had been clear-felled by the government to plant eucalyptus for the Birla's Grasim Rayon Factory, set up in 1958. A huge mass of incriminating data accuses the factory of devastating the bamboo forests in the region, polluting the Chaliyar River, emitting toxins into the air, and causing a great deal of suffering to a great number of people.[26] In the name of employing 3000 people, it destroyed the livelihood of what has been estimated to be about 300,000 bamboo workers, sand miners, and fisherfolk. The state government did nothing to control the pollution or the destruction of forests and rivers. There were no police firing at the owners or managers of Grasim. But then, they had not committed the crime of being poor, being Adivasi, or being on the brink of starvation. When the natural resources (bamboo, eucalyptus pulp) ran out, the factory closed down. The workers were abandoned.[27]

Crisis reportage elides these facts and forces people to make uninformed choices.

The real crisis—the dispossession, the disempowerment, the daily violation of the democratic rights and the dignity of not thousands but millions of people, which has been set into motion not by accident but by deliberate design—does not fit into the predetermined format of crisis reporting.

Fifteen years ago, the corrupt, centralized Indian state was too grand, too top-heavy, and too far away for its poor to have access to it—to its institutions of education, of health, of water supply, and of electricity. Even its sewage system was inaccessible, too good for most. Today, the project of corporate globalization has increased the distance between those who take the decisions and those who must suffer them even more. For the poor, the uneducated, the displaced and dispossessed, that distance puts justice out of reach.

So the unrelenting daily grind of injustice goes unreported and the silent, unformatted battle spreads subcutaneously through our society, ushering us toward a future that doesn't bear thinking about.

But we continue sailing on our *Titanic* as it tilts slowly into the darkened sea. The deckhands panic. Those with cheaper tickets have begun to be washed away. But in the banquet halls, the music plays on. The only signs of trouble are slightly slanting waiters, the kebabs and canapés sliding to one side of their silver trays, the somewhat exaggerated sloshing of the wine in the crystal wineglasses. The rich are comforted by the knowledge that the lifeboats on the deck are reserved for club-class passengers. The tragedy is that they are probably right.

March 2003

an ordinary person's
guide to empire

Mesopotamia. Babylon. The Tigris and Euphrates. How many children, in how many classrooms, over how many centuries, have hang-glided through the past, transported on the wings of these words?

And now the bombs are falling, incinerating and humiliating that ancient civilization.

On the steel torsos of their missiles, adolescent American soldiers scrawl colourful messages in childish handwriting: *For Saddam, from the Fat Boy Posse.*[1] A building goes down. A marketplace. A home. A girl who loves a boy. A child who only ever wanted to play with his older brother's marbles.

On 21 March, the day after American and British troops began their illegal invasion and occupation of Iraq, an 'embedded' CNN correspondent interviewed an American soldier. 'I wanna get in there and get my nose dirty,' Private AJ said. 'I wanna take revenge for 9/11.'[2]

To be fair to the correspondent, even though he *was* 'embedded' he *did* sort of weakly suggest that so far there was no real evidence that linked the Iraqi government to the 11 September attacks. Private AJ stuck his teenage tongue out all the way down to the end of his chin. 'Yeah, well that stuff's way over my head,' he said.[3]

According to a New York Times/CBS News survey, 42 per cent of the American public believes that Saddam Hussein is directly responsible for the 11 September attacks on the World Trade Centre and the Pentagon.[4] And an ABC news poll says that 55 per cent of Americans believe that Saddam Hussein directly supports the Al-Qaeda.[5] What percentage of America's armed forces believe these fabrications is anybody's guess.

It is unlikely that British and American troops fighting in Iraq are aware that their governments supported Saddam Hussein both politically and financially through his worst excesses.

But why should poor AJ and his fellow soldiers be burdened with these details? It doesn't matter any more, does it? Hundreds of thousands of men, tanks, ships, choppers, bombs, ammunition, gas masks, high protein food, whole aircrafts ferrying toilet paper, insect repellent, vitamins and bottled mineral water, are on the move. The phenomenal logistics of Operation Iraqi Freedom make it a universe unto itself. It doesn't need to justify its existence anymore. It exists. It *is*.

President George W. Bush, Commander in Chief of the US army, navy, airforce and marines has issued clear instructions 'Iraq. Will. Be. Liberated'.[6] (Perhaps he means that even if Iraqi people's bodies are killed, their souls will be liberated.) American and British citizens owe it to the Supreme Commander to forsake thought and rally behind their troops. Their countries are at war.

And what a war it is.

After using the 'good offices' of UN diplomacy (economic sanctions and weapons inspections) to ensure that Iraq was brought to its knees, its people starved, half a million of its children killed, its infrastructure severely damaged, *after making sure that most of its weapons have been destroyed,* in an act of cowardice that must surely be unrivalled in history, the 'Allies'/'Coalition of the Willing' (better known as the Coalition of the Bullied and Bought) sent in an invading army!

Operation Iraqi Freedom? I don't think so. It's more like Operation Let's Run a Race, but First Let Me Break Your Knees.

So far the Iraqi army, with its hungry, ill-equipped soldiers, its old guns and ageing tanks, has somehow managed to temporarily confound and occasionally even out-manoeuvre the 'Allies'. Faced with the richest, best-equipped, most-powerful armed forces the world has ever seen, Iraq has shown spectacular courage and has even managed to put up what actually amounts to a *defence*: a defence which the Bush/Blair pair has immediately denounced as deceitful and cowardly. (But then deceit is an old tradition with us natives. When we're invaded/colonized/occupied and stripped of all dignity, we turn to guile and opportunism.)

Even allowing for the fact that Iraq and the 'Allies' are at war, the extent to which the 'Allies' and their media cohorts are prepared to go is astounding to the point of being counter-productive to their own objectives.

When Saddam Hussein appeared on national TV to address the Iraqi people following the failure of the most elaborate assassination attempt in history —'Operation Decapitation'—we had Geoff Hoon, British Defence Secretary deriding him for not having the courage to stand up and be killed, calling him a coward who hides in trenches.[7] We then had a flurry of Coalition speculation—Was it really Saddam Hussein, was it his double? Or was it Osama with a shave? Was it pre-recorded? Was it a speech? Was it black magic? Will it turn into a pumpkin if we really, really want it to?

After dropping not hundreds, but thousands of bombs on Baghdad, when a marketplace was mistakenly blown up and civilians killed—a US army spokesman implied that the Iraqis were blowing themselves up! 'They're using very old stock. Their missiles go up and come down.'[8]

If so, may we ask how this squares with the accusation that the Iraqi regime is a paid-up member of the Axis of Evil and a threat to world peace?

When the Arab TV station Al-Jazeera shows civilian casualties it's denounced as 'emotive' Arab propaganda aimed at orchestrating hostility towards the 'Allies', as though Iraqis are dying only in order to make the 'Allies' look bad. Even French Television has come in for some stick for similar reasons. But the awed, breathless footage of aircraft carriers, stealth bombers and cruise missiles arcing across the desert sky on American and British TV is described as the 'terrible beauty' of war.[9]

When invading American soldiers (from the army 'that's only here to help') are taken prisoner and shown on Iraqi TV, George Bush says it violates the Geneva convention and 'exposes the evil at the heart of the regime'.[10] But it is entirely acceptable for US television stations to show the hundreds of prisoners being held by the US government in Guantanamo Bay, kneeling on the ground with their hands tied behind their backs, blinded with opaque goggles and with earphones clamped on their ears, to ensure complete visual and aural deprivation.[11] When questioned about the treatment of prisoners in Guantanamo Bay, US government officials don't deny that they're being ill-treated. They deny that they're 'prisoners of war'! They call them 'unlawful combatants',[12] implying that their ill-treatment is legitimate! (So what's the Party Line on the massacre of prisoners in Mazar-e-Sharif, Afghanistan?[13] Forgive and Forget? And what of the prisoner tortured to death by the Special Forces at the Bagram Airforce Base? Doctors have formally called it homicide.[14])

When the 'Allies' bombed the Iraqi Television

station (also, incidentally, a contravention of the Geneva convention), there was vulgar jubilation in the American media. In fact Fox TV had been lobbying for the attack for a while.[15] It was seen as a righteous blow against Arab propaganda. But mainstream American and British TV continue to advertise themselves as 'balanced' when their propaganda has achieved hallucinatory levels.

Why should propaganda be the exclusive preserve of the western media? Just because they do it better?

Western journalists 'embedded' with troops are given the status of heroes reporting from the frontlines of war. Non-'embedded' journalists (like the BBC's Rageh Omaar, reporting from besieged and bombed Baghdad, witnessing, and clearly affected by the sight of bodies of burned children and wounded people[16]) are undermined even before they begin their reportage: 'We have to tell you that he is being monitored by the Iraqi Authorities.'

Increasingly, on British and American TV, Iraqi soldiers are being referred to as 'militia' (that is, rabble). One BBC correspondent portentously referred to them as 'quasi-terrorists'. Iraqi defence is 'resistance' or worse still, 'pockets of resistance',

Iraqi military strategy is deceit. (The US government bugging the phone lines of UN Security Council delegates, reported by the London *Observer*, is hard-headed pragmatism.[17]) Clearly for the 'Allies', the only morally acceptable strategy the Iraqi army can pursue is to march out into the desert and be bombed by B-52s or be mowed down by machine-gun fire. Anything short of that is cheating.

And now we have the siege of Basra. About a million and a half people, 40 per cent of them children.[18] Without clean water, and with very little food. We're still waiting for the legendary Shia 'uprising', for the happy hordes to stream out of the city and rain roses and hosannas on the 'liberating' army. Where are the hordes? Don't they know that television productions work to tight schedules? (It may well be that if the Saddam Hussein regime falls there *will* be dancing on the streets of Basra. But then, if the Bush regime were to fall, there would be dancing on the streets the world over.)

After days of enforcing hunger and thirst on the citizens of Basra, the Allies have brought in a few trucks of food and water and positioned them tantalizingly on the outskirts of the city. Desperate people flock to the trucks and fight each other for food. (The water we hear, is being *sold*.[19] To revitalize the dying economy, you understand.) On top of the trucks, desperate photographers fight each other to get pictures of desperate people fighting each other for food. Those pictures will go out through photo agencies to newspapers and glossy magazines that pay extremely well. Their message: The messiahs are at hand, distributing fishes and loaves.

As of July last year the delivery of $5.4 billion worth of supplies to Iraq was blocked by the Bush/Blair pair.[20] It didn't really make the news. But now under the loving caress of live TV, 450 tonnes of humanitarian aid—a miniscule fraction of what's actually needed (call it a script prop)— arrived on a British ship, the 'Sir Galahad'.[21] Its arrival in the port of Umm Qasr merited a whole day of live TV broadcasts. Barf bag, anyone?

Nick Guttmann, Head of Emergencies for Christian Aid, writing for *Independent on Sunday* said that it would take *thirty-two* Sir Galahad's a *day* to match the amount of food Iraq was receiving before the bombing began.[22]

We oughtn't to be surprised though. It's old tactics. They've been at it for years. Consider this moderate proposal by John McNaughton from the Pentagon Papers published during the Vietnam War:

> Strikes at population targets (per se) are likely not only to create a counterproductive wave of revulsion abroad and at home, but greatly to increase the risk of enlarging the war with China or the Soviet Union. Destruction of locks and dams, however—if handled right—might . . . offer promise. It should be studied. Such destruction does not kill or drown people. By shallow-flooding the rice, it leads after time to widespread starvation (more than a million?) unless food is provided—which we could offer to do 'at the conference table'.[23]

Times haven't changed very much. The technique has evolved into a doctrine. It's called 'Winning Hearts and Minds'.

So, here's the moral math as it stands: 200,000 Iraqis estimated to have been killed in the first

Gulf War.[24] Hundreds of thousands dead because of the economic sanctions. (At least that lot has been saved from Saddam Hussein.) More being killed every day. Tens of thousands of US soldiers who fought the 1991 war officially declared 'disabled' by a disease called the Gulf War Syndrome believed in part to be caused by exposure to Depleted Uranium.[25] It hasn't stopped the 'Allies' from continuing to use Depleted Uranium.[26]

And now this talk of bringing the UN back into the picture.

But that old UN girl—it turns out that she just ain't what she was cracked up to be. She's been demoted (although she retains her high salary). Now she's the world's janitor. She's the Philippino cleaning lady, the Indian jamadarni, the postal bride from Thailand, the Mexican household help, the Jamaican au pair. She's employed to clean other peoples' shit. She's used and abused at will.

Despite Tony Blair's earnest submissions, and all his fawning, George Bush has made it clear that the UN will play no independent part in the administration of post-war Iraq. The US will decide who gets those juicy 're-construction' contracts.[27] But Bush has appealed to the international community not to 'politicize' the issue of humanitarian aid. On 28 March, after Bush called for the immediate resumption of the UN's Oil for Food programme, the UN Security Council voted unanimously for the resolution.[28] This means that everybody agrees that Iraqi money (from the sale of Iraqi oil) should be used to feed Iraqi people who are starving because of US-led sanctions and the illegal US-led war.

Contracts for the 're-construction' of Iraq we're told, in discussions on the business news, could jump-start the world economy. It's funny how the interests of American corporations are so often, so successfully and so deliberately confused with the interests of the world economy. While the American people will end up paying for the war, oil companies, weapons manufacturers, arms dealers, and corporations involved in 're-construction' work will make direct gains from the war. Many of them are old friends and former employers of the Bush/Cheney/Rumsfeld/Rice cabal. Bush has already asked Congress for $75 billion.[29] Contracts for 're-construction' are already being negotiated. The news doesn't hit the stands because much of the US corporate media is owned and managed by the same interests.

Operation Iraqi Freedom, George Bush assures us, is about returning Iraqi oil to the Iraqi people. That is, returning Iraqi oil to the Iraqi people via corporate multinationals. Like Shell, like Chevron, like Halliburton. Or are we missing the plot here? Perhaps Halliburton is actually an Iraqi company? Perhaps US Vice-President Dick Cheney (who was a former Director of Halliburton) is a closet Iraqi?

As the rift between Europe and America deepens, there are signs that the world could be entering a new era of economic boycotts. CNN reported that Americans are emptying French wine into gutters, chanting 'We don't want your stinking wine.'[30] We've heard about the re-baptism of French fries. Freedom fries they're called now.[31] There's news trickling in about Americans boycotting German goods.[32] The thing is that if the fallout of the war takes this turn, it is the US who will suffer the most. Its homeland may be defended by border patrols and nuclear weapons, but its economy is strung out across the globe. Its economic outposts are exposed and vulnerable to attack in every direction. Already the internet is buzzing with elaborate lists of American and British government products and companies that should be boycotted. Apart from the usual targets, Coke, Pepsi and McDonald's, government agencies like USAID, the British DFID, British and American banks, Arthur Andersen, Merrill Lynch, American Express, corporations like Bechtel, General Electric, and companies like Reebok, Nike and Gap, could find themselves under siege. These lists are being honed and refined by activists across the world. They could become a practical guide that directs and channelizes the amorphous, but growing fury in the world. Suddenly, the 'inevitability' of the project of corporate globalization is beginning to seem more than a little evitable.

It's become clear that the War against Terror is not really about terror, and the War on Iraq not only about oil. It's about a superpower's self-destructive impulse towards supremacy, global hegemony. The argument is being made that the people of Argentina and Iraq have both been decimated by the same process. Only the weapons used against them differ: In one case it's an IMF cheque book, in the other, cruise missiles.

Finally, there's the matter of Saddam Hussein's arsenal of Weapons of Mass Destruction. (Oops, nearly forgot about those!)

One thing's for sure—if the Saddam Hussein regime indeed has Weapons of Mass Destruction, it is showing an astonishing degree of responsibility and restraint in the teeth of extreme provocation. Under similar circumstances, (say if Iraqi troops were bombing New York and laying siege to Washington DC) could we expect the same of the Bush regime? Would it keep its thousands of nuclear warheads in their wrapping paper? What about its chemical and biological weapons? Its stocks of anthrax, smallpox and nerve gas? Would it?

Excuse me while I laugh.

In the fog of war we're forced to speculate: either Saddam Hussein is an extremely responsible tyrant, or he simply does not possess Weapons of Mass Destruction. Either way, regardless of what happens next, Iraq comes out of the argument smelling sweeter than the US government.

So here's Iraq—Rogue State, grave threat to world peace, paid up member of the Axis of Evil. Here's Iraq, invaded, bombed, besieged, bullied, its sovereignty shat upon, its children killed by cancers, its people blown up on the streets. And here's all of us watching. CNN-BBC, BBC-CNN late into the night. Here's all of us, enduring the horror of the war, enduring the horror of the propaganda and enduring the slaughter of language as we know and understand it. Freedom now means mass murder (or, in the US, fried potatoes). When someone says 'humanitarian aid' we automatically go looking for induced starvation. 'Embedded' I have to admit, is a great find. It's what it sounds like. And what about 'arsenal of tactics?' Nice!

In most parts of the world, the invasion of Iraq is being seen as a racist war. The real danger of a racist war unleashed by racist regimes is that it engenders racism in everybody—perpetrators, victims, spectators. It sets the parameters for the debate, it lays out a grid for a particular way of thinking. There is a tidal wave of hatred for the United States rising from the ancient heart of the world. In Africa, Latin America, Asia, Europe, Australia. I encounter it every day. Sometimes it comes from the most unlikely sources. Bankers, businessmen, yuppie students, and they bring to it all the crassness of their conservative, illiberal politics. That absurd inability to separate governments from people: America is a nation of morons, a nation of murderers, they say, (with the same carelessness with which they say, 'All muslims are terrorists'). Even in the grotesque universe of racist insult, the British make their entry as add-ons. Arse-lickers, they're called.

Suddenly, I, who have been vilified for being 'anti-American' and 'anti-West', find myself in the extraordinary position of defending the people of America. And Britain.

Those who descend so easily into the pit of racist abuse would do well to remember the hundreds of thousands of American and British citizens who protested against their country's stockpile of nuclear weapons. And the thousands of American war resistors who forced their government to withdraw from Vietnam. They should know that the most scholarly, scathing, hilarious critiques of the US government and the 'American Way of Life' come from American citizens. And that the funniest, most bitter condemnation of their prime minister comes from the British media. Finally they should remember that right now, hundreds of thousands of British and American citizens are on the streets protesting the war. The Coalition of the Bullied and Bought consists of governments, not people. More than one third of America's citizens have survived the relentless propaganda they've been subjected to and many thousands are actively fighting their own government. In the ultra-patriotic climate that prevails in the US, that's as brave as any Iraqi fighting for his or her homeland.

While the 'Allies' wait in the desert for an uprising of Shia Muslims on the streets of Basra, the real uprising is taking place in hundreds of cities across the world. It has been the most spectacular display of public morality ever seen.

Most courageous of all, are the hundreds of thousands of American people on the streets of America's great cities—Washington, New York, Chicago, San Francisco. The fact is that the only institution in the world today that is more powerful than the American government, is American civil society. American citizens have a huge responsibility riding on their shoulders. How can we not salute and support those who not only acknowledge but act upon that responsibility? They are our allies, our friends.

At the end of it all, it remains to be said that

dictators like Saddam Hussein, and all the other despots in the Middle East, in the Central Asian Republics, in Africa and Latin America, many of them installed, supported and financed by the US government, are a menace to their own people. Other than strengthening the hand of civil society (instead of weakening it as has been done in the case of Iraq), there is no easy, pristine way of dealing with them. (It's odd how those who dismiss the peace movement as utopian, don't hesitate to proffer the most absurdly dreamy reasons for going to war: to stamp out terrorism, install democracy, eliminate fascism, and most entertainingly, to 'rid the world of evil-doers'.[33])

Regardless of what the propaganda machine tells us, these tinpot dictators are not the greatest threat to the world. The real and pressing danger, the *greatest threat of all* is the locomotive force that drives the political and economic engine of the US government, currently piloted by George Bush. Bush-bashing is fun, because he makes such an easy, sumptuous target. It's true that he is a dangerous, almost suicidal pilot, but the machine he handles is far more dangerous than the man himself.

Despite the pall of gloom that hangs over us today,

I'd like to file a cautious plea for hope: in times of war, one wants one's weakest enemy at the helm of his forces. And President George W. Bush is certainly that. Any other even averagely intelligent US president would have probably done the very same things, but would have managed to smoke up the glass and confuse the opposition. Perhaps even carry the UN with him. George Bush's tactless imprudence and his brazen belief that he can run the world with his riot squad, has done the opposite. He has achieved what writers, activists and scholars have striven to achieve for decades. He has exposed the ducts. He has placed on full public view the working parts, the nuts and bolts of the apocalyptic apparatus of the American Empire.

Now that the blueprint, The Ordinary Person's Guide to Empire, has been put into mass circulation, it could be disabled quicker than the pundits predicted.

Bring on the spanners.

April 2003

instant-mix imperial democracy
(buy one, get one free)

instant-mix imperial democracy
(buy one, get one free)

In these times when we have to race to keep abreast of the speed at which our freedoms are being snatched from us, and when few can afford the luxury of retreating from the streets for a while in order to return with an exquisite, fully formed political thesis replete with footnotes and references, what profound gift can I offer you tonight?

As we lurch from crisis to crisis, beamed directly into our brains by satellite TV, we have to think on our feet. On the move. We enter histories through the rubble of war. Ruined cities, parched fields, shrinking forests and dying rivers are our archives. Craters left by daisy cutters, our libraries.

So what can I offer you tonight? Some uncomfortable thoughts about money, war, empire, racism and democracy. Some worries that flit around my brain like a family of persistent moths that keep me awake at night.

Some of you will think it bad manners for a person like me, officially entered in the Big Book of Modern Nations as an 'Indian citizen', to come here and criticize the US government. Speaking for myself, I'm no flag-waver, no patriot, and am fully aware that venality, brutality, and hypocrisy are imprinted on the leaden soul of every state. But when a country ceases to be merely a country and becomes an empire, then the scale of operations changes dramatically. So may I clarify that tonight I speak as a subject of the American Empire? I speak as a slave who presumes to criticize her king.

Since lectures must be called something, mine tonight is called Instant-Mix Imperial Democracy (Buy One, Get One Free).

Way back in 1988, on the 3rd of July, the USS Vincennes, a missile cruiser stationed in the Persian Gulf, accidentally shot down an Iranian airliner and killed 290 civilian passengers.[1] George Bush the First, who was at the time on his presidential campaign, was asked to comment on the incident. He said quite subtly, 'I will never apologize for the United States. I don't care what the facts are.'[2]

I don't care what the facts are. What a perfect maxim for the New American Empire. Perhaps a slight variation on the theme would be more apposite: *The facts can be whatever we want them to be.*

When the United States invaded Iraq, a *New York Times*/CBS News survey estimated that 42 per cent of the American public believed that Saddam Hussein was directly responsible for the 11 September attacks on the World Trade Centre and the Pentagon.[3] And an ABC news poll said that 55 per cent of Americans believed that Saddam Hussein directly supported Al-Qaeda.[4] None of this opinion is based on evidence (because there isn't any). All of it is based on insinuation, auto-suggestion and outright lies circulated by the US corporate media, known otherwise as the 'Free Press', that hollow pillar on which contemporary American democracy rests.

Public support in the US for the war against Iraq was founded on a multi-tiered edifice of falsehood and deceit, coordinated by the US government and faithfully amplified by the corporate media.

Apart from the invented links between Iraq and Al-Qaeda, we had the manufactured frenzy about Iraq's Weapons of Mass Destruction. George Bush the Lesser went to the extent of saying it would be 'suicidal' for the US *not* to attack Iraq.[5] We once again witnessed the paranoia that a starved, bombed, besieged country was about to annihilate almighty America. (Iraq was only the latest in a succession of countries—earlier there were Cuba, Nicaragua, Libya, Grenada, Panama.) But this time it wasn't just your ordinary brand of friendly neighbourhood frenzy. It was Frenzy with a Purpose. It ushered in an old doctrine in a new bottle: the Doctrine of Pre-emptive Strike, a.k.a. The United States Can Do Whatever the Hell It Wants, and That's Official.

The war against Iraq has been fought and won and no Weapons of Mass Destruction have been found. Not even a little one. Perhaps they'll have to be planted before they're discovered. And then, the more troublesome amongst us will need an explanation for why Saddam Hussein didn't use them when his country was being invaded.

Of course, there'll be no answers. True Believers will make do with those fuzzy TV reports about the discovery of a few barrels of banned chemicals in an old shed. There seems to be no consensus yet about whether they're really chemicals, whether they're actually banned and whether the vessels they're contained in can technically be called barrels. (There were unconfirmed rumours that a teaspoonful of potassium permanganate and an old harmonica were found there too.)

Meanwhile, in passing, an ancient civilization has been casually decimated by a very recent, casually brutal nation.

Then there are those who say, so what if Iraq had no chemical and nuclear weapons? So what if there is no Al-Qaeda connection? So what if Osama bin Laden hates Saddam Hussein as much as he hates the United States? Bush the Lesser has said Saddam Hussein was a 'Homicidal Dictator'.[6] And so, the reasoning goes, Iraq needed a 'regime change'.

Never mind that forty years ago, the CIA, under President John F. Kennedy, orchestrated a regime change in Baghdad. In 1963, after a successful coup, the Ba'ath party came to power in Iraq. Using lists provided by the CIA, the new Ba'ath regime systematically eliminated hundreds of doctors, teachers, lawyers and political figures known to be leftists.[7] An entire intellectual community was slaughtered. (The same technique was used to massacre hundreds of thousands of people in Indonesia and East Timor.[8]) The young Saddam Hussein was said to have had a hand in supervising the bloodbath. In 1979, after factional infighting within the Ba'ath Party, Saddam Hussein became the president of Iraq. In April 1980, while he was massacring Shias, the US National Security Adviser Zbigniew Brzezinksi declared, 'We see no fundamental incompatibility of interests between the United States and Iraq.'[9] Washington and London overtly and covertly supported Saddam Hussein. They financed him, equipped him, armed him and provided him with dual-use materials to manufacture Weapons of Mass Destruction.[10] They supported his worst excesses financially, materially and morally. They supported the eight-year war against Iran and the 1988 gassing of Kurdish people in Halabja, crimes which fourteen years later were re-heated and served up as reasons to justify invading Iraq.[11] After the first Gulf War, the 'Allies' fomented an uprising of Shias in Basra and then looked away while Saddam Hussein crushed the revolt and slaughtered thousands in an act of vengeful reprisal.[12]

The point is, if Saddam Hussein was evil enough to merit the most elaborate, openly declared assassination attempt in history (the opening move of Operation Shock & Awe), then surely those who supported him ought at least to be tried for war crimes? Why aren't the faces of US and UK government officials on the infamous pack of cards of wanted men and women?

Because when it comes to Empire, facts don't matter.

Yes, but all that's in the past we're told. Saddam Hussein is a monster who must be stopped *now*. And only the US can stop him. It's an effective technique, this use of the urgent morality of the present to obscure the diabolical sins of the past and the malevolent plans for the future. Indonesia, Panama, Nicaragua, Iraq, Afghanistan—the list goes on and on. Right now there are brutal regimes being groomed for the future—Egypt, Saudi Arabia, Turkey, Pakistan, the Central Asian Republics.

US Attorney General John Ashcroft recently declared that US freedoms are 'not the grant of any government or document, but . . . our endowment from God'.[13] (Why bother with the United Nations when God himself is on hand?)

So here we are, the people of the world, confronted with an Empire armed with a mandate from heaven (*and,* as added insurance, the most formidable arsenal of Weapons of Mass Destruction in history). Here we are, confronted with an Empire that has conferred upon itself the right to go to war at will, and the right to deliver people from corrupting ideologies, from religious fundamentalists, dictators, sexism, and poverty by the age-old, tried-and-tested practice of extermination. Empire is on the move, and Democracy is its sly new war cry. Democracy, home-delivered to your doorstep by daisy-cutters. Death is a small price for people to pay for the privilege of sampling this new product: Instant-Mix Imperial Democracy (bring to a boil, add oil, then bomb).

But then perhaps chinks, negroes, dinks, gooks and wogs don't really qualify as real people. Perhaps our deaths don't qualify as real deaths. Our histories don't qualify as history. They never have.

Speaking of history, in these past months, while the world watched, the US invasion and occupation of Iraq was broadcast on live TV. Like Osama bin Laden and the Taliban in Afghanistan, the regime of Saddam Hussein simply disappeared. This was followed by what analysts called a 'power vacuum'.[14] Cities that had been under siege, without food, water and electricity for days, cities that had been bombed relentlessly, people who had been starved and systematically impoverished by the UN sanctions regime for more than a decade, were suddenly left with no semblance of urban administration. A seven-thousand-year-old civilization slid into anarchy. On live TV.

Vandals plundered shops, offices, hotels and hospitals.[15] American and British soldiers stood by and watched. They said they had no orders to act. In effect, they had orders to kill people, but not to protect them. Their priorities were clear. The safety and security of Iraqi people was not their business. The security of whatever little remained of Iraq's infrastructure was not their business. But the security and safety of Iraq's oil fields were. Of course they were. The oil fields were 'secured' almost before the invasion began.[16]

On CNN and BBC the scenes of the rampage were played and replayed. TV commentators, army and government spokespersons portrayed it as 'liberated people' venting their rage at a despotic regime. US Defence Secretary Donald Rumsfeld said: 'It's untidy. Freedom's untidy and free people are free to commit crimes and make mistakes and do bad things.'[17] Did anybody know that Donald Rumsfeld was an anarchist? I wonder—did he hold the same view during the riots in Los Angeles following the beating of Rodney King? Would he care to share his thesis about the Untidiness of Freedom with the two million people being held in US prisons right now?[18] (The world's 'freest' country has the highest number of prisoners in the world.[19]) Would he discuss its merits with young African American men, 28 per cent of whom will spend some part of their adult lives in jail?[20] Could he explain why he serves under a president who oversaw 152 executions when he was governor of Texas?[21]

Before the war on Iraq began, the Office of Reconstruction and Humanitarian Assistance (ORHA) sent the Pentagon a list of sixteen crucial sites to protect. The National Museum was second on that list.[22] Yet the Museum was not just looted, it was desecrated. It was a repository of an ancient cultural heritage. Iraq, as we know it today, was part of the river valley of Mesopotamia. The civilization that grew along the banks of the Tigris and the Euphrates produced the world's first writing, first calendar, first library, first city, and, yes, the world's first democracy. King Hammurabi of Babylon was the first to codify laws governing the social life of citizens.[23] It was a code in which abandoned women, prostitutes, slaves, and even animals had rights. The Hammurabi code is acknowledged not just as the birth of legality, but the beginning of an understanding of the concept of social justice. The US government could not have chosen a more inappropriate land in which to stage its illegal war and display its grotesque disregard for justice.

At a Pentagon briefing during the days of looting, Secretary Rumsfeld, Prince of Darkness, turned on his media cohorts who had served him so loyally through the war. 'The images you are seeing on television, you are seeing over and over and over, and it's the same picture, of some person walking out of some building with a vase, and you see it twenty times and you say, "My god, were there that many vases? Is it possible that there were that many vases in the whole country?"'[24]

Laughter rippled through the press room. Would it be all right for the poor of Harlem to loot the Metropolitan Museum? Would it be greeted with similar mirth?

The last building on the ORHA list of sixteen sites to be protected was the Ministry of Oil.[25] It was the only one that was given protection.[26] Perhaps the occupying army thought that in Muslim countries lists are read upside down?

Television tells us that Iraq has been 'liberated' and that Afghanistan is well on its way to becoming a paradise for women—thanks to Bush and Blair, the twenty-first century's leading feminists. In reality, Iraq's infrastructure has been destroyed. Its people brought to the brink of starvation. Its food stocks depleted. And its cities devastated by a complete administrative breakdown. Iraq is being ushered in the direction of a civil war between Shias and Sunnis. Meanwhile, Afghanistan has lapsed into the pre-Taliban era of anarchy, and its territory has been carved up into fiefdoms by hostile warlords.[27]

Undaunted by all this, on 2 May George Bush launched his 2004 campaign hoping to be finally elected US president. In what probably constitutes the shortest flight in history, a military jet landed on an aircraft carrier, the USS Abraham Lincoln, which was so close to shore that, according to the Associated Press, administration officials acknowledged 'positioning the massive ship to provide the best TV angle for Bush's speech, with the sea as his background instead of the San Diego coastline'.[28] President Bush, who never served his term in the military,[29] emerged from the cockpit in fancy dress—a US military bomber jacket, combat boots, flying goggles, helmet. Waving to his cheering troops, he officially proclaimed victory over Iraq. He was careful to say that it was 'just one victory in a war on terror . . . [which] still goes on'.[30]

It was important to avoid making a straightforward victory announcement, because under the Geneva Convention a victorious army is bound by legal obligations of an occupying force, a responsibility that the Bush administration does not want to burden itself with.[31] Also, closer to the 2004 elections, in order to woo wavering voters, another victory in the 'War on Terror' might become necessary. Syria is being fattened for the kill.

It was Herman Goering, that old Nazi, who said, 'People can always be brought to the bidding of the leaders . . . All you have to do is tell them they're being attacked and denounce the pacifists for a lack of patriotism and exposing the country to danger. It works the same way in any country.'[32]

He's right. It's dead easy. That's what the Bush

regime banks on. The distinction between election campaigns and war, between democracy and oligarchy, seems to be closing fast.

The only caveat in these campaign wars is that US lives must not be lost. It shakes voter confidence. But the problem of US soldiers being killed in combat has been licked. More or less.

At a media briefing before 'Operation Shock & Awe' was unleashed, General Tommy Franks announced, 'This campaign will be like no other in history.'[33] Maybe he's right.

I'm no military historian, but when was the last time a war was fought like this?

After using the 'good offices' of UN diplomacy (economic sanctions and weapons inspections) to ensure that Iraq was brought to its knees, its people starved, half a million children dead, its infrastructure severely damaged, *after making sure that most of its weapons had been destroyed,* in an act of cowardice that must surely be unrivalled in history, the 'Coalition of the Willing' (better known as the Coalition of the Bullied and Bought)—sent in an invading army!

Operation Iraqi Freedom? I don't think so. It was more like Operation Let's Run a Race, but First

Let Me Break Your Knees.

As soon as the war began, the governments of France, Germany and Russia, which refused to allow a final resolution legitimizing the war to be passed in the UN Security Council, fell over each other to say how much they wanted the United States to win. President Jacques Chirac offered French airspace to the Anglo-American air force.[34] US military bases in Germany were open for business.[35] German Foreign Minister Joschka Fischer publicly hoped for the 'rapid collapse' of the Saddam Hussein regime.[36] Vladimir Putin publicly hoped for the same.[37] These are governments that colluded in the enforced disarming of Iraq before their dastardly rush to take the side of those who attacked it. Apart from hoping to share the spoils, they hoped Empire would honour their pre-war oil contracts with Iraq. Only the very naïve could expect old Imperialists to behave otherwise.

Leaving aside the cheap thrills and the lofty moral speeches made in the UN during the run-up to the war, eventually, at the moment of crisis, the unity of Western governments—despite the opposition from the majority of their people—was overwhelming.

When the Turkish government temporarily bowed to the views of 90 per cent of its population, and turned down the US government's offer of billions of dollars of blood money for the use of Turkish soil, it was accused of lacking 'democratic credentials'.[38] According to a Gallup International poll, in no European country was support for a war carried out 'unilaterally by America and its allies' higher than 11 per cent.[39] But the governments of England, Italy, Spain, Hungary and other countries of eastern Europe were praised for disregarding the views of the majority of their people and supporting the illegal invasion. That, presumably, was fully in keeping with democratic principles. What's it called? New Democracy? (Like Britain's New Labour?)

In stark contrast to the venality displayed by their governments, on 15 February, weeks before the invasion, in the most spectacular display of public morality the world has ever seen, more than ten million people marched against the war on five continents.[40] Many of you I'm sure, were among them. They—we—were disregarded with utter disdain. When asked to react to the anti-war demonstrations, President Bush said, 'It's like deciding, well, I'm going to decide policy based upon a focus group. The role of a leader is to decide policy based upon the security, in this case the security of the people.'[41]

Democracy, the modern world's holy cow, is in crisis. And the crisis is a profound one. Every kind of outrage is being committed in the name of democracy. It has become little more than a hollow word, a pretty shell, emptied of all content or meaning. It can be whatever you want it to be. Democracy is the Free World's whore, willing to dress up, dress down, willing to satisfy a whole range of taste, available to be used and abused at will.

Until quite recently, right up to the 1980s, democracy did seem as though it might actually succeed in delivering a degree of real social justice.

But modern democracies have been around for long enough for neoliberal capitalists to learn how to subvert them. They have mastered the technique of infiltrating the instruments of democracy—the 'independent' judiciary, the 'free' press, the parliament—and moulding them to their purpose. The project of corporate globalization has cracked the code. Free elections, a free press and an independent judiciary mean little when the free market has reduced them to commodities on sale to the highest bidder.

To fully comprehend the extent to which Democracy is under siege, it might be an idea to look at what goes on in some of our contemporary democracies. The world's largest: India (which I have written about at some length and therefore will not speak about tonight). The world's most interesting: South Africa. The world's most powerful: the USA. And, most instructive of all, the plans that are being made to usher in the world's newest: Iraq.

In South Africa, after 300 years of brutal domination of the black majority by a white minority through colonialism and apartheid, a non-racial, multi-party democracy came to power in 1994. It was a phenomenal achievement. Yet, within two years of coming to power, the African National Congress had genuflected with no caveats to the Market God. Its massive programme of structural adjustment, privatization and liberalization has only increased the hideous disparities between the rich and the poor. More than a million people have lost their jobs. The corporatization of basic services—electricity, water and housing—has meant that ten million South Africans, almost a quarter of the population, have been disconnected from water and electricity.[42] Two million have been evicted from their homes.

Meanwhile, a small white minority that has been historically privileged by centuries of brutal exploitation, are more secure than ever before. They continue to control the land, the farms, the factories and the abundant natural resources of that country. For them the transition from apartheid to neoliberalism barely disturbed the grass. It's apartheid with a clean conscience. And it goes by the name of Democracy.

Democracy has become Empire's euphemism for neoliberal capitalism.

In countries of the first world, too, the machinery of democracy has been effectively subverted. Politicians, media barons, judges, powerful corporate lobbies and government officials are imbricated in an elaborate underhand configuration that completely undermines the lateral arrangement of checks and balances between the constitution, courts of law, parliament, the administration and, perhaps most important of all, the independent media that form the structural basis of a parliamentary democracy. Increasingly, the imbrication is neither subtle nor elaborate.

Italian Prime Minister Silvio Berlusconi, for instance, has a controlling interest in major Italian newspapers, magazines, television channels and publishing houses. The *Financial Times* reported that he controls about 90 per cent of Italy's TV viewership.[43] Recently, during a trial on bribery charges, while insisting he was the only person who could save Italy from the Left, he said, 'How much longer do I have to keep living this life of sacrifices?'[44] That bodes ill for the remaining 10 per cent of Italy's TV viewership. What price Free Speech? Free Speech for *whom?*

In the United States, the arrangement is more complex. Clear Channel Worldwide Incorporated is the largest radio station owner in the country. It runs more than 1200 channels, which together account for 9 per cent of the market.[45] Its CEO contributed hundreds of thousands of dollars to Bush's election campaign. When hundreds of thousands of American citizens took to the streets to protest against the war on Iraq, Clear Channel organized pro-war patriotic 'Rallies for America' across the country.[46] It used its radio stations to advertise the events and then sent correspondents to cover them as though they were breaking news. The era of manufacturing consent has given way to the era of manufacturing news. Soon media newsrooms will drop the pretence, and start hiring theatre directors instead of journalists.

As America's show business gets more and more violent and war-like, and America's wars get more and more like show business, some interesting cross-overs are taking place. The designer who built the $250,000 set in Qatar from which General Tommy Franks stage-managed news coverage of Operation Shock & Awe also built sets for Disney, MGM and 'Good Morning America'.[47]

It is a cruel irony that the US, which has the most ardent, vociferous defenders of the idea of Free Speech, and (until recently) the most elaborate legislation to protect it, has so circumscribed the space in which that freedom can be expressed. In a strange, convoluted way, the sound and fury that accompanies the legal and *conceptual* defence of Free Speech in America serves to mask the process of the rapid erosion of the possibilities of actually *exercising* that freedom.

The news and entertainment industry in the US is for the most part controlled by a few major corporations—AOL–Time Warner, Disney, Viacom, News Corporation.[48] Each of these corporations owns and controls TV stations, film studios, record companies and publishing ventures. Effectively, the exits are sealed.

America's media empire is controlled by a tiny coterie of people. Chairman of the Federal Communications Commission Michael Powell, the son of Secretary of State Colin Powell, has proposed even further deregulation of the communication industry, which will lead to even greater consolidation.[49]

So here it is—the world's greatest democracy, led by a man who was not legally elected. America's Supreme Court gifted him his job. What price have American people paid for this spurious presidency?

In the three years of George Bush's term, the American economy has lost more than two million jobs.[50] Outlandish military expenses, corporate welfare and tax giveaways to the rich have created a financial crisis for the US educational system. According to a survey by the National Council of State Legislatures, US states cut $49 billion in public services, health, welfare benefits and education in 2002. They plan to cut another $25.7 billion this year.[51] That makes a total of $75 billion. Bush's initial budget request to Congress to finance the war in Iraq was $80 billion.[52]

So who's paying for the war? America's poor. Its students, its unemployed, its single mothers, its hospital and home-care patients, its teachers and health workers.

And who's actually fighting the war? Once again, America's poor. The soldiers who are baking in Iraq's desert sun are not the children of the rich. Only one of all the representatives in Congress and the Senate has a child fighting in Iraq.[53] America's 'volunteer' army in fact depends on a poverty draft of poor Whites, Blacks, Latinos and Asians looking for a way to earn a living and get an education. Federal statistics show that African Americans make up 21 per cent of the total armed forces and 29 per cent of the US army. They count for only 12 per cent of the population.[54] It's ironic, isn't it—the disproportionately high representation of African Americans in the army and prison? Perhaps we should take a positive view, and look at this as affirmative action at its effective best. Nearly four million Americans (2 per cent of the population) have lost the right to vote because of felony convictions.[55] Of that number, 1.4 million are African Americans, which means that 13 per cent of all voting-age Black people have been disenfranchised.[56]

For African Americans there's also affirmative action in death. A study by the economist Amartya Sen shows that African Americans as a group have a lower life expectancy than people born in China, in the Indian State of Kerala (where I come from), Sri Lanka or Costa Rica.[57] Bangladeshi men have a better chance of making it to the age of forty than African American men from here in Harlem.[58]

This year on what would have been Martin Luther King Jr's seventy-fourth birthday, President Bush denounced the University of Michigan's affirmative action programme favouring Blacks and Latinos. He called it 'divisive', 'unfair' and 'unconstitutional'.[59] The successful effort to keep Blacks off the voting rolls in the state of Florida in order that George Bush be elected was of course neither unfair nor unconstitutional. I don't suppose affirmative action for White Boys From Yale ever is.

So we know who's paying for the war. We know who's fighting it. But who will benefit from it? Who is homing in on the reconstruction contracts estimated to be worth up to $100 billion ?[60] Could it be America's poor and unemployed and sick? Could it be America's single mothers? Or America's Black and Latino minorities?

Operation Iraqi Freedom, George Bush assures us, is about returning Iraqi oil to the Iraqi people. That is, returning Iraqi oil to the Iraqi people via corporate multinationals. Like Bechtel, like Chevron, like Halliburton.

Once again it is a small, tight circle that connects corporate, military, and government leadership to one another. The promiscuousness, the cross-pollination is outrageous.

Consider this: the Defence Policy Board is a government appointed group that advises the Pentagon on defence policy. Its members are appointed by the under secretary of defence and approved by Donald Rumsfeld. Its meetings are classified. No information is available for public scrutiny.

The Washington-based Centre for Public Integrity found that nine out of the thirty members of the Defence Policy Board are connected to companies that were awarded defence contracts worth $76 billion between the years 2001 and 2002.[61] One of them, Jack Sheehan, a retired

Marine Corps general, is a senior vice president at Bechtel, the giant international engineering outfit.[62] Riley Bechtel, the company chairman, is on the president's Export Council.[63] Former Secretary of State George Shultz, who is also on the Board of Directors of the Bechtel Group, is the chairman of the advisory board of the Committee for the Liberation of Iraq.[64] When asked by the *New York Times* whether he was concerned about the appearance of a conflict of interest, he said, 'I don't know that Bechtel would particularly benefit from it. But if there's work to be done, Bechtel is the type of company that could do it.'[65]

Bechtel has been awarded a $680 million reconstruction contract in Iraq.[66] According to the Centre for Responsive Politics, Bechtel contributed $1.3 million towards the 1999-2000 Republican campaign.[67]

Arcing across this subterfuge, dwarfing it by the sheer magnitude of its malevolence, is America's anti-terrorism legislation. The USA Patriot Act, passed on 13 October 2001, has become the blueprint for similar anti-terrorism bills in countries across the world. It was passed in the House of Representatives by a majority vote of

337 to 79. According to the *New York Times,* 'Many lawmakers said it had been impossible to truly debate, or even read, the legislation.'[68]

The Patriot Act ushers in an era of systemic automated surveillance. It gives the government the authority to monitor phones and computers and spy on people in ways that would have seemed completely unacceptable a few years ago.[69] It gives the FBI the power to seize all of the circulation, purchasing and other records of library users and bookstore customers on the suspicion that they are part of a terrorist network.[70] It blurs the boundaries between speech and criminal activity, creating the space to construe acts of civil disobedience as violating the law.

Already hundreds of people are being held indefinitely as 'unlawful combatants'.[71] (In India, the number is in the thousands.[72] In Israel, 5000 Palestinians are now being detained.[73]) Non-citizens, of course, have no rights at all. They can simply be 'disappeared' like the people of Chile under Washington's old ally, General Pinochet. More than 1000 people, many of them Muslim or of Middle Eastern origin, have been detained, some without access to legal representatives.[74]

Apart from paying the actual economic costs of

war, American people are paying for these wars of 'liberation' with their own freedoms. For the ordinary American, the price of 'New Democracy' in other countries is the death of real democracy at home.

Meanwhile, Iraq is being groomed for 'liberation'. (Or did they mean 'liberalization' all along?) The *Wall Street Journal* reports that 'the Bush administration has drafted sweeping plans to remake Iraq's economy in the US image'.[75]

Iraq's constitution is being redrafted. Its trade laws, tax laws and intellectual property laws are being rewritten in order to turn it into an American-style capitalist economy.[76]

The United States Agency for International Development has invited US companies to bid for contracts that range between road building, water systems, textbook distribution and cell-phone networks.[77]

Soon after junior George Bush announced that he wanted American farmers to feed the world, Dam Amstutz, a former senior executive of Cargill, the biggest grain exporter in the world, was put in charge of agricultural reconstruction in Iraq. Kevin Watkin, Oxfam's policy director, said, 'Putting Dam Amstutz in charge of agricultural reconstruction in Iraq is like putting Saddam Hussein in the chair of a human rights commission.'[78]

The two men who have been shortlisted to run operations for managing Iraqi oil have worked with Shell, BP and Fluer. Fluer is embroiled in a lawsuit by black South African workers who have accused the company of exploiting and brutalizing them during the apartheid era.[79] Shell, of course, is well known for its devastation of the Ogoni tribal lands in Nigeria.[80]

Tom Brokaw (one of America's best-known TV anchors) was inadvertently succinct about the process. 'One of the things we don't want to do,' he said, 'is to destroy the infrastructure of Iraq because in a few days we're going to own that country.'[81]

Now that the ownership deeds are being settled, Iraq is ready for New Democracy.

So, as Lenin used to ask: What Is To Be Done?

Well . . .

We might as well accept the fact that there is no conventional military force that can successfully challenge the American war machine. Terrorist strikes only give the US government an opportunity that it is eagerly awaiting to further tighten its stranglehold. Within days of an attack you can bet that Patriot II would be passed. To argue against US military aggression by saying that it will increase the possibilities of terrorist strikes is futile. It's like threatening Brer Rabbit that you'll throw him into the bramble bush. The document called 'The Project for the New American Century', the government's suppression of the Congressional Committee Report on September 11 which found that there was intelligence warning of the strikes that was ignored,[82] makes that obvious. For all their posturing, the terrorists and the Bush regime might as well be working as a team. They both hold people responsible for the actions of their governments. They both believe in the doctrine of collective guilt and collective punishment. Their actions benefit each other greatly.

The US government has already displayed in no uncertain terms the range and extent of its capability for paranoid aggression. In human psychology, paranoid aggression is usually an indicator of nervous insecurity. It could be argued that it's no different in the case of the psychology of nations. Empire is paranoid because it has a soft underbelly.

Its homeland may be defended by border patrols and nuclear weapons, but its economy is strung out across the globe. Its economic outposts are exposed and vulnerable. Already the Internet is buzzing with elaborate lists of American and British government products and companies that should be boycotted. Apart from the usual targets,—Coke, Pepsi, McDonald's—government agencies like US AID, the British DFID, British and American banks, Arthur Andersen, Merrill Lynch, American Express could find themselves under siege. These lists are being honed and refined by activists across the world. They could become a practical guide that directs the amorphous but growing fury in the world. Suddenly, the 'inevitability' of the project of Corporate Globalization is beginning to seem more than a little evitable.

It would be naïve to imagine that we can directly confront Empire. Our strategy must be to isolate Empire's working parts and disable them one by one. No target is too small. No victory too insignificant. We could reverse the idea of the economic sanctions imposed on poor countries by Empire and its Allies. We could impose a regime of Peoples' Sanctions on every corporate house that has been awarded a contract in postwar Iraq, just as activists in this country and around the world targeted institutions of apartheid. Each one of them should be named, exposed and boycotted. Forced out of business. That could be our response to the Shock & Awe campaign. It would be a great beginning.

Another urgent challenge is to expose the corporate media for the boardroom bulletin that it really is. We need to create a universe of alternative information. We need to support independent media like Democracy Now, Alternative Radio, South End Press.

The battle to reclaim democracy is going to be a difficult one. Our freedoms were not granted to us by any governments. They were wrested *from* them by us. And once we surrender them, the battle to retrieve them is called a revolution. It is a battle that must range across continents and countries. It must not acknowledge national boundaries, but, if it is to succeed, has to begin here. In America. The only institution more powerful than the US government is American civil society. The rest of us are subjects of slave nations. We are by no means powerless, but you have the power of proximity. You have access to the Imperial Palace and the Emperor's chambers. Empire's conquests are being carried out in your name, and you have the right to refuse. You could refuse to fight. Refuse to move those missiles from the warehouse to the dock. Refuse to wave that flag. Refuse the victory parade.

You have a rich tradition of resistance. You need only read Howard Zinn's *A People's History of the United States* to remind yourself of this.[83]

Hundreds of thousands of you have survived the relentless propaganda you have been subjected to, and are actively fighting your own government. In the ultra-patriotic climate that prevails in the United States, that's as brave as any Iraqi or Afghan or Palestinian fighting for his or her homeland.

If you join the battle, not in your hundreds of thousands, but in your millions, you will be greeted joyously by the rest of the world. And you will see how beautiful it is to be gentle instead of brutal, safe instead of scared. Befriended instead of isolated. Loved instead of hated.

I hate to disagree with your president. Yours is

by no means a great nation. But you could be a great people.

History is giving you the chance.

Seize the time.

May 2003

when the saints go
marching out

The Strange Fate of Martin, Mohandas and Mandela

We're coming up to the fortieth anniversary of the March on Washington, when Martin Luther King gave his famous 'I have a dream' speech. Perhaps it's time to reflect—again—on what has become of that dream.

It's interesting how icons, when their time has passed, are commodified and appropriated (some voluntarily, others involuntarily) to promote the prejudice, bigotry and inequity they battled against. But then in an age when everything's up for sale, why not icons? In an era when all of humanity, when every creature on God's earth, is trapped between the IMF cheque book and the American cruise missile, can icons stage a getaway?

Martin Luther King is part of a trinity. So it's hard to think of him without two others elbowing their way into the picture: Mohandas Gandhi and Nelson Mandela. The three high priests of non-violent resistance. Together they represent (to a greater or lesser extent) the twentieth century's non-violent liberation struggles (or should we say 'negotiated settlements'?): of colonized against colonizer, former slave against slave owner.

Today the elites of the very societies and peoples in whose name the battles for freedom were waged, use them as mascots to entice new masters.

Mohandas, Mandela, Martin.
India, South Africa, the United States.
Broken dreams, betrayal, nightmares.
A quick snapshot of the supposedly 'Free World' today.

Last March in India, in Gujarat—*Gandhi's* Gujarat—right-wing Hindu mobs murdered 2000 Muslims in a chillingly efficient orgy of violence. Women were gang-raped and burned alive. Muslim tombs and shrines were razed to the ground. More than 150,000 Muslims have been driven from their homes. The economic base of the community has been destroyed. Eyewitness accounts and several fact-finding commissions have accused the state government and the police of collusion in the violence.[1] I was present at a meeting where a group of victims kept wailing, 'Please save us from the police! That's all we ask . . .'

In December 2002, the same state government was voted back to office. Narendra Modi, who was widely accused of having orchestrated the riots, has embarked on his second term as chief minister of Gujarat. On 15 August, Independence Day, he hoisted the Indian flag before thousands of cheering people. In a gesture of menacing symbolism he wore the black RSS cap—which proclaims him as a member of the Hindu nationalist guild that has not been shy of admiring Hitler and his methods.[2]

One hundred and thirty million Muslims—not to mention the other minorities, Dalits, Christians, Sikhs, Adivasis—live in India under the shadow of Hindu nationalism.

As his confidence in his political future brims over, Narendra Modi, master of seizing the political moment, invited Nelson Mandela to Gujarat to be the chief guest at the celebration of Gandhi's birth anniversary on 2 October.[3] Fortunately the invitation was turned down.[4]

And what of Mandela's South Africa? Otherwise known as the Small Miracle, the Rainbow Nation of God? South Africans say that the only miracle they know of is how quickly the rainbow has been privatized, sectioned off and auctioned to the highest bidders. Within two years of taking office in 1994, the African National Congress genuflected with hardly a caveat to the Market God. In its rush to replace Argentina as neoliberalism's poster boy, it has instituted a massive programme of privatization and structural adjustment. The government's promise to re-distribute agricultural land to twenty-six million landless people has remained in the realm of dark humour.[5] While 60 per cent of the population remains landless, almost all agricultural land is owned by 60,000 White farmers.[6] (Small wonder that George Bush on his recent visit to South Africa referred to Thabo Mbeki as his 'point man' on the Zimbabwe issue.)

Post-apartheid, the income of 40 per cent of the poorest Black families has diminished by about 20 per cent.[7] Two million have been evicted from their homes.[8] Six hundred die of AIDS every day. Forty per cent of the population is unemployed and that number is rising sharply.[9] The corporatization of basic services has meant that millions have been disconnected from water and electricity.[10]

A fortnight ago I visited the home of Teresa Naidoo in Chatsworth, Durban. Her husband had died the previous day of AIDS. She had no money for a coffin. She and her two small children are HIV-positive. The government disconnected her water supply because she was unable to pay her water bills and her rent arrears for her tiny council flat. The government dismisses her troubles and those of millions like her as a 'culture of non-payment'.[11]

In what ought to be an international scandal, this same government has officially asked the judge in a US court case to rule *against* forcing companies to pay reparations for the role they played during apartheid.[12] It's reasoning is that reparations—in other words justice—will discourage foreign investment.[13] So South Africa's poorest must pay apartheid's debts, so that those who amassed profit by exploiting Black people during apartheid can profit even more from the goodwill generated by Nelson Mandela's Rainbow Nation of God. President Thabo Mbeki is still called 'comrade' by his colleagues in government. In South Africa, Orwellian parody goes under the genre of Real Life.

What's left to say about Martin Luther King's America? Perhaps it's worth asking a simple question: Had he been alive today, would he have chosen to stay warm in his undisputed place in the pantheon of Great Americans? Or would he have stepped off his pedestal, shrugged off the empty hosannas and walked out onto the streets to rally his people once more?

On 4 April 1967, one year before he was assassinated, Martin Luther King spoke at the Riverside Church in New York City. That evening he said: 'I could never again raise my voice against the violence of the oppressed in the ghettos without having first spoken clearly to the greatest purveyor of violence in the world today—my own government.'[14]

Has anything happened in the thirty-six years between 1967 and 2003 that would have made him change his mind? Or would he be doubly confirmed in his opinion after the overt and covert wars and acts of mass killing that successive governments of his country, both Republican and Democrat, have engaged in since then?

Let's not forget that Martin Luther King Jr didn't start out as a militant. He began as a Persuader, a Believer. In 1964 he won the Nobel Peace Prize. He was held up by the media as an exemplary Black leader, unlike, say, the more militant Malcolm X. It was only three years later that Martin Luther King publicly connected the US government's racist war in Vietnam with its racist policies at home.

In 1967 in an uncompromising, militant speech he denounced the American invasion of Vietnam. He said:

> We have repeatedly been faced with the cruel irony of watching Negro and White boys on TV screens as they kill and die together for a nation that has been unable to seat them together in the same schools. So we watch them in brutal solidarity burning the huts of a poor village, but we realize they would hardly live on the same block in Detroit.[15]

The *New York Times* had some wonderful

counter-logic to offer the growing anti-war sentiment among Black Americans: 'In Vietnam,' it said, 'the Negro for the first time has been given the chance to do his share of fighting for his country.'[16]

It omitted to mention Martin Luther King's remark that '[t]here are twice as many Negroes dying in Vietnam as Whites in proportion to their size in the population'.[17] It omitted to mention that when the body bags came home, some of the Black soldiers were buried in segregated graves in the deep south.

What would Martin Luther King Jr say today about the fact that federal statistics show that African Americans, who account for 12 per cent of America's population, make up 21 per cent of the total armed forces and 29 per cent of the US army?[18]

Perhaps he would take a positive view and look at this as affirmative action at its most effective?

What would he say about the fact that having fought so hard to win the right to vote, today 1.4 million African Americans, which means 13 per cent of all voting-age Black people, have been disenfranchised because of felony convictions?[19]

But the most pertinent question of all is: What would Martin Luther King Jr say to those Black men and women who make up a fifth of America's armed forces and close to a third of the US army?

To Black soldiers fighting in Vietnam, Martin Luther King Jr said, 'As we counsel young men concerning military service we must clarify for them our nation's role in Vietnam and challenge them with the alternative of conscientious objection'.[20]

In April 1967 at a massive anti-war demonstration in Manhattan, Stokely Carmichael described the draft as 'White people sending Black people to make war on yellow people in order to defend land they stole from red people'.[21]

What's changed? Except of course the compulsory draft has become a poverty draft—a different kind of compulsion.

Would Martin Luther King say today that the invasion and occupation of Iraq and Afghanistan are in any way morally different from the US government's invasion of Vietnam? Would he say that it was just and moral to participate in these wars? Would he say that it was right for the US

government to have supported a dictator like
Saddam Hussein politically and financially for
years while he committed his worst excesses
against Kurds, Iranians and Iraqis in the 1980s
when he was an ally against Iran?

And that when that dictator began to chafe at the
bit, as Saddam Hussein did, would he say it was
right to go to war against Iraq, to fire several
hundred tonnes of depleted uranium into its
fields, to degrade its water supply systems, to
institute a regime of economic sanctions that
results in the death of half a million children, to
use UN weapons inspectors to force it to disarm,
to mislead the public about an arsenal of weapons
of mass destruction that could be deployed in a
matter of minutes, and then, when the country
was on its knees, to send in an invading army to
conquer it, occupy it, humiliate its people, take
control of its natural resources and infrastructure,
and award contracts worth hundreds of millions
of dollars to American corporations like Bechtel?

When he spoke out against the Vietnam War,
Martin Luther King drew some connections that
many these days shy away from making. He said,
'The problem of racism, the problem of economic
exploitation, and the problem of war are all tied

together. These are the triple evils that are inter-related.'[22] Would he tell people today that it is right for the US government to export its cruelties—its racism, its economic bullying and its war machine to poorer countries?

Would he say that Black Americans must fight for their fair share of the American pie and the bigger the pie, the better their share—never mind the terrible price that the people of Africa, Asia, the Middle East and Latin America are paying for the American Way of Life? Would he support the grafting of the Great American Dream onto his own dream, which was a very different, very beautiful sort of dream? Or would he see that as a desecration of his memory and everything that he stood for?

The Black American struggle for civil rights gave us some of the most magnificent political fighters, thinkers, public speakers and writers of our times. Martin Luther King Jr, Malcolm X, Fannie Lou Hamer, Ella Baker, James Baldwin, and of course the marvellous, magical, mythical Muhammad Ali.

Who has inherited their mantle?

Could it be the likes of Colin Powell? Condoleezza Rice? Michael Powell?

They're the exact opposite of icons or role models. They *appear* to be the embodiment of Black peoples' dreams of material success, but in actual fact they represent the Great Betrayal. They are the liveried doormen guarding the portals of the glittering ballroom against the press and swirl of the darker races. Their role and purpose is to be trotted out by the Bush administration looking for brownie points in its racist wars and African safaris.

If these are Black America's new icons, then the old ones must be dispensed with because they do not belong in the same pantheon. If these are Black America's new icons, then perhaps the haunting image that Mike Marqusee describes in his beautiful book *Redemption Song*—an old Muhammad Ali afflicted with Parkinson's disease, advertising a retirement pension— symbolizes what has happened to Black Power, not just in the United States but the world over.[23]

If Black America genuinely wishes to pay homage to its real heroes, and to all those unsung people who fought by their side, if the world wishes to pay homage, then its time to march on Washington. Again. Keeping hope alive—for all of us.

August 2003

in memory of
shankar guha niyogi

in memory of shankar guha niyogi

We are gathered here today exactly twelve years after the murder of your beloved leader Shankar Guha Niyogi. All these years have gone by and we are still waiting for those who murdered him to be brought to justice.

I'm a writer, but in this time of urgent, necessary battle, it is important for everybody, even for writers, not usually given to public speaking, to stand before thousands of people and share their thoughts.

I am here on this very important day to say that I support and respect the spectacular struggle of the Chhattisgarh Mukti Morcha.

Yesterday, I visited the settlement around the iron-ore mines of Dalli Rajhara where the Chhattisgarh Mukti Morcha's battle began. Now

Shankar Guha Niyogi was a popular trade union leader of Chhattisgarh.

it has spread across the whole of Chhattisgarh. I was deeply moved by what I saw and the people I met. What inspired me most of all was the fact that yours is and always has been a struggle not just for workers' rights and farmers' rights, not just about wages and bonuses and jobs, but a struggle that has dared to dream about what it means to be human. Whenever people's rights have been assaulted, whether they are women or children, whether they are Sikhs or Muslims during communal killings, whether they are workers or farmers who were denied irrigation, you have always stood by them.

This sharp, compelling sense of humanity will have to be our weapon in times to come, when everything—our homes, our fields, our jobs, our rivers, our electricity, our right to protest, and our dignity—is being taken from us.

This is happening not just in India but in poor countries all over the world, and in response to this the poor are rising in revolt across the world.

The culmination of the process of corporate globalization is taking place in Iraq.

Imagine if you can what we would feel if thousands of armed American soldiers were patrolling the streets of India, of Chhattisgarh, deciding where we may go, who we may meet, what we must think.

It is of utmost importance that we understand that the American occupation of Iraq and the snatching away of our fields, homes, rivers, jobs, infrastructure, and resources are products of the very same process. For this reason, any struggle against corporate globalization, any struggle for the rights and dignity of human beings must support the Iraqi people who are resisting the American occupation.

After India won independence from British rule in 1947, perhaps many of your lives did not undergo radical material change for the better. Even so, we cannot deny that it was a kind of victory, it was a kind of freedom. But today, fifty years on, even this is being jeopardized. The process of selling this country back into slavery began in the mid-1980s. The Chhattisgarh Mukti Morcha was one of the first people's resistance movements to recognize this, and so today you are an example, a beacon of light, a ray of hope for the rest of the country—and perhaps the rest of the world.

Exactly at the time when the government of India

was busy undermining labour laws and dismantling the formal structures that protected workers' rights, the Chhattisgarh Mukti Morcha intensified its struggle for the rights of all workers—formal, informal, and contract labourers. For this Shankar Guha Niyogi and at least sixteen others lost their lives, killed by assassins and police bullets.[1]

When the government of India has made it clear that it is not concerned with public health, the Chhattisgarh Mukti Morcha, with contributions from workers, built the wonderful Shaheed Hospital and drew attention to the urgent necessity of providing health care to the poor.

When the state made it clear that it was more than happy to keep the poor of India illiterate and vulnerable, the Chhattisgarh Mukti Morcha started schools for the children of workers. These schools don't just educate children, but inculcate in them revolutionary thought and create new generations of activists. Today these children led our rally, tomorrow they'll lead the resistance. It is of immense significance that this movement is led by the workers and farmers of Chhattisgarh.

To belong to a people's movement that recognized and struggled against the project of neo-imperialism as early as the Chhattisgarh Mukti Morcha did is to shoulder a great responsibility.

But you have shown, with your courage, your wisdom, and your perseverance that you are more than equal to this task. You know better than me that the road ahead is long and hard.

As a writer, as a human being, I salute you.

Lal Johar.

October 2003

do turkeys enjoy thanksgiving?

do turkeys enjoy thanksgiving?

Last January thousands of us from across the world gathered in Porto Allegre in Brazil and declared—reiterated—that 'Another World is Possible'. A few thousand miles north, in Washington, George Bush and his aides were thinking the same thing.

Our project was the World Social Forum (WSF). Theirs—to further what many call The Project for the New American Century.[1]

In the great cities of Europe and America, where a few years ago these things would only have been whispered, now people are openly talking about the good side of Imperialism and the need for a strong Empire to police an unruly world. The new missionaries want order at the cost of justice. Discipline at the cost of dignity. And ascendancy at any price. Occasionally some of us are invited to 'debate' the issue on 'neutral' platforms provided by the corporate media. Debating

Imperialism is a bit like debating the pros and cons of rape. What can we say? That we really miss it?

In any case, New Imperialism is already upon us. It's a remodelled, streamlined version of what we once knew. For the first time in history, a single Empire with an arsenal of weapons that could obliterate the world in an afternoon, has complete, unipolar, economic and military hegemony. It uses different weapons to break open different markets. There isn't a country on God's earth that is not caught in the cross hairs of the American cruise missile and the IMF chequebook. Argentina's the model if you want to be the poster-boy of neoliberal capitalism, Iraq if you're the black sheep.

Poor countries that are geopolitically of strategic value to Empire, or have a 'market' of any size, or infrastructure that can be privatized, or, God forbid, natural resources of value—oil, gold, diamonds, cobalt, coal—must do as they're told, or become military targets. Those with the greatest reserves of natural wealth are most at risk. Unless they surrender their resources willingly to the corporate machine, civil unrest will be fomented, or war will be waged. In this new age of Empire, when nothing is as it appears to be, executives of concerned companies are allowed to influence foreign policy decisions. The Centre for Public Integrity in Washington found that nine out of the thirty members of the Defense Policy Board of the US government were connected to companies that were awarded defence contracts for $76 billion between 2001 and 2002. George Shultz, former US Secretary of State was Chairman of the Committee for the Liberation of Iraq. He is also on the Board of Directors of the Bechtel Group. When asked about a conflict of interest, in the case of a war in Iraq, he said, ' I don't know that Bechtel would particularly benefit from it. But if there's work to be done, Bechtel is the type of company that could do it. But nobody looks at it as something you benefit from.' After the war, Bechtel signed a $680 million contract for reconstruction in Iraq.

This brutal blueprint has been used over and over again, across Latin America, Africa, Central and Southeast Asia. It has cost millions of lives. It goes without saying that every war Empire wages becomes a Just War. This, in large part, is due to the role of the corporate media. It's important to understand that the corporate media doesn't just support the neoliberal project. It *is* the neoliberal project. This is not a moral position it has chosen to take, it's structural. It's intrinsic to the economics of how the mass media works.

Most nations have adequately hideous family secrets. So it isn't often necessary for the media to lie. It's what's emphasized and what's ignored. Say for example, India was chosen as the target for a righteous war. The fact that about 80,000 people have been killed in Kashmir since 1989, most of them Muslims, most of them by Indian Security Forces (making the average death toll about 6000 a year); the fact that in February and March of 2002 more than 2000 Muslims were murdered on the streets of Gujarat, that women were gang-raped and children were burned alive and 150,000 people driven from their homes while the police and administration watched, and sometimes actively participated; the fact that no one has been punished for these crimes and the government that oversaw them was re-elected . . . all of this would make perfect headlines in international newspapers in the run-up to war.

Next we know, our cities will be levelled by cruise missiles, our villages fenced in with razor wire, US soldiers will patrol our streets and, Narendra

Modi, Pravin Togadia or any of our popular bigots will, like Saddam Hussein, be in US custody, having their hair checked for lice and the fillings in their teeth examined on prime-time TV.

But as long as our 'markets' are open, as long as corporations like Enron, Bechtel, Halliburton, Arthur Andersen are given a free hand, our 'democratically elected' leaders can fearlessly blur the lines between democracy, majoritarianism and fascism.

Our government's craven willingness to abandon India's proud tradition of being Non-aligned, its rush to fight its way to the head of the queue of the Completely Aligned (the fashionable phrase is 'natural ally'—India, Israel and the US are 'natural allies'), has given it the leg room to turn into a repressive regime without compromising its legitimacy.

A government's victims are not only those it kills and imprisons. Those who are displaced and dispossessed and sentenced to a lifetime of starvation and deprivation must count among them too. Millions of people have been dispossessed by 'development' projects. In the past fifty-five years, Big Dams alone have displaced between thirty-three and fifty-five million people in India. They have no recourse to justice.

In the last two years there has been a series of incidents when police have opened fire on peaceful protestors, most of them Adivasi and Dalit. When it comes to the poor, and in particular Dalit and Adivasi communities, they get killed for encroaching on forest land, and killed when they're trying to protect forest land from encroachments—by dams, mines, steel plants and other 'development' projects.[2] In almost every instance in which the police opened fire, the government's strategy has been to say the firing was provoked by an act of violence. Those who have been fired upon are immediately called militants.

Across the country, thousands of innocent people including minors have been arrested under POTA (Prevention of Terrorism Act) and are being held in jail indefinitely and without trial. In the era of the War against Terror, poverty is being slyly conflated with terrorism. In the era of corporate globalization, poverty is a crime. Protesting against further impoverishment is terrorism. And now, our Supreme Court says that going on strike is a crime.[3] Criticizing the court of course is a crime, too.[4] They're sealing the exits.

Like Old Imperialism, New Imperialism too relies for its success on a network of agents—corrupt, local elites who service Empire. We all know the sordid story of Enron in India. The then Maharashtra government signed a power-purchase agreement which gave Enron profits that amounted to 60 per cent of India's entire rural development budget. A single American company was guaranteed a profit equivalent to funds for infrastructural development for about 500 million people!

Unlike in the old days the New Imperialist doesn't need to trudge around the tropics risking malaria or diarrhoea or early death. New Imperialism can be conducted on e-mail. The vulgar, hands-on racism of Old Imperialism is outdated. The cornerstone of New Imperialism is New Racism.

The tradition of 'turkey pardoning' in the US is a wonderful allegory for New Racism. Every year since 1947, the National Turkey Federation presents the US president with a turkey for Thanksgiving. Every year, in a show of ceremonial magnanimity, the president spares that particular bird (and eats another one). After receiving the presidential pardon, the chosen one is sent to Frying Pan Park in Virginia to live out its natural life. The rest of the fifty million turkeys raised for Thanksgiving are slaughtered and eaten on Thanksgiving Day. ConAgra Foods, the company that has won the presidential turkey contract, says it trains the lucky birds to be sociable, to interact with dignitaries, school children and the press. (Soon they'll even speak English!)

That's how New Racism in the corporate era works. A few carefully bred turkeys—the local elites of various countries, a community of wealthy immigrants, investment bankers, the occasional Colin Powell, or Condoleezza Rice, some singers, some writers (like myself)—are given absolution and a pass to Frying Pan Park. The remaining millions lose their jobs, are evicted from their homes, have their water and electricity connections cut, and die of AIDS. Basically they're for the pot. But the fortunate fowls in Frying Pan Park are doing fine. Some of them even work for the IMF and the WTO—so who can accuse those organizations of being anti-turkey? Some serve as board members on the turkey choosing committee—so who can say that turkeys are against Thanksgiving? They participate in it! Who can say the poor are anti-corporate globalization? There's a stampede to get into Frying Pan Park. So what if most perish on the way?

Part of the project of New Racism is New Genocide. In this new era of economic interdependence, New Genocide can be facilitated by economic sanctions. It means creating conditions that lead to mass death without actually going out and killing people. Denis Halliday, the UN humanitarian coordinator in Iraq between 1997 and 1998 (after which he resigned in disgust), used the term genocide to describe the sanctions in Iraq.[5] In Iraq the sanctions outdid Saddam Hussein's best efforts by claiming more than half a million children's lives.[6]

In the new era, apartheid as formal policy is antiquated and unnecessary. International instruments of trade and finance oversee a complex system of multilateral trade laws and financial agreements that keep the poor in their Bantustans anyway. Its whole purpose is to institutionalize inequity. Why else would it be that the US taxes a garment made by a Bangladeshi manufacturer twenty times more than it taxes a garment made in the UK?[7] Why else would it be that countries that grow 90 per cent of the world's cocoa bean produce only 5 per cent of the world's chocolate? Why else would it be that countries that grow cocoa bean, like the Ivory Coast and Ghana, are taxed out of the market if they try and turn it into chocolate?[8] Why else would it be that rich countries that spend over $1 billion a day on subsidies to farmers demand that poor countries like India withdraw all agricultural subsidies, including subsidized electricity? Why else would it be that after having been plundered by colonizing regimes for more than half a century, former colonies are steeped in debt to those same regimes, and repay them some $382 *billion* a year?[9]

For all these reasons, the derailing of trade agreements at Cancún was crucial for us.[10] Though our governments try to take the credit, we know that it was the result of years of struggle by millions of people in many, many countries. What Cancún taught us is that in order to inflict real damage and force radical change, it is vital for local resistance movements to make international alliances. From Cancún we learned the importance of globalizing resistance.

No individual nation can stand up to the project of corporate globalization on its own. Time and again we have seen that when it comes to the neoliberal project, the heroes of our times are suddenly diminished. Extraordinary, charismatic men, giants in opposition, when they seize power and become heads of state are rendered powerless on the global stage. I'm thinking here of President Lula of Brazil. Lula was the hero of the World Social Forum last year. This year he's busy implementing IMF guidelines, reducing pension benefits and purging radicals from the Workers' Party. I'm thinking also of ex-president of South Africa, Nelson Mandela. Within two years of taking office in 1994, his government genuflected with hardly a caveat to the Market God. It instituted a massive programme of privatization and structural adjustment that has left millions of people homeless, jobless and without water and electricity.

Why does this happen? There's little point in beating our breasts and feeling betrayed. Lula and Mandela are, by any reckoning, magnificent men. But the moment they cross the floor from the opposition into government they become hostage to a spectrum of threats—most malevolent among them the threat of capital flight, which can destroy any government overnight. To imagine that a leader's personal charisma and a cv of struggle will dent the corporate cartel is to have no understanding of how capitalism works, or for that matter, how power works. Radical change will not be negotiated by governments; it can only be enforced by people.

At the WSF, some of the best minds in the world come together to exchange ideas about what is happening around us. These conversations refine our vision of the kind of world we're fighting for. It is a vital process that must not be undermined. However, if all our energies are diverted into this process at the cost of real political action, then the WSF, which has played such a crucial role in the movement for global justice, runs the risk of becoming an asset to our enemies. What we need to discuss urgently is strategies of resistance. We need to aim at real targets, wage real battles and inflict real damage. Gandhi's Salt March was not just political theatre; when, in a simple act of defiance, thousands of Indians marched to the sea and made their own salt, they broke the salt tax laws. It was a direct strike at the economic underpinning of the British Empire. It was *real*. While our movement has won some important victories, we must not allow non-violent resistance to atrophy into ineffectual, feel-good political theatre. It is a very precious weapon that needs to be constantly honed and re-imagined. It cannot be allowed to become a mere spectacle, a photo opportunity for the media.

It was wonderful that on 15 February last year, in a spectacular display of public morality, ten million people in five continents marched against the war on Iraq. It was wonderful, but it was not enough. February 15th was a weekend. Nobody had to so much as miss a day of work. Holiday protests don't stop wars. George Bush knows that. The confidence with which he disregarded overwhelming public opinion should be a lesson to us all. Bush believes that Iraq can be occupied and colonized—as Afghanistan has been, as Tibet has been, as Chechnya is being, as East Timor once was and Palestine still is. He thinks that all he has to do is hunker down and wait until a crisis-driven media, having picked this crisis to the bone, drops it and moves on. Soon the carcass will slip off the best-seller charts, and all of us outraged folks will lose interest. Or so he hopes.

This movement of ours needs a major, global victory. It's not good enough to be right. Sometimes, if only in order to test our resolve, it's important to win something. In order to win something, we need to agree on something. That something does not need to be an over-arching pre-ordained ideology into which we force-fit our delightfully factious, argumentative selves. It does not need to be an unquestioning allegiance to one or another form of resistance to the exclusion of everything else. It could be a minimum agenda.

If all of us are indeed against Imperialism and against the project of neoliberalism, then let's turn our gaze on Iraq. Iraq is the inevitable culmination of both. Plenty of anti-war activists have retreated in confusion since the capture of Saddam Hussein. Isn't the world better off without Saddam Hussein? they ask timidly.

Let's look this thing in the eye once and for all. To applaud the US army's capture of Saddam Hussein and therefore, in retrospect, justify its invasion and occupation of Iraq, is like deifying Jack the Ripper for disembowelling the Boston Strangler. And that after a quarter century partnership in which the Ripping and Strangling was a joint enterprise. It's an in-house quarrel.

They're business partners who fell out over a dirty deal. Jack's the CEO.

So if we are against Imperialism, shall we agree that we are against the US occupation and that we believe that the US must withdraw from Iraq and pay reparations to the Iraqi people for the damage that the war has inflicted?

How do we begin to mount our resistance? Let's start with something really small. The issue is not about *supporting* the resistance in Iraq against the occupation or discussing who exactly constitutes the resistance. (Are they old killer Ba'athists, are they Islamic fundamentalists?)

We have to *become* the global resistance to the occupation.

Our resistance has to begin with a refusal to accept the legitimacy of the US occupation of Iraq. It means acting to make it materially impossible for Empire to achieve its aims. It means soldiers should refuse to fight, reservists should refuse to serve, workers should refuse to load ships and aircraft with weapons. It certainly means that in countries like India and Pakistan we must block the US government's plans to have Indian and Pakistani soldiers sent to Iraq to clean up after them.

I suggest we choose, by some means, two of the major corporations that are profiting from the destruction of Iraq. We could then list every project they are involved in. We could locate their offices in every city and every country across the world. We could go after them. We could shut them down. It's a question of bringing our collective wisdom and experience of past struggles to bear on a single target. It's a question of the desire to win.

The Project For The New American Century seeks to perpetuate inequity and establish American hegemony at any price, even if it's apocalyptic. The WSF demands justice and survival.

For these reasons, we must consider ourselves at war.

January 2003

how deep shall we dig?

how deep shall we dig?

Recently, a young Kashmiri friend was talking to me about life in Kashmir. Of the morass of political venality and opportunism, the callous brutality of the security forces, of the osmotic, inchoate edges of a society saturated in violence, where militants, police, intelligence officers, government servants, businessmen and even journalists encounter each other, and gradually, over time, *become* each other. He spoke of having to live with the endless killing, the mounting 'disappearances', the whispering, the fear, the unresolved rumours, the insane disconnection between what is actually happening, what Kashmiris know is happening and what the rest of us are told is happening in Kashmir. He said 'Kashmir used to be a business. Now it's a mental asylum.'

The more I think about that remark, the more apposite a description it seems for all of India.

Admittedly, Kashmir and the Northeast are separate wings that house the more perilous wards in the asylum. But in the heartland too, the schism between knowledge and information, between what we know and what we're told, between what is unknown and what is asserted, between what is concealed and what is revealed, between fact and conjecture, between the 'real' world and the virtual world, has become a place of endless speculation and potential insanity. It's a poisonous brew which is stirred and simmered and put to the most ugly, destructive, political purpose.

Each time there is a so-called 'terrorist strike', the government rushes in, eager to assign culpability with little or no investigation. The burning of the Sabarmati Express in Godhra, the 13 December attack on the Parliament building, or the massacre of Sikhs by so-called 'terrorists' in Chittisinghpura are only a few, high profile examples. (The so-called terrorists who were later killed by security forces turned out to be innocent villagers. The state government subsequently admitted that fake blood samples were submitted for DNA testing.[1]) In each of these cases, the evidence that eventually surfaced raised very disturbing questions and so was immediately put into cold storage. Take the case of Godhra: as soon as it happened the home minister announced it was an ISI plot. The VHP says it was the work of a Muslim mob throwing petrol bombs.[2] Serious questions remain unanswered. There is endless conjecture. Everybody believes what they want to believe, but the incident is used to cynically and systematically whip up communal frenzy.

The US government used the lies and disinformation generated around the 11 September attacks to invade not just one country, but two—and heaven knows what else is in store.

The Indian government uses the same strategy not with other countries, but against its own people.

Over the last decade, the number of people who have been killed by the police and security forces runs into the tens of thousands. Recently several Bombay policemen spoke openly to the press about how many 'gangsters' they had eliminated on 'orders' from their senior officers.[3] Andhra Pradesh chalks up an average of about 200 'extremists' in 'encounter' deaths a year.[4] In Kashmir in a situation that almost amounts to war, an estimated 80,000 people have been killed since

1989. Thousands have simply 'disappeared'.[5]
According to the records of the Association of
Parents of Disappeared People (APDP) in
Kashmir more than 3000 people have been killed
in 2003, of which 463 were soldiers.[6] Since the
Mufti Mohammed Sayeed government came to
power in October 2002 on the promise of
bringing a 'healing touch', the APDP says there
have been fifty-four custodial deaths.[7] In this age
of hyper-nationalism, as long as the people who
are killed are labelled gangsters, terrorists,
insurgents or extremists, their killers can strut
around as crusaders in the national interest, and
are answerable to no one. Even if it were true
(which it most certainly isn't) that every person
who has been killed was in fact a gangster,
terrorist, insurgent or extremist—it only tells us
there is something terribly wrong with a society
that drives so many people to take such desperate
measures.

The Indian State's proclivity to harass and
terrorize people has been institutionalized,
consecrated, by the enactment of the Prevention
of Terrorism Act (POTA). It has been
promulgated in ten states. A cursory reading of
POTA will tell you that it is draconian and

ubiquitous. It's a versatile, hold-all law that could apply to anyone—from an Al-Qaeda operative caught with a cache of explosives to an Adivasi playing his flute under a neem tree, to you or me. The genius of POTA is that it can be anything the government wants it to be. We live on the sufferance of those who govern us. In Tamil Nadu it has been used to stifle criticism of the state government.[8] In Jharkhand 3200 people, mostly poor Adivasis accused of being Maoists have been named in FIRs under POTA.[9] In eastern Uttar Pradesh the Act is used to clamp down on those who dare to protest about the alienation of their land and livelihood rights.[10] In Gujarat and Mumbai it is used almost exclusively against Muslims.[11] In Gujarat after the 2002 state-assisted pogrom in which an estimated 2000 Muslims were killed and 150,000 driven from their homes, 287 people have been acccused under POTA. Of these, 286 are *Muslims* and one is a Sikh![12] POTA allows confessions extracted in police custody to be admitted as judicial evidence. In effect, under the POTA regime, police torture tends to replace police investigation. It's quicker, cheaper and ensures results. Talk of cutting back on public spending.

Last month I was a member of a peoples' tribunal on POTA. Over a period of two days we listened to harrowing testimonies of what goes on in our wonderful democracy. Let me assure you that in our police stations it's everything: from people being forced to drink urine, to being stripped, humiliated, given electric shocks, burned with cigarette butts, having iron rods put up their anuses, to being beaten and kicked to death.

Across the country hundreds of people, including some very young children charged under POTA have been imprisoned and are being held without bail, awaiting trial in special POTA courts that are not open to public scrutiny. A majority of those booked under POTA are guilty of one of two crimes. Either they're poor—for the most part Dalits and Adivasis. Or they're Muslims. POTA inverts the accepted dictum of criminal law—that a person is innocent until proven guilty. Under POTA you cannot get bail unless you can prove you are innocent—of a crime that you have not been formally charged with. Essentially, you have to prove you're innocent even if you're unaware of the crime you are supposed to have committed. And that applies to all of us. Technically, we are a nation waiting to be accused.

It would be naïve to imagine that POTA is being 'misused'. On the contrary. It is being used for precisely the reasons it was enacted. Of course if the recommendations of the Malimath Committee are implemented, POTA will soon become redundant. The Malimath Committee recommends that in certain respects normal criminal law be brought in line with the provisions of POTA.[13] There'll be no more criminals then. Only terrorists. It's kind of neat.

Today in Jammu and Kashmir and many Northeastern states the Armed Forces Special Powers Act allows not just officers but even junior commissioned officers and non-commissioned officers of the army to use force on (and even kill) any person on suspicion of disturbing public order or carrying a weapon.[14] On *suspicion* of! Nobody who lives in India can harbour any illusions about what that leads to. The documentation of instances of torture, disappearances, custodial deaths, rape and gang-rape (by security forces) is enough to make your blood run cold. The fact that despite all this India retains its reputation as a legitimate democracy in the international community and amongst its own middle class is a triumph.

The Armed Forces Special Powers Act is a harsher version of the Ordinance that Lord Linlithgow passed in 1942 to handle the Quit India Movement. In 1958 it was clamped on parts of Manipur which were declared 'disturbed areas'. In 1965 the whole of Mizoram, then still part of Assam, was declared 'disturbed'. In 1972 the Act was extended to Tripura. By 1980 the whole of Manipur had been declared 'disturbed'.[15] What more evidence does anybody need to realize that repressive measures are counter-productive and only exacerbate the problem?

Juxtaposed against this unseemly eagerness to repress and eliminate people, is the Indian State's barely hidden reluctance to investigate and bring to trial cases in which there is plenty of evidence: the massacre of 3000 Sikhs in Delhi in 1984; the massacre of Muslims in Bombay in 1993 and in Gujarat in 2002 (not one conviction to date!); the murder a few years ago of Chandrashekhar, former president of the JNU students union; the murder twelve years ago of Shankar Guha Nyogi of the Chattisgarh Mukti Morcha are just a few examples.[16] Eyewitness accounts and masses of incriminating evidence are not enough when all of the State machinery is stacked against you.

Meanwhile, economists cheering from the pages of corporate newspapers inform us that the GDP Growth Rate is phenomenal, unprecedented. Shops are overflowing with consumer goods. Government storehouses are overflowing with foodgrain. Outside this circle of light, farmers steeped in debt are committing suicide in their hundreds. Reports of starvation and malnutrition come in from across the country. Yet the government allowed 63 million tonnes of grain to rot in its granaries.[17] Twelve million tonnes were exported and sold at a subsidized price the Indian government was not willing to offer the Indian poor.[18] Utsa Patnaik, the well-known agricultural economist, has calculated foodgrain availability and foodgrain absorption in India for nearly a century, based on official statistics. She calculates that in the period between the early nineties and 2001, foodgrain absorption has dropped to levels lower than during the World War II years, including during the Bengal famine in which three million people died of starvation.[19] As we know from the work of Professor Amartya Sen, democracies don't take kindly to starvation deaths. They attract too much adverse publicity from the 'free press'.[20]

So dangerous levels of malnutrition and permanent hunger are the preferred model these days. Forty-seven per cent of India's children below three suffer from malnutrition, 46 per cent are stunted.[21] Utsa Patnaik's study reveals that about 40 per cent of the rural population in India has the same foodgrain absorption level as sub-Saharan Africa.[22] Today, an average rural family eats about 100 kg less food in a year than it did in the early 1990s.[23] The last five years have seen the most violent increase in rural–urban income inequalities since independence.

But in urban India, wherever you go, shops, restaurants, railway stations, airports, gymnasiums, hospitals, you have TV monitors in which election promises have already come true. India's Shining, Feeling Good. You only have to close your ears to the sickening crunch of the policeman's boot on someone's ribs, you only have to raise your eyes from the squalor, the slums, the ragged broken people on the streets and seek a friendly TV monitor and you will be in that other beautiful world. The singing–dancing world of Bollywood's permanent pelvic thrusts, of permanently privileged, permanently happy Indians waving the tri-colour and Feeling

Good. It's becoming harder and harder to tell which one's the real world and which one's virtual. Laws like POTA are like buttons on a TV. You can use it to switch off the poor, the troublesome, the unwanted.

There is a new kind of secessionist movement taking place in India. Shall we call it New Secessionism? It's an inversion of Old Secessionism. It's when people who are actually part of a whole different economy, a whole different country, a whole different *planet*, pretend they're part of this one. It is the kind of secession in which a relatively small section of people become immensely wealthy by appropriating everything—land, rivers, water, freedom, security, dignity, fundamental rights including the right to protest—from a large group of people. It's a vertical secession, not a horizontal, territorial one. It's the real structural adjustment—the kind that separates India Shining from India. India Pvt Ltd from India the Public Enterprise.

It's the kind of secession in which public infrastructure, productive public assets—water, electricity, transport, telecommunications, health services, education, natural resources—assets that the Indian State is supposed to hold in trust for the people it represents, assets that have been built and maintained with public money over decades—are sold by the State to private corporations. In India 70 per cent of the population—seven hundred million people—live in rural areas.[24] Their livelihoods depend on access to natural resources. To snatch these away and sell them as stock to private companies is beginning to result in dispossession and impoverishment on a barbaric scale.

India Pvt Ltd is on its way to being owned by a few corporations and major multinationals. The CEOs of these companies will control this country, its infrastructure and its resources, its media and its journalists, but will owe nothing to its people. They are completely unaccountable—legally, socially, morally, politically. Those who say that in India a few of these CEOs are more powerful than the prime minister know exactly what they're talking about.

Quite apart from the economic implications of all this, even if it were all that it is cracked up to be (which it isn't)—miraculous, efficient, amazing, etc.—is the *politics* of it acceptable to us? If the Indian State chooses to mortgage its responsibilities to a handful of corporations, does it mean that this theatre of electoral democracy that is unfolding around us right now in all its shrillness is entirely meaningless? Or does it still have a role to play?

The Free Market (which is actually far from free) needs the State and needs it badly. As the disparity between the rich and poor grows, in poor countries States have their work cut out for them. Corporations on the prowl for 'sweetheart deals' that yield enormous profits cannot push through those deals and administer those projects in developing countries without the active connivance of State machinery. Today corporate globalization needs an international confederation of loyal, corrupt, preferably authoritarian governments in poorer countries, to push through unpopular reforms and quell the mutinies. It's called 'creating a good investment climate'.

When we vote in these elections we will be voting to choose which political party we would like to invest the coercive, repressive powers of the State in.

Right now in India we have to negotiate the dangerous cross-currents of neoliberal capitalism and communal neo-fascism. While the word capitalism hasn't completely lost its sheen yet, using the word fascism often causes offence. So we must ask ourselves, are we using the word loosely? Are we exaggerating our situation? Does what we are experiencing on a daily basis qualify as fascism?

When a government more or less openly supports a pogrom against members of a minority community in which upto 2000 people are brutally killed, is it fascism? When women of that community are publicly raped and burned alive, is it fascism? When authorities collude to see to it that nobody is punished for these crimes, is it fascism? When 150,000 people are driven from their homes, ghettoized and economically and socially boycotted, is it fascism? When the cultural guild that runs hate camps across the country commands the respect and admiration of the prime minister, the home minister, the law minister, the disinvestment minister, is it fascism? When painters, writers, scholars and filmmakers who protest are abused, threatened and have their work burned, banned and destroyed, is it fascism? When a government issues an edict requiring the arbitrary alteration of school history textbooks, is it fascism? When mobs attack and burn archives of ancient historical documents, when every minor politician masquerades as a professional medieval historian and archaeologist, when painstaking scholarship is rubbished using baseless populist assertion, is it fascism? When murder, rape, arson and mob justice are condoned by the party in power and its stable of stock intellectuals as an appropriate response to a real or perceived historical wrong committed centuries ago, is it fascism? When the middle class and the well-heeled pause a moment, tut-tut and then go on with their lives, is it fascism? When the prime minister who presides over all of this is hailed as a statesman and visionary, are we not laying the foundations for full-blown fascism?

That the history of oppressed and vanquished people remains for the large part unchronicled is a truism that does not apply only to Savarna Hindus. If the politics of avenging historical wrong is our chosen path, then surely the Dalits and Adivasis of India have the right to murder, arson and wanton destruction?

In Russia they say the past is unpredictable. In India, from our recent experience with school history textbooks, we know how true that is. Now all 'pseudo-secularists' have been reduced to hoping that archaeologists digging under the Babri Masjid wouldn't find the ruins of a Ram temple. But even if it were true that there is a Hindu temple under every mosque in India, what was under the temple? Perhaps another Hindu temple to another god. Perhaps a Buddhist stupa. Most likely an Adivasi shrine. History didn't begin with Savarna Hinduism, did it? How deep shall we dig? How much should we overturn? And why is it that while Muslims who are socially, culturally and economically an unalienable part of India are called outsiders and invaders and cruelly targeted, the government is busy signing corporate deals and contracts for development aid with a government who colonized us for centuries? Between 1876 and 1892, during the great famines, millions of Indians died of starvation while the British government continued to export food and raw materials to England. Historical records put the figure between 12 and 29 million people.[25] That should figure somewhere in the politics of revenge, should it not? Or is vengeance only fun when its victims are vulnerable and easy to target?

Successful fascism takes hard work. And so does 'creating a good investment climate'. Do the two work well together? Historically, corporations have not been shy of fascists. Corporations like Siemens, I.G. Farben, Bayer, IBM, and Ford did business with the Nazis.[26] We have the more recent example of our own Confederation of Indian Industry (CII) abasing itself to the Gujarat government after the pogrom in 2002.[27] As long as our markets are open, a little homegrown fascism won't come in the way of a good business deal.

It's interesting that just around the time Manmohan Singh, the then finance minister, was preparing India's markets for neoliberalism, L.K. Advani was making his first rath yatra, fuelling communal passion and preparing us for neo-fascism. In December 1992, rampaging mobs destroyed the Babri Masjid. In 1993, the Congress government of Maharashtra signed a power-purchase agreement with Enron. It was the first private power project in India. The Enron contract, disastrous as it has turned out, kick-started the era of privatization in India. Now, as the Congress whines from the sidelines, the BJP has wrested the baton from its hands. The government is conducting an extraordinary dual orchestra. While one arm is busy selling the nation's assets off in chunks, the other, to divert attention, is arranging a baying, howling, deranged chorus of cultural nationalism. The inexorable ruthlessness of one process feeds directly into the insanity of the other.

Economically too, the dual orchestra is a viable model. Part of the enormous profits generated by the process of indiscriminate privatization (and the accruals of 'India Shining') goes into financing Hindutva's vast army—the RSS, the VHP, the Bajrang Dal, and the myriad other charities and trusts which run schools, hospitals and social services. Between them they have tens of thousands of shakhas across the country. The hatred they preach, combined with the unmanageable frustration generated by the relentless impoverishment and dispossession of the corporate globalization project, fuels the violence of poor on poor—the perfect smokescreen to keep the structures of power intact and unchallenged.

However, directing peoples' frustrations into violence is not always enough. In order to 'create a good investment climate' the State often needs to intervene directly.

In recent years the police has repeatedly opened

fire on unarmed people, mostly Adivasis, at peaceful demonstrations. In Nagarnar, Jharkhand; in Mehndi Kheda, Madhya Pradesh; in Umergaon, Gujarat; in Rayagara and Chilika, Orissa; in Muthanga, Kerala; people have been killed.[28]

When it comes to the poor, and in particular Dalit and Adivasi communities, they get killed for encroaching on forest land (Muthanga), as well as when they're trying to protect forest land from dams, mining operations, steel plants (Koel Karo, Nagarnar). The repression goes on and on— Jambudweep, Kashipur, Maikanj.

In almost every instance of police firing, those who have been fired upon are immediately called militants (PWG, MCC, ISI, LTTE).

When victims refuse to be victims, they are called terrorists and are dealt with as such. POTA is the broad-spectrum antibiotic for the disease of dissent. There are other, more specific steps that are being taken—court judgements that in effect curtail free speech, the right to strike, the right to life and livelihood. The exits are being sealed. This year 181 countries voted in the UN for increased protection of human rights in the era of the War on Terror. Even the US voted in favour of it. India abstained.[29] The stage is being set for a full-scale assault on human rights.

So how can ordinary people counter the assault of an increasingly violent state?

The space for non-violent civil disobedience has atrophied. After struggling for several years, several non-violent peoples' resistance movements have come up against a wall and feel, quite rightly, they have to now change direction. Views about what that direction should be are deeply polarized. There are some who believe that an armed struggle is the only avenue left. Leaving aside Kashmir and the Northeast, huge swathes of territory, whole districts in Jharkhand, Bihar, Uttar Pradesh and Madhya Pradesh are controlled by those who hold that view. Others, increasingly, are beginning to feel they must participate in electoral politics—enter the system, negotiate from within. (Similar, is it not, to the choices people faced in Kashmir?) The thing to remember is that while their methods differ radically, both sides share the belief that—to put it crudely—enough is enough. *Ya Basta.*

There is no debate taking place in India that is more crucial than this one. Its outcome will, for better or for worse, change the quality of life in this country. For everyone. Rich, poor, rural, urban.

Armed struggle provokes a massive escalation of violence from the State. We have seen the morass it has led to in Kashmir and across the Northeast.

So then, should we do what our prime minister suggests we do? Renounce dissent and enter the fray of electoral politics? Join the roadshow? Participate in the shrill exchange of meaningless insults which serve only to hide what is otherwise an almost absolute consensus? Let's not forget that on every major issue—nuclear bombs, Big Dams, the Babri Masjid controversy, and privatization—the Congress sowed the seeds and the BJP swept in to reap the hideous harvest.

This does not mean that the Parliament is of no consequence and elections should be ignored. Of course there is a difference between an overtly communal party with fascist leanings and an opportunistically communal party. Of course there is a difference between a politics that openly, proudly preaches hatred and a politics that slyly pits people against each other.

And of course we know that the legacy of one has led us to the horror of the other. Between them they have eroded any real choice that parliamentary democracy is supposed to provide. The frenzy, the fair-ground atmosphere created around elections takes centre stage in the media because everybody is secure in the knowledge that regardless of who wins, the status quo will essentially remain unchallenged. (After the impassioned speeches in Parliament, repealing POTA doesn't seem to be a priority in any party's election campaign. They all know they need it, in one form or another.) Whatever they say during elections or when they're in the opposition, no government at the state or centre, no political party right/left/centre/sideways has managed to stay the hand of neo-liberalism. There will be no radical change from 'within'.

Personally, I don't believe that entering the electoral fray is a path to alternative politics. Not because of that middle-class squeamishness— 'politics is dirty' or 'all politicians are corrupt'— but because I believe that strategically battles must be waged from positions of strength, not weakness.

The targets of the dual assault of communal fascism and neoliberalism are the poor and the minority communities (who, as time goes by, are gradually being impoverished). As neoliberalism drives its wedge between the rich and the poor, between India Shining and India, it becomes increasingly absurd for any mainstream political party to pretend to represent the interests of both the rich and the poor, because the interests of one can only be represented at the *cost* of the other. My 'interests' as a wealthy Indian (were I to pursue them) would hardly coincide with the interests of a poor farmer in Andhra Pradesh.

A political party that represents the poor will be a poor party. A party with very meagre funds. Today it isn't possible to fight an election without funds. Putting a couple of well-known social activists into Parliament is interesting, but not really politically meaningful. Not a process worth channelizing all our energies into. Individual charisma, personality politics, cannot effect radical change.

However, being poor is not the same as being weak. The strength of the poor is not indoors in office buildings and courtrooms. It's outdoors, in the fields, the mountains, the river valleys, the city streets and university campuses of this country. That's where negotiations must be held. That's where the battle must be waged.

Right now those spaces have been ceded to the
Hindu Right. Whatever anyone might think of
their politics, it cannot be denied that they're out
there, working extremely hard. As the State
abrogates its responsibilities and withdraws funds
from health, education and essential public
services, the foot soldiers of the Sangh Parivar
have moved in. Alongside their tens of thousands
of shakhas disseminating deadly propaganda, they
run schools, hospitals, clinics, ambulance
services, disaster management cells. They
understand powerlessness. They also understand
that people, and particularly powerless people,
have needs and desires that are not only practical,
humdrum day-to-day needs, but emotional,
spiritual, recreational. They have fashioned a
hideous crucible into which the anger, the
frustration, the indignity of daily life, and dreams
of a different future can be decanted and directed
to deadly purpose. Meanwhile the traditional,
mainstream Left, still dreams of 'seizing power',
but remains strangely unbending, unwilling to
address the times. It has laid siege to itself and
retreated into an inaccessible intellectual space,
where ancient arguments are proffered in an
archaic language that few can understand.

The only ones who present some semblance of a challenge to the onslaught of the Sangh Parivar are the grass-roots resistance movements scattered across the country, fighting the dispossession and violation of fundamental rights caused by our current model of 'development'. Most of these movements are isolated and (despite the relentless accusation that they are 'foreign-funded foreign agents') they work with almost no money and no resources at all. They're magnificent firefighters, they have their backs to the wall. But they *do* have their ears to the ground. They *are* in touch with grim reality. If they got together, if they were supported and strengthened, they could grow into a force to reckon with. Their battle, when it is fought, will have to be an idealistic one—not a rigidly ideological one.

At a time when opportunism is everything, when hope seems lost, when everything boils down to a cynical business deal, we must find the courage to dream. To reclaim romance. The romance of believing in justice, in freedom and in dignity. For everybody. We have to make common cause, and to do this we need to understand how this big old machine works—who it works for and who it works against. Who pays, who profits.

Many non-violent resistance movements fighting isolated, single-issue battles across the country have realized that their kind of special interest politics which had its time and place, is no longer enough. That they feel cornered and ineffectual is not good enough reason to abandon non-violent resistance as a strategy. It is, however, good enough reason to do some serious introspection. We need vision. We need to make sure that those of us who say we want to reclaim democracy are egalitarian and democratic in our own methods of functioning. If our struggle is to be an idealistic one, we cannot really make caveats for the internal injustices that we perpetrate on one another, on women, on children. For example, those fighting communalism cannot turn a blind eye to economic injustices. Those fighting dams or development projects cannot elide issues of communalism or caste politics in their spheres of influence—*even at the cost of short-term success in their immediate campaigns*. If opportunism and expediency come at the cost of our beliefs, then there is nothing to separate us from mainstream politicians. If it is justice that we want, it must be justice and equal rights for all—not only for special interest groups with special interest prejudices. That is non-negotiable.

We have allowed non-violent resistance to atrophy into feel-good political theatre, which at its most successful is a photo opportunity for the media, and at its least successful, simply ignored.

We need to look up and urgently discuss strategies of resistance, wage real battles and inflict real damage. We must remember that the Dandi March was not just fine political theatre. It was a strike at the economic underpinning of the British Empire.

We need to re-define the meaning of politics. The 'NGO'ization of civil society initiatives is taking us in exactly the opposite direction. It's de-politicizing us. Making us dependant on aid and handouts. We need to re-imagine the meaning of civil disobedience.

Perhaps we need an elected shadow Parliament *outside* the Lok Sabha, without whose support and affirmation Parliament cannot easily function. A shadow Parliament that keeps up an underground drumbeat, that shares intelligence and information (all of which is increasingly unavailable in the mainstream media). Fearlessly, but *non-violently* we must disable the working parts of this machine that is consuming us.

We're running out of time. Even as we speak the circle of violence is closing in. Either way, change will come. It could be bloody, or it could be beautiful. It depends on us.

April 2004

the road to harsud

Villages die by night. Quietly. Towns die by day, shrieking as they go.

Since independence, Big Dams have displaced more than thirty-five million people in India alone.[1] What is it about our understanding of nationhood that allows governments to crush their own people with such impunity? What is it about our understanding of 'progress' and 'national interest' that allows (applauds) the violation of human rights on a scale so vast that it takes on the texture of everyday life and is rendered virtually invisible?

But every now and then something happens to make the invisible visible, the incomprehensible comprehensible. Harsud is that something. It is literature. Theatre. History.

Harsud is a seven-hundred-year-old town in Madhya Pradesh, slated to be submerged by the reservoir of the Narmada Sagar Dam (sometimes called the Indira Sagar). The same Harsud where in 1989, 30,000 people gathered from across India, held hands in a ring around the town, and vowed to collectively resist destruction masquerading as 'development'.[2] Fifteen years on, while Harsud waits to drown, that dream endures on slender moorings.

The 92 metre high Narmada Sagar (262 metres above Mean Sea Level, which is the way dam heights are usually referred to) is the second highest of the many large dams on the Narmada.[3] The Sardar Sarovar in Gujarat is the highest. The reservoir of the Narmada Sagar is designed to be the largest in India. In order to irrigate 123,000 hectares of land it will submerge 91,000 hectares![4] This includes 41,000 hectares of prime dry deciduous forest, 249 villages and the town of Harsud.[5] According to the Detailed Project Report, 30,000 hectares of the land in the Narmada Sagar command was already irrigated in 1982.[6] Odd math, wouldn't you say? Those who have studied the Narmada Sagar Project—Ashish Kothari of Kalpvriksh, Claude Alvarez and Ramesh Billorey[7]—have warned us for years that of all the high dams on the Narmada, the Narmada Sagar would be the most destructive.

The Indian Institute of Science, Bangalore, estimated that up to 40 per cent of the composite command areas of the Omkareshwar and Narmada Sagar could become severely waterlogged.[8] In a note prepared in 1993 for the Review Committee, the Ministry of Environment and Forests estimated the value of the forest that would be submerged as Rs 33,923 crore.[9] It went on to say that if this cost was included it would make the project unviable. The Wild Life Institute, Dehradun, warned of the loss of a vast reservoir of biodiversity, wildlife and rare medicinal plants. Its 1994 Impact Assessment Report to the Ministry of Environment said: 'The compensation of the combined adversarial impacts of the Narmada Sagar Project and the Omkareshwar Project is neither possible nor is being suggested. These will have to be reckoned as the price for the perceived socio-economic benefit.'[10]

As always, all the warnings were ignored.

Construction of the dam began in 1985. For the first few years it proceeded slowly. It ran into trouble with finance and land acquisition. In 1999, after a fast by activists of the Narmada Bachao Andolan (NBA or Save the Narmada Movement), work was suspended altogether.[11]

On 16 May 2000, in keeping with the central government's push to privatize the power sector and open it to global finance, the government of Madhya Pradesh signed a memorandum of understanding with the government of India[12] to 'affirm the joint commitment of the two parties to the reform of the power sector in Madhya Pradesh'. The 'reforms' involved 'rationalizing' power tariffs and slashing cross-subsidies that would (and did) inevitably lead to political unrest. The same memorandum of understanding promised central government support for the Narmada Sagar and Omkareshwar dams by setting up a joint venture with the National Hydroelectric Power Corporation (NHPC). That contract was signed on the same day, 16 May 2000.[13]

Both agreements will inevitably lead to the pauperization and dispossession of people in the state.

The NHPC boasts that the Narmada Sagar will eventually take care of the 'power needs' of the state. That's not a claim that stands up to scrutiny.

The installed capacity of the Narmada Sagar Dam is 1000 megawatts.[14] Which means what it sounds like—that the power-generating machinery that has been installed is *capable* of producing 1000 megawatts of electricity. What is produced—firm power—depends on actually available water flows. (A fancy Ferrari may be *capable* of doing 300 kilometres per hour. But what would it do without fuel?) The Detailed Project Report puts the actual firm power at 212 megawatts, coming down to 147 megawatts when the irrigation canals become operational.[15]

According to the NHPC's own publicity, the cost of power at the bus bar (factory gate) is Rs 4.59 per unit.[16] Which means at consumer point it will cost about Rs 9. Who can afford that? It's even more expensive than Enron's electricity in Dabhol!

When (if) the project is fully built, the NHPC says it will generate an annual average of 1950 million units of power.[17] For the sake of argument, let's accept that figure. Madhya Pradesh currently loses 44.2 per cent of its electricity—12 billion units a year in transmission and distribution losses.[18] That's the equivalent of six Narmada Sagars. If the Madhya Pradesh government could work towards saving even half its current transmission and distribution losses, it could generate power equal to three Narmada Sagar projects, at a third of the cost, with none of the social and ecological devastation.[19]

But instead, once again we have a Big Dam with questionable benefits and unquestionably cruel, unviable costs.

After the memorandum of understanding for the Narmada Sagar was signed, the NHPC set to work with its customary callousness. The dam wall began to go up at an alarming pace. At a press conference in March 2004 (after the BJP won the assembly elections and Uma Bharati became chief minister of Madhya Pradesh), Yogendra Prasad, chairman and managing director of the NHPC boasted that the project was eight to ten months ahead of schedule.[20] He said that because of better management the costs of the project would be substantially lower. Asked to comment on the objections being raised by the NBA about rehabilitation, he said the objections were irrelevant.

'Better management' it now turns out, is a euphemism for cheating thousands of poor people.

Yogendra Prasad, Digvijay Singh and Uma Bharati are criminally culpable, and in any society in which the powerful are accountable, would find themselves in jail. The fact that the NHPC is a central government body makes the union government culpable too. They have wilfully violated the terms of their own memorandum of understanding, which legally binds them to comply with the principles of the Narmada Water Disputes Tribunal Award (NWDTA).[21] The Award specifies that in no event can submergence precede rehabilitation. (Which is about as self-evident as saying child abuse is a crime.) They have violated the government of Madhya Pradesh's Rehabilitation Policy. They have violated the conditions of environmental and forest clearance. They have violated the terms of several international covenants that India has signed: the Universal Declaration of Human Rights, the International Covenant on Civil Economic and Political Rights and the International Labour Organization Convention. The Supreme Court says that any International Treaty signed by India becomes part of our domestic and municipal law. Not a single family has been resettled according to the NWDTA or the Madhya Pradesh rehabilitation policy.[22]

There is no excuse, no mitigating argument for the horror they have unleashed.

■

The road from Khandwa to Harsud is a toll road. A smooth, new private highway, littered with the carcasses of trucks, motorcycles and cars whose drivers were clearly unused to such luxury. On the outskirts of Harsud you pass row upon row of cruel, corrugated tin sheds. Tin roofs, tin walls, tin doors, tin windows. As blindingly bright on the outside as they are blind dark inside. A sign says *Baad Raahat Kendra* (Flood Relief Centre). It's largely empty except for the bulldozers, jeeps, government officers and police, who stroll around unhurried, full of the indolent arrogance that comes with power. The Flood Relief Centre has been where only a few weeks ago the government college stood.

And then, under the lowering, thundery sky, Harsud . . . like a scene out of a Marquez novel.

The first to greet us was an old buffalo, blind, green-eyed with cataract. Even before we entered the town we heard the announcement repeated over and over again on loudspeakers attached to a roving matador van. 'Please tether your cattle and livestock. Please do not allow them to roam free. The government will make arrangements to transport them.' (Where to?) People with nowhere to go are leaving. They have let loose their livestock onto Harsud's ruined streets. And the government doesn't want drowning cattle on its hands.

Behind the blind buffalo, silhouetted against the sky, the bare bones of a broken town. A town turned inside out, its privacy ravaged, its innards exposed. Personal belongings, beds, cupboards, clothes, photographs, pots and pans lie on the street. In several houses caged parakeets hang from broken beams. An infant swaddled in a sari-crib sways gently, fast asleep in a doorway in a free-standing wall. Leading from nowhere to nowhere. Live electric cables hang down like dangerous aerial roots. The insides of houses lie rudely exposed. It's strange to see how a bleached, colourless town on the outside, was vibrant on the inside, the walls every shade of turquoise, emerald, lavender, fuchsia.

Perched on the concrete frames of wrecked buildings, men, like flightless birds, are hammering, sawing, smoking, talking. If you didn't know what was happening, you could be forgiven for thinking that Harsud was being built, not broken. That it had been hit by an earthquake and its citizens were re-building it. But then, you notice that the old, grand trees, mahua, neem, peepul, jamun, are all still standing. And outside every house you see the order in the chaos. The doorframes stacked together. Iron grills in a separate pile. Tin sheets in another. Broken bricks still flecked with coloured plaster piled up in a heap. Tin boards, shop signs, leaning against lampposts. 'Ambika Jewellers', 'Lovely Beauty Parlour', 'Shantiniketan Dharamshala', 'Blood and Urine Tested Here'. On more than one house there are insanely optimistic signs: *This house is for sale*. Every house, every tree has a code number on it. Only the people are un-coded. The local cartoonist is exhibiting his work on a pile of stones. Every cartoon is about how the government cheated and deceived people. A group of spectators discuss the details of various on-going rackets in town—from tenders for the tin sheets for the tin sheds, to the megaphones on the matador, to the bribes being demanded from parents for School TCs (Transfer Certificates) to a non-existent school in a non-existent rehabilitation site. Parents are distraught and children are delighted because their school building has been torn down. Many children will lose a whole school year. The poorer ones will drop out.

The people of Harsud are razing their town to the ground. Themselves. The very young and the very old sit on heaps of broken brick. The able-bodied are frenetically busy. They're tearing apart their homes, their lives, their past, their stories. They're carting the debris away in trucks and tractors and bullock carts. Harsud is hectic. Like a frontier town during the Gold Rush. The demise of a town is lucrative business. People have arrived from nearby towns. Trucks, tractors, dealers in scrap iron, timber and old plastic, throng the streets, beating down prices, driving hard bargains, mercilessly exploiting distress sales. Migrant workers camp in makeshift hovels on the edge of the town. They are the poorest of the poor. They have come from Jhabua, and the villages around Omkareshwar, displaced by the other Big Dams on the Narmada, the Sardar Sarovar and the Omkareshwar. The better off in Harsud hire them as labour. A severely malnutritioned demolition squad. And so the circle of relentless impoverishment closes in upon itself.

In the midst of the rubble, life goes on. Private things are now public. People are cooking, bathing, chatting, (and yes, crying) in their wall-less homes. Iridescent orange jalebis and gritty pakoras are being deep fried in stoves surrounded by mounds of debris. The barber has a broken mirror on a broken wall. (Perhaps the man he's shaving has a broken heart.) The man who is demolishing the mosque is trying to save the coloured glass. Two men are trying to remove the Shivling from a small shrine without chipping it. There is no method to the demolition. No safety precautions. Just a mad hammering. A house collapses on four labourers. When they are extricated one of them is unconscious and has a steel rod sticking into his temple. But they're only Adivasis. They don't matter. The show must go on.

There is an eerie, brittle numbness to the bustle. It masks the government's ruthlessness and people's despair. Everyone knows that nearby, in the Kalimachak tributary, the water has risen. The bridge on the road to Badkeshwar is already under water.

There are no proper estimates of how many villages will be submerged in the Narmada Sagar Reservoir, when (if) the monsoon comes to the Narmada Valley. The Narmada Control Authority website uses figures from the 1981 Census! In newspaper reports government officials estimate it will submerge more than a hundred villages and Harsud town. Most estimates suggest that this year 30,000 families will be uprooted from their homes. About 5,600 of these families (22,000 people) are from Harsud.[23] Remember, these are 1981 figures.

When the reservoir of the first dam on the Narmada—the Bargi Dam—was filled in 1989, it submerged three times more land than government engineers said it would. One hundred and one villages were slated for submergence, but in the monsoon of 1989, when the sluice gates were finally closed and the reservoir was filled, 162 villages (including some of the government's own resettlement sites) were submerged.[24] There was no rehabilitation. Tens of thousands of people slid into destitution and abject poverty. Today, fifteen years later, irrigation canals have still not been built. So the Bargi Dam irrigates less land than it submerged *and only 6 per cent of the land that its planners claimed it would irrigate.*[25] All indicators suggest that the Narmada Sagar could be an even bigger disaster.

Farmers who usually pray for rain, now trapped between drought and drowning, have grown to dread the monsoon.

Oddly enough, after the 1989 rally, when the anti-dam movement was at its peak, the town of Harsud never became a major site of struggle.

The people chose the option of conventional, mainstream politics, and divided themselves acrimoniously between the Congress Party and the Bharatiya Janata Party (BJP). Like most people, they believed that dams were not intrinsically bad, provided displaced people were resettled. So they didn't oppose the Dam, hoping their political mentors would see that they received just compensation. Villages in the submergence zone did try to organize resistance, but were brutally and easily suppressed. Time and again they appealed to the NBA (located further downstream, fighting against the Sardar Sarovar and Maheshwar Dams) for help. The NBA, absurdly overstretched and under-resourced, did make sporadic interventions, but was not able to expand its zone of influence to the Narmada Sagar.

With no NBA to deal with, bolstered by the Supreme Court's hostile judgements on the Sardar Sarovar and Tehri Dams,[26] the Madhya Pradesh government and its partner the NHPC, have rampaged through the region with a callousness that would shock even a seasoned cynic. The lie of rehabilitation has been punctured once and for all. Planners who peddle it do so for the most

cruel, opportunistic reasons. It gives them cover.
It *sounds* so reasonable

In the absence of organized resistance, the media
in Madhya Pradesh has done a magnificent job.
Local journalists have doggedly exposed the
outrage for what it is. Editors have given the story
the space it deserves. *Sahara Samay* has its OB
Van parked in Harsud. Newspapers and television
channels carry horror stories every day. A
normally anesthetized, unblinking public has
been roused to anger. Every day groups of people
arrive to see for themselves what is happening,
and to express their solidarity. The state
government and the NHPC remain unmoved.
Perhaps a decision has been taken to exacerbate
the tragedy and wait out the storm once and for
all. Perhaps they're gambling on the fickleness of
public memory and the media's need for a crisis
turnover. But a crime of this proportion is not
going to be forgotten so easily. If it goes
unpunished, it cannot but damage India's image
as a benign destination for international finance:
thousands of people, evicted from their homes
with nowhere to go. And its not war. It's *policy*.

Can it really be that 30,000 families have nowhere
to go? Can it really be that a whole town has

nowhere to go? Ministers and government officials assure the press that a whole new township—New Harsud—has been built near Chhanera, 12 kilometres away. On 12 July in his budget presentation, Madhya Pradesh Finance Minister Shri Raghavji announced: 'Rehabilitation of Harsud town which was pending for years has been completed in six months.'[27]

Lies.

New Harsud is nothing but mile upon mile of stony, barren land in the middle of nowhere. A few hundred of the poorest families of Harsud have moved there and live under tarpaulin and tin sheets. (The rest have placed themselves at the mercy of relatives in nearby towns, or are using up their meagre compensation on rented accommodation. In and around Chhanera rents have skyrocketed.) In New Harsud there's no water, no sewage system, no shelter, no school, no hospital. Plots have been marked out like cells in a prison, with mud roads that criss-cross at right angles. They get water from a tanker. Sometimes they don't. There are no toilets and there is not a tree or a bush in sight for them to piss or shit behind. When the wind rises it takes the tin sheets with it. When it rains, the scorpions come out of the wet earth. Most important of all, there's no work in New Harsud. No means of earning a livelihood.

People can't leave their possessions in the open and go off in search of work. So the little money they have been paid, dwindles. Of course cash compensation is only given to the Head of the Family, that is, to men. What a travesty for the thousands of women who are hit hardest by the violence of displacement.

In Chhanera the booze shops are doing brisk business.

When media attention trails away so will the water tankers. People will be left in a stony desert with no option but to flee. Again.

And this is what is being done to people from a town. You don't need to be a rocket scientist to imagine what is happening to the villages.

In circumstances such as these, how does a government get people to not just move, but to humiliate themselves by tearing apart their own lives? With their own hands? In Harsud so far, there has been no bulldozing, no police firing, no coercion. Only cold, brilliant strategy.

The people of Harsud have known for years that their town lay in the submergence zone of the Narmada Sagar Dam. Like all 'oustees' of all dams, they were promised compensation and rehabilitation. There was no sign of either. And now, while people's lives are being devastated, Uma Bharati and Digvijay Singh accuse each other of criminal negligence. Let's look at some basic facts.

In September 2003, just before the assembly elections, the Digvijay Singh government granted the NHPC permission to raise the dam wall to 245 metres. At 10 o'clock in the morning on 18 November 2003, the diversion tunnel was closed and water began to be impounded in the reservoir. Downstream the river dried up, fish died and for days the riverbed was exposed.[28] By mid-December, when Uma Bharati took over as the new CM, the height of the dam was already 238 metres.[29] Eager to partake of some of the 'credit' for the Narmada Sagar, without bothering to check on how rehabilitation was progressing, she allowed the dam height to be increased from 238 to 245 metres.[30] In January 2004 she congratulated the NHPC for its 'achievements'. In April 2004 the NHPC began to install the radial crest gates, which will take the dam to its full height of 262 metres. Six of the twenty gates are in place.[31] The NHPC has announced that the project will be completed by March 2004.[32]

The responsibility of surveying the submergence zone for the purposes of compensation and rehabilitation had been transferred to the NHPC. The responsibility for actual Land Acquisition and Rehabilitation still rests with the government. The NHPC holds 51 per cent of the equity in the project.[33] Between the two 'interested parties,' they're in a hurry to get the job done and keep the costs down.

The first, most deadly sleight of hand involves the computation of compensation. In other words, fiddling with the definition of who counts as Project Affected and who doesn't. The absolute poorest, in the villages are sloughed off at this stage. Essentially those who are landless— fisherpeople, boatpeople, sand quarriers, daily wage workers and those who are considered 'encroachers' do not qualify as Project Affected and are done away with. In some cases whole villages have fallen prey to this process. For example, the 1982 Detailed Project Report says that 255 villages will be submerged by the reservoir.[34] Somewhere along the way six of those villages were taken off the list and the number came down to 249. The Narmada Control Authority now says only 211 villages will be eligible for compensation. Thirty-eight villages have been designated as 'encroachers' and are not eligible for compensation.

The next lethal blow is when rates of compensation are fixed. The fortunate people who actually qualify as Project Affected, asked, quite reasonably, to be compensated for their land according to the prevailing land prices in the villages in the command area of the dam. They received almost exactly half of that: Rs 40,000 an acre for unirrigated land, Rs 60,000 for irrigated land. The market price for irrigated land is over Rs 100,000. As a result, farmers who had 10 acres of land will barely manage 5. Small farmers with a couple of acres, become landless labourers. Rich become poor. Poor become destitute. It's called Better Management.

And it gets worse.

Patwaris and revenue inspectors descended on Harsud and the 'notified' villages like a terminator virus. They held thousands of people's futures in their grasping fists. Every single person we spoke to, every farmer, every labourer, every villager, every citizen of Harsud, rich and poor, man and woman, told the same story.

The technique they described is as diabolical as it is simple. Basically the patwaris and revenue inspectors undervalued everything. Irrigated land was entered as unirrigated. Pucca houses were shown as kuccha. A 5-acre farm became 4 acres. And so on. This was done indiscriminately, to rich and poor alike. People had the option of challenging the award in a civil court (and spending more on lawyers' fees than the compensation they hoped to receive). The other option was to bribe the patwaris and revenue inspectors. The poor simply did not have the liquid cash to pay the going rate—'*Hum feelgood nahin kar paaye.*' So they fell out of the basket. Those who managed to make the Patwaris 'feelgood', managed to get even their cattle sheds entered as palatial homes and received handsome compensation (in lakhs) for them. Of course, much of this made its way back to the officials as more 'feelgood'.

Even this unfair, absurd compensation that was promised has not been fully disbursed. So in the villages and in Harsud, thousands of people continued to cling to their homes.

On 14 May Uma Bharati announced a grant of a minimum of Rs 25,000[35] (or 10 per cent of the allotted compensation going up to a maximum of five lakhs) to people who demolished their houses and moved out of town before 30 June. Still people didn't move.

On 8 June two representatives of the Sangharsh Morcha filed a petition in the Jabalpur high court asking that water not be impounded in the reservoir until proper compensation is paid and rehabilitation completed. Annexed to their petition were carefully compiled documents that clearly showed the extent of criminal malfeasance that took place in Harsud. The townspeople's hopes were pinned on the court's response. At the first hearing government lawyers cautioned the judge that there was nothing anybody could do about the fact that the water was rising and the situation could turn dangerous. It cautioned the judge that if the court intervened, it could have a disaster on its hands.

The state government knew that if it could break Harsud, the despair and resignation would spread to the villages. To break Harsud once and for all, to ensure that people never came back even if the monsoon failed and the town was not fully submerged, meant demolishing the town *physically*. In order to create panic they simulated a flood, by releasing water from the Bargi reservoir upstream. On 23 June the water in the Kalimachak tributary rose by a metre and a half. Still people didn't move. On 27 June more than 300 police and paramilitary forces staged a flag march through the terrified town. Companies of mounted police, the Rapid Action Force, the paramilitary, and armed constabulary paraded through the streets.

On 29 June the high court issued a tepid, cautious interim order.[36] Morale in Harsud sank. Still the deadline of 30 June passed without event. On the morning of 1 July loudspeakers mounted on vehicles criss-crossed the town announcing that the Rs 25,000 grant would only be given to those who demolished their homes that very night.

Harsud broke.

All night people smashed away at their own homes with crowbars, hammers, iron rods . . . By morning it looked like a suburb of modern-day Baghdad.

The panic spread to the villages. Away from the

gaze of the media, in place of the lure of Rs 25,000, the government resorted to good old-fashioned repression. In fact repression in the villages had begun a while ago. In village after village—Amba Khaal, Bhawarli, Jetpur—people told us in precise, heartbreaking detail how they had been cheated by patwaris and revenue inspectors. Fearing what lay in store for them, many had sent their children and their stocks of grain away to relatives. Families who had lived together for generations did not know when they would ever see each other again. A whole fragile economy had begun to unravel. People described how a posse of policemen would arrive in a village, dismantle handpumps and cut electricity connections.[37] Those who dared to resist were beaten. (This was the same technique the Digvijay Singh government used two years ago in the submergence zone of the Maan Dam.) In each of the villages we visited, the schools had either been demolished or occupied by the police. In Amba Khaal small children studied in the shade of a peepul tree while the police lay about in their classrooms.

As we travelled further inland towards the reservoir, the road got worse and eventually disappeared. At Malud there was a boat tethered to the police assistance booth overlooking a rocky outcrop. The policeman said he was waiting for the flood. Beyond Malud we passed ghost villages reduced to rubble. A boy with two goats told us about twenty monkeys that were marooned on a clump of trees surrounded by water. We passed Gannaur, the last village where a lone man was loading the last few bricks of his home onto a tractor. Beyond Gannaur, the land slopes down towards the edge of the reservoir.

As we approached the water it began to rain. It was quiet except for the alarm calls of frightened lapwings. In my mind, the man loading his tractor in the distance was Noah building his ark, waiting for the Deluge. The sound of the water lapping against the shore was full of menace. The violence of what we had seen and heard, robbed beautiful things of their beauty. A pair of dragonflies mated in the air. I caught myself wondering if it was rape. There was a line of froth that marked the level up to which the water had risen before it receded in the government-induced Bargi flood. There was a small child's shoe in it.

On our way back we took another route.

We drove down a red gravel road built by the

Forest Department and travelled deep into the forest. We arrived at a village that looked as though it had been evacuated some years ago. Broken houses had been reclaimed by trees and creepers. A herd of feral cows grazed in the ruins.

There was no one around to tell us the name of the village—this village that must have been loved and lived in. That must *still* be loved. And dreamt about.

As we turned to go we saw a man walking towards us. His name was Baalak Ram. He was a Banjara. He told us the name of the village—Jamunia. It had been uprooted two years ago. My friend Chittaroopa from the NBA was visibly disturbed when she heard this. She remembered tractor loads of people from Jamunia who came to support NBA's rallies against the Maheshwar Dam. And now they were gone. Swallowed by their own, more terrible dam.

Baalak Ram was a labourer who had been sent back by the land-owning Patels of Jamunia to try and round up their cows. But the cows wouldn't go. 'They pay me, but it's not easy, the cattle have become wild. They refuse to go. They have grass and water here, the river and the forest are close by. Why should they go?'

He told us how cows and dogs had returned to Jamunia from distant places. He seemed happy, alone in the forest with the almost-wild cows. We asked him if he ever felt lonely. 'This is my village,' he said. And then, after a moment 'Only sometimes . . . when I think where has everyone gone? Are they all dead?'

A tiny boy arrived. Dark. Glowing. He attached himself to Baalak Ram's legs. He clutched a bunch of beautiful wildflowers. We asked him who they were for.

'*Khubsurat the.*' They *were* beautiful. As though Beautiful was someone who had died recently.

At a meeting in Harsud, desperate people discussed the possibility of filing a Public Interest Litigation (PIL) in the Supreme Court. I realized with some sadness that I no longer associate that institution with the idea of Justice. Power, yes. Strategy, maybe. But Justice? Phrases from Justices A.S Anand and B.N Kirpal's majority judgement on the Sardar Sarovar[38] flashed through my mind:

> Public Interest Litigation should not be allowed to degenerate into becoming

Publicity Interest Litigation or Private Inquisitiveness Litigation.

Though these villages comprise a significant population of tribals and people of weaker sections, but majority will not be a victim of displacement. Instead, they will gain from shifting.

The displacement of tribals and other persons would not per se result in the violation of their fundamental or other rights.

Thus were the thousands displaced by the Sardar Sarovar Dam doomed to destitution.

I thought of how the same Justice B.N. Kirpal, one day before he retired as India's chief justice, while he was the sitting judge on another, entirely unconnected case, ordered the government of India to begin work on the river linking project![39] In an affidavit submitted in response, the central government said the project would take forty-three years to complete and would cost Rs 560,000 crore. Justice Kirpal didn't quibble about the cost, only asked that the project be completed in ten years! And so, a project of Stalinist proportions, potentially more destructive than all of India's dams put together, was given the Supreme Court's stamp of approval. Justice Kirpal subsequently clarified that it was not an order— just a 'suggestion'. Meanwhile, the government began to treat it like a Supreme Court order. How could the ecology of a whole sub-continent be irreversibly altered in such an arbitrary way? Who has the jurisdiction to do that? How can a country that calls itself a democracy function like this?

(Today Justice Kirpal heads the Indian Environmental Council of Hindustan Coca-Cola Beverage Pvt. Ltd. Earlier this year, he publicly criticized a Kerala High Court order which refused to grant a stay on the Kerala government's directive restraining Coke from mining groundwater in Plachimada.[40] A contempt of court case has been filed against him.)

So. Should the people of Harsud approach the courts? It's not an easy question to answer.

What should they ask for? What could they hope to achieve?

The concrete section of the Narmada Sagar Dam is 245 metres high. The radial crest gates take the dam wall up to its full height of 262.13 metres

According to the Narmada Control Authority's own figures, a huge part of the submergence will take place between 245 metres and 262 metres.[41]

Can we look to the courts to explore the possibility of blasting open the sluice-gates (as was done in the case of the Maan Dam), keeping them open until the rehabilitation process is complete according to the NWDTA stipulations?

Can we look to the courts to order the re-opening of the diversion tunnel so that water is not impounded in the reservoir this monsoon?

Can we look to the courts to arraign every politician, bureaucrat, and NHPC official that has been involved in criminal malfeasance?

Can we look to the courts to order the removal of the four existing gates (and stay the installation of the rest) until every displaced family has been rehabilitated?

Will the courts consider these options or will they give us more of the same? A pseudo-rap on the government's knuckles for shoddy rehabilitation (Bad boy Fido! Naughty dog!) and a stamp of approval for project upon project that violate the fundamental rights of fellow human beings? What should we expect? The charade of yet another retired judge setting up yet another Grievance Redressal Authority to address the woes of yet another 100,000 people?

If so, the question must be asked. Which institution in our wonderful democracy remains accountable to people and not to power? What are people supposed to do? Are they on their own now? Have they fallen through the grid?

We left Harsud at dusk. On the way we stopped at the *Baad Raahat Kendra*. There were very few people around, although a couple of families had moved into the tin sheds. One of the tin doors had a sticker that said Export Quality. It was hard to make out the man sitting on the floor in the dark. He said his name was Kallu Driver. I'm glad I met him. He was sitting on the floor. He had unstrapped his wooden leg. He used to be a driver, fifteen years ago he lost his leg in an accident. He lived alone in Harsud. He had been given a check for Rs 25,000 in exchange for demolishing his mud hut. His pregnant daughter had come from her husband's village to help him move. He had been to Chhanera three times to try and cash his cheque. He ran out of money for bus fare. The fourth time he walked. The bank sent him away and asked him to come back after three days. He showed us how his wooden leg had chipped and splintered. He said every night officials threatened him and tried to make him move to New Harsud. They said that the *Baad Raahat Kendra* was for emergencies only. Kallu was incoherent with rage. 'What will I do in that desert?' he said. 'How will I live? There's nothing there.' A crowd gathered at the door. His anger fuelled theirs.

Kallu Driver does not need to read news reports or court affidavits or sly editorials (or fly-by-night Ph.D's pretending to be on the inside-track of people's movements) to know which side he's on. Each time anybody mentioned government officials, or Digvijay Singh or Uma Bharati, he cursed. He made no gender distinctions.

Maaderchod. He said. Motherfuckers.

He is not aware of feminist objections to derogatory references to women's bodies.

The World Bank however, disagrees with Kallu Driver. It has singled the NHPC out for high praise. In December 2003 a team of senior World Bank officers visited the Narmada Sagar Project. In its Draft Country Assistance Strategy (CAS),[42] the Bank said: 'While for many years the hydropower business had a poor reputation, some major actors (including the NHPC) have started to improve their environmental and social practices.'

Interestingly, this is the third time in six months that the Bank has singled the NHPC out for praise since January 2004. Why? Read the next sentence in the CAS[43]: 'Given this . . . the Bank will work with the government of India and its PSUs to seek possible new areas of support on a modest scale for hydropower development.'

Then again, on 15 February 2004, in a report that praises the NHPC for 'completing projects like the Narmada Sagar within time and within budget', the *Economic Times* quoted a World Bank official saying, 'The NHPC is moving towards global corporate performance standards and is improving its financial performance. We have done due diligence on the corporation and are impressed by the performance.'

What makes the World Bank so very solicitous?

Power and Water 'Reforms' in developing countries are the twenty-first century's version of the Great Game. All the usual suspects, beginning of course, with the World Bank, the big private banks and multinational corporations are cruising around, looking for sweetheart deals. But overt privatization has run into bad weather. It has been widely discredited and is now looking for ways in which to re-incarnate itself in a new avatar. From overt invasion to covert insurgency.

Over the last few years the reputation of Big Dams (both public and private) has been badly mauled. The World Bank was publicly humiliated and forced to withdraw from the Sardar Sarovar Project. But now, encouraged by the Supreme Court judgements on the Sardar Sarovar and Tehri Dams, it's back on the block, and is looking for a back-door entry into the industry. Who better to cozy up to than the biggest player in India's hydropower industry—the NHPC? The NHPC which is eyeing a number of other dam projects (including the Maheshwar Dam) and aims to install 32,000 megawatts of power over the next thirteen years.[44] That's the equivalent of thirty-two Narmada Sagars.

The World Bank is by no means the only shark in the water.[45] Here's a list of international banks who have financed NHPC projects: ABN Amro, ANZ, Barclays, Emirates, Natwest, Standard

Chartered, Sumitomo. And a list of bilateral export credit and financing agencies who support it: COFACE France, EDC & CIDA Canada, NEXI & JBIC Japan, the former ODA (now DFID) UK, and SIDA & AKN Sweden.

What's a few human rights abuses among friends? We're deep into the Great Game.

It is dark on the highway back to Khandwa. We pass truck upon truck carrying unmarked, illegal timber.

Trucks carrying away the forest. Tractors carrying away the town. The night carrying away the dreams of hundreds of thousands of people.

I agree with Kallu Driver.

But I have a problem with derogatory references to women's bodies.

July 2004

**public power
in the age of empire**

public power in the age of empire

When language has been butchered and bled of meaning, how do we understand 'public power'? When freedom means occupation, when democracy means neoliberal capitalism, when reform means repression, when words like 'empowerment' and 'peacekeeping' make your blood run cold—why, then, 'public power' could mean whatever you want it to mean. A biceps building machine, or a Community Power Shower. So, I'll just have to define 'public power' as I go along, in my own self-serving sort of way.

In India, the word *public* is now a Hindi word. It means *people*. In Hindi, we have sarkar and public, the government and the people. Inherent in this use is the underlying assumption that the government is quite separate from 'the people'. This distinction has to do with the fact that India's freedom struggle, though magnificent, was by no means revolutionary. The Indian elite stepped easily and elegantly into the shoes of the British imperialists. A deeply impoverished, essentially feudal society became a modern, independent nation state. Even today, fifty-seven years on to the day, the truly vanquished still look upon the government as mai-baap, the parent and provider. The somewhat more radical, those who still have fire in their bellies, see it as chor, the thief, the snatcher-away of all things.

Either way, for most Indians, sarkar is very separate from public. However, as you make your way up India's complex social ladder, the distinction between sarkar and public gets blurred. The Indian elite, like the elite anywhere in the world, finds it hard to separate itself from the state. It sees like the state, thinks like the state, speaks like the state.

In the United States, on the other hand, the blurring of the distinction between sarkar and public has penetrated far deeper into society. This could be a sign of a robust democracy, but unfortunately, it's a little more complicated and less pretty than that. Among other things, it has to do with the elaborate web of paranoia generated by the US sarkar and spun out by the corporate media and Hollywood. Ordinary people in the

United States have been manipulated into imagining they are a people under siege whose sole refuge and protector is their government. If it isn't the Communists, it's Al-Qaeda. If it isn't Cuba, it's Nicaragua. As a result, this, the most powerful nation in the world—with its unmatchable arsenal of weapons, its history of having waged and sponsored endless wars, and the only nation in history to have actually used nuclear bombs—is peopled by a terrified citizenry, jumping at shadows. A people bonded to the state not by social services, or public health care, or employment guarantees, but by fear.

This synthetically manufactured fear is used to gain public sanction for further acts of aggression. And so it goes, building into a spiral of self-fulfilling hysteria, now formally calibrated by the US government's Amazing Technicoloured Terror Alerts: fuchsia, turquoise, salmon pink.

To outside observers, this merging of sarkar and public in the United States sometimes makes it hard to separate the actions of the government from the people. It is this confusion that fuels anti-Americanism in the world. Anti-Americanism is then seized upon and amplified by the US government and its faithful media outlets. You know the routine: 'Why do they hate us? They hate our freedoms,' et cetera. This enhances the sense of isolation among people in the United States and makes the embrace between sarkar and public even more intimate. Like Red Riding Hood looking for a cuddle in the wolf's bed.

2001 was not the first year that the US government declared a 'war on terrorism'. As Noam Chomsky reminds us, the first 'war on terrorism' was declared by President Ronald Reagan in the 1980s during the US-sponsored terrorist wars across Central America, the Middle East, and Africa.[1] The Reagan administration called terrorism a 'plague spread by depraved opponents of civilization itself'.[2] In keeping with this sentiment, in 1987, the United Nations General Assembly proposed a strongly worded condemnation of terrorism. One hundred and fifty-three countries voted for it. Only the United Stares and Israel voted against it. They objected to a passage that referred to 'the right to self-determination, freedom, and independence . . . of people forcibly deprived of that right . . . particularly peoples under colonial and racist regimes and foreign occupation'.[3] Remember that in 1987, the United States was a staunch ally of apartheid South Africa. The African National Congress and Nelson Mandela were listed as 'terrorists'. The term 'foreign occupation' was taken to mean Israel's occupation of Palestine.[4]

Over the past few years, the 'war on terrorism' has mutated into the more generic 'war on terror'. Using the threat of an external enemy to rally people behind you is a tired old horse that politicians have ridden into power for centuries. But could it be that ordinary people are fed up with that poor old horse and are looking for something different? There's an old Hindi film song that goes *Yeh public hai, yeh sab jaanti hai* (the public, she knows it all). Wouldn't it be lovely if the song were right and the politicians wrong?

Before Washington's illegal invasion of Iraq, a Gallup International poll showed that in no European country was the support for a unilateral war higher than 11 per cent.[5] On 15 February 2003, weeks before the invasion, more than 10 million people marched against the war on different continents, including North America.[6] And yet the governments of many supposedly democratic countries went to war.

The question is: Is 'democracy' still democratic? Are democratic governments accountable to the people who elected them? And, critically, is the public in democratic countries responsible for the actions of its sarkar?

If you think about it, the logic that underlies the war on terrorism and the logic that underlies terrorism are exactly the same. Both make ordinary citizens pay for the actions of their government. Al-Qaeda made the people of the United States pay with their lives for the actions of their government in Palestine, Saudi Arabia, Iraq, and Afghanistan. The US government has made the people of Afghanistan pay in the thousands for the actions of the Taliban and the people of Iraq pay in the hundreds of thousands for the actions of Saddam Hussein.

The crucial difference is that nobody really elected Al-Qaeda, the Taliban, or Saddam Hussein. But the president of the United States was elected (well . . . in a manner of speaking). The prime ministers of Italy, Spain, and the United Kingdom were elected. Could it then be argued that citizens of these countries are more responsible for the actions of their governments than Iraqis were for the actions of Saddam Hussein or Afghans for the Taliban?

Whose God decides which is a 'just war' and

which isn't? George Bush Sr once said: 'I will never apologize for the United States. I don't care what the facts are.'[7] When the president of the most powerful country in the world doesn't *need* to care what the facts are, then we can at least be sure we have entered the Age of Empire.

So what does public power mean in the Age of Empire? Does it mean anything at all? Does it actually *exist*?

In these allegedly democratic times, conventional political thought holds that public power is exercised through the ballot. Scores of countries in the world will go to the polls this year. Most (not all) of them will get the governments they vote for. But will they get the governments they want?

In India this year, we voted the Hindu nationalists out of office. But even as we celebrated, we knew that on nuclear bombs, neoliberalism, privatization, censorship, Big Dams—on every major issue other than overt Hindu nationalism— the Congress and the BJP have no major ideological differences. We know that it is the fifty-year legacy of the Congress Party that prepared the ground culturally and politically for the far right. It was also the Congress Party that first opened India's markets to corporate globalization. It passed legislation that encouraged the privatization of water and power, the dismantling of the public sector, and the denationalization of public companies. It enforced cutbacks in government spending on education and health, and weakened labour laws that protected workers' rights. The BJP took this process forward with pitiless abandon.

In its election campaign, the Congress Party indicated that it was prepared to rethink some of its earlier economic policies. Millions of India's poorest people came out in strength to vote in the elections. The spectacle of the great Indian democracy was telecast live—the poor farmers, the old and infirm, the veiled women with their beautiful silver jewellery, making quaint journeys to election booths on elephants and camels and bullock carts. Contrary to the predictions of all India's experts and pollsters, the Congress Party won more votes than any other party. India's communist parties won the largest share of the vote in their history.[8] India's poor had clearly voted against neoliberalism's economic 'reforms' and growing fascism. As soon as the votes were counted, the corporate media dispatched them like badly paid extras on a film set. Television channels featured split screens. Half the screen showed the chaos outside the home of Sonia Gandhi, the leader of the Congress Party, as the coalition government was cobbled together. The other half showed frenzied stockbrokers outside the Bombay Stock Exchange, panicking at the thought that the Congress Party might actually honour its promises and implement its electoral mandate. We saw the Sensex stock index move up and down and sideways. The media, whose own publicly listed stocks were plummeting, reported the stock market crash as though Pakistan had launched Intercontinental Ballistic Missiles on New Delhi.

Even before the new government was formally sworn in, senior Congress politicians made public statements reassuring investors and the media that privatization of public utilities would continue. Meanwhile the BJP, now in opposition, has cynically, and comically, begun to oppose foreign direct investment and the further opening of Indian markets.

This is the spurious, evolving dialectic of electoral democracy.

As for the Indian poor, once they've provided the

votes, they are expected to bugger off home.
Policy will be decided despite them.

■

And what of the US elections? Do US voters have
a real choice?

It's true that if John Kerry becomes president, some
of the oil tycoons and Christian fundamentalists
in the White House will change. Few will be sorry
to see the backs of Dick Cheney or Donald
Rumsfeld or John Ashcroft or an end to their
blatant thuggery. But the real concern is that in
the new administration their policies will continue.
That we will have Bushism without Bush.

Those in positions of real power—the bankers,
the CEOs—are not vulnerable to the vote (and
in any case, they fund both sides).

Unfortunately, US elections have deteriorated
into a sort of personality contest, a squabble over
who would do a better job of overseeing empire.
John Kerry believes in the idea of empire as
fervently as George Bush does. The US political
system has been carefully crafted to ensure that
no one who questions the natural goodness of
the military-industrial-corporate structure will be
allowed through the portals of power.

Given this, it's no surprise that in this election you have two Yale University graduates, both members of Skull and Bones, the same secret society, both millionaires, both playing at soldier-soldier, both talking up war, and arguing almost childishly about who will lead the war on terror more effectively.

Like President Bill Clinton before him, Kerry will continue the expansion of US economic and military penetration into the world. He says he would have voted to authorize Bush to go to war in Iraq even if he had known that Iraq had no weapons of mass destruction.[9] He promises to commit more troops to Iraq.[10] He said recently that he supports Bush's policies toward Israel and Ariel Sharon 'completely'.[11] He says he'll retain 98 per cent of Bush's tax cuts.[12]

So, underneath the shrill exchange of insults, there is almost absolute consensus. It looks as though even if people in the United States vote for Kerry, they'll still get Bush. President John Kerbush or President George Berry. It's not a real choice. It's an *apparent* choice. Like choosing a brand of detergent. Whether you buy Ivory Snow or Tide, they're both owned by Proctor & Gamble.

This doesn't mean that one takes a position that

is without nuance, that the Congress and the BJP, New Labour and the Tories, the Democrats and Republicans are the same. Of course, they're not.

Neither are Tide and Ivory Snow. Tide has oxy-boosting and Ivory Snow is a gentle cleanser.

In India, there is a difference between an overtly fascist party (the BJP) and a party that slyly pits one community against another (Congress) and sows the seeds of communalism that are then so ably harvested by the BJP. There are differences in the IQs and levels of ruthlessness between this year's US presidential candidates. The anti-war movement in the United States has done a phenomenal job of exposing the lies and venality that led to the invasion of Iraq, despite the propaganda and intimidation it faced. This was a service not just to people here, but to the whole world.

But why is it that the Democrats do not even have to pretend to be against the invasion and occupation of Iraq? If the anti-war movement openly campaigns for Kerry, the rest of the world will think that it approves of his policies of 'sensitive' imperialism.[13] Is US imperialism preferable if it is supported by the United Nations and European countries? Is it preferable if the

UN asks Indian and Pakistani soldiers to do the killing and dying in Iraq instead of US soldiers? Is the only change that Iraqis can hope for that French, German, and Russian companies will share in the spoils of the occupation of their country?

Is this actually better or worse for those of us who live in subject nations? Is it better for the world to have a smarter emperor in power or a stupider one? Is that our only choice?

I'm sorry, I know that these are uncomfortable, even brutal questions, but they must be asked.

The fact is that electoral democracy has become a process of cynical manipulation. It offers us a very reduced political space today. To believe that this space constitutes real choice would be naïve.

The crisis in modern democracy is a profound one. Free elections, a free press, and an independent judiciary mean little when the free market has reduced them to commodities available on sale to the highest bidder.

On the global stage, beyond the jurisdiction of sovereign governments, international instruments of trade and finance oversee a complex web of multilateral laws and agreements that have entrenched a system of appropriation that puts colonialism to shame. This system allows the unrestricted entry and exit of massive amounts of speculative capital—hot money—into and out of third world countries, which then effectively dictates their economic policy. Using the threat of capital flight as a lever, international capital insinuates itself deeper and deeper into these economies. Giant transnational corporations are taking control of their essential infrastructure and natural resources, their minerals, their water, their electricity. The World Trade Organization, the World Bank, the International Monetary Fund (IMF), and other financial institutions like the Asian Development Bank, virtually write economic policy and parliamentary legislation. With a deadly combination of arrogance and ruthlessness, they take their sledgehammers to fragile, interdependent, historically complex societies, and devastate them.

All this goes under the fluttering banner of 'reform'. As a consequence of this reform, in Africa, Asia, and Latin America, thousands of small enterprises and industries have closed down, millions of workers and farmers have lost their jobs and land. Anyone who criticizes this process is mocked for being anti-reform, anti-progress, anti-development. Somehow a Luddite.

The *Spectator* newspaper in London assures us that '[w]e live in the happiest, healthiest and most peaceful era in human history'.[14]

Billions wonder: who's 'we'? Where does he live? What's his Christian name?

Once the economies of third world countries are controlled by the free market, they are enmeshed in an elaborate, carefully calibrated system of economic inequality. For example, Western countries that together spend more than $1 billion a *day* on subsidies to farmers demand that poor countries withdraw all agricultural subsidies, including subsidized electricity.[15] Then they flood the markets of poor countries with their subsidized agricultural goods and other products with which local producers cannot possibly compete.

Countries that have been plundered by colonizing regimes are steeped in debt to these same powers, and have to repay them at the rate of about $382 *billion* a year.[16] Ergo, the rich get richer and the poor get poorer—not accidentally, but by *design*. By *intention*.

To put a vulgar point on all of this—the truth is

getting more vulgar by the minute—the combined wealth of the world's billionaires in 2004 (587 'individuals and family units'), according to *Forbes* magazine, is $1.9 trillion. This is more than the gross domestic product of the world's 135 poorest countries combined.[17] The good news is that there are 111 more billionaires this year than there were in 2003.[18] Isn't that fun?

The thing to understand is that modern democracy is safely premised on an almost religious acceptance of the nation state. But corporate globalization is not. Liquid capital is not. So, even though capital needs the coercive powers of the nation state to put down revolts in the servants' quarters, this setup ensures that no individual nation can oppose corporate globalization on its own.

Time and again we have seen the heroes of our times, giants in opposition, suddenly diminished. President Lula of Brazil was the hero of the World Social Forum (WSF) in January 2002. Now he's busy implementing IMF guidelines, reducing pension benefits and purging radicals from the Workers' Party.[19] Lula has a worthy predecessor in the former president of South Africa, Nelson Mandela, who instituted a massive programme of privatization and structural adjustment that has left thousands of people homeless, jobless, and without water and electricity.[20] When Harry Oppenheimer died in August 2000, Mandela called him 'one of the great South Africans of our time'.[21] Oppenheimer was the head of Anglo-American, one of South Africa's largest mining companies, which made its money exploiting cheap black labour made available by the repressive apartheid regime.

Why does this happen? It is neither true nor useful to dismiss Mandela or Lula as weak or treacherous people. It's important to understand the nature of the beast they were up against. The moment they crossed the floor from the opposition into government they became hostage to a spectrum of threats—most malevolent among them the threat of capital flight, which can destroy any government overnight. To imagine that a leader's personal charisma and history of struggle will dent the corporate cartel is to have no understanding of how capitalism works, or for that matter, how power works.

Radical change cannot and will not be negotiated by governments; it can only be enforced by people. By the public. A public who can link hands *across* national borders.

So when we speak of public power in the age of Empire, I hope it's not presumptuous to assume that the only thing that is worth discussing seriously is the power of a *dissenting* public. A public that *disagrees* with the very concept of empire. A public that has set itself against incumbent power—international, national, regional, or provincial governments and institutions that support and service Empire.

Of course those of us who live in Empire's subject nations are aware that in the great cities of Europe and the United States, where a few years ago these things would only have been whispered, there is now open talk about the benefits of imperialism and the need for a strong empire to police an unruly world. It wasn't long ago that colonialism also sanctified itself as a 'civilizing mission'. So we can't give these pundits high marks for originality.

We are aware that New Imperialism is being marketed as a 'lesser evil' in a less-than-perfect world.[22] Occasionally some of us are invited to 'debate' the merits of imperialism on 'neutral' platforms provided by the corporate media. It's like debating slavery. It isn't a subject that deserves the dignity of a debate.

What are the avenues of protest available to people who wish to resist empire? By resist I don't mean only to *express* dissent, but to effectively force change.

Empire has a range of calling cards. It uses different weapons to break open different markets. There isn't a country on God's earth that is not caught in the cross hairs of the US cruise missile and the IMF chequebook. Argentina's the model if you want to be the poster boy of neoliberal capitalism, Iraq if you're the black sheep.

For poor people in many countries, Empire does not always appear in the form of cruise missiles and tanks, as it has in Iraq or Afghanistan or Vietnam. It appears in their lives in very local avatars—losing their jobs, being sent unpayable electricity bills, having their water supply cut, being evicted from their homes and uprooted from their land. All this overseen by the repressive machinery of the state, the police, the army, the judiciary. It is a process of relentless impoverishment with which the poor are historically familiar. What Empire does is to further entrench and exacerbate already existing inequalities.

Even until quite recently, it was sometimes difficult for people to see themselves as victims of Empire. But now local struggles have begun to see their role with increasing clarity. However grand it might sound, the fact is, they *are* confronting Empire in their own, very different ways. Differently in Iraq, in South Africa, in India, in Argentina, and differently, for that matter, on the streets of Europe and the United States.

Mass resistance movements, individual activists, journalists, artists, and film makers have come together to strip Empire of its sheen. They have connected the dots, turned cash-flow charts and boardroom speeches into real stories about real people and real despair. They have shown how the neoliberal project has cost people their homes, their land, their jobs, their liberty, their dignity. They have made the intangible tangible. The once seemingly incorporeal enemy is now corporeal.

This is a huge victory. It was forged by the coming together of disparate political groups, with a variety of strategies. But they all recognized that the target of their anger, their activism, and their doggedness is the same. This was the beginning of *real* globalization. The globalization of dissent.

Broadly speaking, there are two kinds of mass resistance movements in third world countries today. The landless people's movement in Brazil, the anti-dam movement in India, the Zapatistas in Mexico, the Anti-Privatization Forum in South Africa, and hundreds of others, are fighting their own sovereign governments, which have become agents of the neoliberal project. Most of these are radical struggles, fighting to change the structure and chosen model of 'development' of their own societies.

Then there are those fighting formal and brutal neocolonial occupations in contested territories whose boundaries and fault lines were often arbitrarily drawn last century by the imperialist powers. In Palestine, Tibet, Chechnya, Kashmir, and several states in India's northeastern provinces, people are waging struggles for self-determination.

Several of these struggles might have been radical, even revolutionary when they began, but often the brutality of the repression they face pushes them into conservative, even retrogressive spaces where they use the same violent strategies and the same language of religious and cultural nationalism used by the states they seek to replace.

Many of the foot soldiers in these struggles will find, like those who fought apartheid in South Africa, that once they overcome overt occupation, they will be left with another battle on their hands—a battle against covert economic colonialism.

Meanwhile, the rift between rich and poor is being driven deeper and the battle to control the world's resources is intensifying. Economic colonialism through formal military aggression is staging a comeback.

Iraq today is a tragic illustration of this process. An illegal invasion. A brutal occupation in the name of liberation. The rewriting of laws that allow the shameless appropriation of the country's wealth and resources by corporations allied to the occupation, and now the charade of a local 'Iraqi government'.

For these reasons, it is absurd to condemn the resistance to the US occupation in Iraq as being masterminded by terrorists or insurgents or supporters of Saddam Hussein. After all, if the United States were invaded and occupied, would everybody who fought to liberate it be a terrorist or an insurgent or a Bushite?

The Iraqi resistance is fighting on the frontlines of the battle against Empire. And therefore that battle is our battle.

Like most resistance movements, it combines a

motley range of assorted factions. Former Baathists, liberals, Islamists, fed-up Collaborationists, communists, etc. Of course, it is riddled with opportunism, local rivalry, demagoguery, and criminality. But if we are only going to support pristine movements, then no resistance will be worthy of our purity.

A whole industry of development experts, academics, and consultants have built an industry on the back of global social movements in which they are not direct participants. Many of these 'experts', who earn their livings studying the struggles of the world's poor, are funded by groups like the Ford Foundation, the World Bank, and wealthy universities such as Harvard, Stanford, and Cornell. From a safe distance, they offer us their insightful critiques. But the same people who tell us that we can reform the World Bank from within, that we can change the IMF by working inside it, would not themselves seek to reform a resistance movement by working within it.

This is not to say that we should never criticize resistance movements. Many of them suffer from a lack of democracy, from the iconization of their 'leaders', a lack of transparency, a lack of vision and direction. But most of all they suffer from vilification, repression, and lack of resources.

Before we prescribe how a pristine Iraqi resistance must conduct a secular, feminist, democratic, non-violent battle, we should shore up our end of the resistance by forcing the US government and its allies to withdraw from Iraq.

■

The first militant confrontation in the United States between the global justice movement and the neoliberal junta took place famously at the WTO conference in Seattle in December 1999. To many mass movements in developing countries that had long been fighting lonely, isolated battles, Seattle was the first delightful sign that their anger and their vision of another kind of world was shared by people in the imperialist countries.

In January 2001, in Porto Alegre, Brazil, 20,000 activists, students, film makers—some of the best minds in the world—came together to share their experiences and exchange ideas about confronting Empire. That was the birth of the now historic WSF. It was the first formal coming together of an exciting, anarchic, unindoctrinated, energetic, new kind of 'public power'. The rallying cry of the WSF is 'Another World is Possible'. The forum has become a platform where hundreds of conversations, debates, and seminars have helped to hone and refine a vision of what kind of world it should be. By January 2004, when the fourth WSF was held in Mumbai, India, it attracted 200,000 delegates. I have never been part of a more electrifying gathering. It was a sign of the social forum's success that the mainstream media in India ignored it completely. But now the WSF is threatened by its own success. The safe, open, restive atmosphere of the forum has allowed politicians and non-governmental organizations that are imbricated in the political and economic systems that the forum opposes to participate and make themselves heard.

Another danger is that the WSF, which has played such a vital role in the movement for global justice, runs the risk of becoming an end unto itself. Just organizing it every year consumes the energies of some of the best activists. If *conversations* about resistance replace real civil disobedience, then the WSF could become an asset to those whom it was created to oppose. The forum must be held and must grow, but we have to find ways to channel our conversations there back into concrete action.

As resistance movements have begun to reach out across national borders and pose a real threat, governments have developed their own strategies of how to deal with them. They range from co-option to repression.

I'm going to speak about three of the contemporary dangers that confront resistance movements: the difficult meeting point between mass movements and the mass media, the hazards of the NGO-ization of resistance, and the confrontation between resistance movements and increasingly repressive states.

The place in which the mass media meets mass movements is a complicated one.

Governments have learned that a crisis-driven media cannot afford to hang about in the same place for too long. Like a business needs cash turnover, the media need crises turnover. Whole countries become old news. They cease to exist, and the darkness becomes deeper than before the light was briefly shone on them. We saw it happen in Afghanistan when the Soviets withdrew. And now, after Operation Enduring Freedom put Hamid Karzai in place, Afghanistan has been thrown to its warlords once more. Another CIA operative, Iyad Allawi, has been installed in

Iraq, so perhaps it's time for the media to move on from there, too.[23]

While governments hone the art of waiting out crises, resistance movements are increasingly being ensnared in a vortex of crisis production, seeking to find ways of manufacturing them in easily consumable, spectator-friendly formats. Every self-respecting people's movement, every 'issue', is expected to have its own hot air balloon in the sky advertising its brand and purpose. For this reason, starvation deaths are more effective advertisements for impoverishment than millions of malnourished people, who don't quite make the cut. Dams are not newsworthy until the devastation they wreak makes good television. (And by then, it's too late.)

Standing in the rising water of a reservoir for days on end, watching your home and belongings float away, to protest against a Big Dam used to be an effective strategy, but isn't any more. The media is dead bored of that one. So the hundreds of thousands of people being displaced by dams are expected to either conjure new tricks or give up the struggle.

Resistance as spectacle, as political theatre, has a history. Gandhi's salt march in 1931 to Dandi is among the most exhilarating examples. But the salt march wasn't theatre alone. It was the symbolic part of a larger act of real civil disobedience. When Gandhi and an army of freedom fighters marched to Gujarat's coast and made salt from sea water, thousands of Indians across the country began to make their own salt, openly defying imperial Britain's salt tax laws, which banned local production in favour of British imports. It was a direct strike at the economic underpinning of the British Empire.

The disturbing thing nowadays is that resistance as spectacle has cut loose from its origins in genuine civil disobedience and is beginning to become more symbolic than real. Colourful demonstrations and weekend marches are vital but alone are not powerful enough to stop wars. Wars will be stopped only when soldiers refuse to fight, when workers refuse to load weapons onto ships and aircraft, when people boycott the economic outposts of Empire that are strung across the globe.

If we want to reclaim the space for civil disobedience, we will have to liberate ourselves from the tyranny of crisis reportage and its fear of the mundane. We have to use our experience, our imagination, and our art to interrogate those instruments of state that ensure that 'normality' remains what it is: cruel, unjust, unacceptable. We have to expose the policies and processes that make ordinary things—food, water, shelter and dignity—such a distant dream for ordinary people. The real pre-emptive strike is to understand that wars are the end result of a flawed and unjust peace.

As far as mass resistance movements are concerned, the fact is that no amount of media coverage can make up for mass strength on the ground. There is no option, really, to old-fashioned, back-breaking political mobilization. Corporate globalization has increased the distance between those who make decisions and those who have to suffer the effects of those decisions. Forums like the WSF enable local resistance movements to reduce that distance and to link up with their counterparts in rich countries. That alliance is a formidable one. For example, when India's first private dam, the Maheshwar Dam, was being built, alliances between the Narmada Bachao Andolan (NBA), the German organization Urgewald, the Berne Declaration in Switzerland, and the International Rivers

Network in Berkeley worked together to push a series of international banks and corporations out of the project. This would not have been possible had there not been a rock solid resistance movement on the ground. The voice of that local movement was amplified by supporters on the global stage, embarrassing investors and forcing them to withdraw.

An infinite number of similar alliances, targeting specific projects and specific corporations would help to make another world possible. We should begin with the corporations who did business with Saddam Hussein and now profit from the devastation and occupation of Iraq.

A second hazard facing mass movements is the NGO-ization of resistance. It will be easy to twist what I'm about to say into an indictment of all NGOs. That would be a falsehood. In the murky waters of fake NGOs, set up to siphon off grant money or as tax dodges (in states like Bihar, they are given as dowry), of course there are NGOs doing valuable work. But it's important to turn our attention away from the positive work being done by some individual NGOs, and consider the NGO phenomenon in a broader political context.

In India, for instance, the funded NGO boom began in the late 1980s and 1990s. It coincided with the opening of India's markets to neoliberalism. At the time, the Indian state, in keeping with the requirements of structural adjustment, was withdrawing funding from rural development, agriculture, energy, transport, and public health. As the state abdicated its traditional role, NGOs moved in to work in these very areas. The difference, of course, is that the funds available to them are a minuscule fraction of the actual cut in public spending. Most large, well-funded NGOs are financed and patronized by aid and development agencies, which are in turn funded by Western governments, the World Bank, the UN, and some multinational corporations. Though they may not be the very same agencies, they are certainly part of the same loose, political formation that oversees the neoliberal project and demands the slash in government spending in the first place.

Why should these agencies fund NGOs? Could it be just old-fashioned missionary zeal? Guilt? It's a little more than that.

NGOs give the *impression* that they are filling the vacuum created by a retreating state. And they are, but in a materially inconsequential way. Their *real* contribution is that they defuse political anger and dole out as aid or benevolence what people ought to have by right. They alter the public psyche. They turn people into dependent victims and blunt the edges of political resistance. NGOs form a sort of buffer between the sarkar and the public. Between Empire and its subjects. They have become the arbitrators, the interpreters, the facilitators of the discourse. They play out the role of the 'reasonable man' in an unfair, unreasonable war.

In the long run, NGOs are accountable to their funders, not to the people they work among. They're what botanists would call an indicator species. It's almost as though the greater the devastation caused by neoliberalism, the greater the outbreak of NGOs. Nothing illustrates this more poignantly than the phenomenon of the United States preparing to invade a country and simultaneously readying NGOs to go in and clean up the devastation.

In order to make sure their funding is not jeopardized and that the governments of the countries they work in will allow them to function, NGOs have to present their work—whether it's in a country devastated by war, poverty or an epidemic of disease—within a shallow framework more or less shorn of a political or historical context. At any rate, an *inconvenient* historical or political context. It's not for nothing that the 'NGO perspective' is becoming increasingly respected.

Apolitical (and therefore, actually, extremely political) distress reports from poor countries and war zones eventually make the (dark) people of those (dark) countries seem like pathological victims. *Another malnourished Indian, another starving Ethiopian, another Afghan refugee camp, another maimed Sudanese* . . . in need of the white man's help. They unwittingly reinforce racist stereotypes and re-affirm the achievements, the comforts, and the compassion (the tough love) of Western civilization, minus the guilt of the history of genocide, colonialism, and slavery. They're the secular missionaries of the modern world.

Eventually—on a smaller scale, but more insidiously—the capital available to NGOs plays the same role in alternative politics as the speculative capital that flows in and out of the economies of poor countries. It begins to dictate the agenda.

It turns confrontation into negotiation. It depoliticizes resistance. It interferes with local peoples' movements that have traditionally been self-reliant. NGOs have funds that can employ local people who might otherwise be activists in resistance movements, but now can feel they are doing some immediate, creative good (and earning a living while they're at it). Charity offers instant gratification to the giver, as well as the receiver, but its side effects can be dangerous. Real political resistance offers no such short cuts.

The NGO-ization of politics threatens to turn resistance into a well-mannered, reasonable, salaried, nine-to-five job. With a few perks thrown in.

Real resistance has real consequences. And no salary.

This brings us to a third danger I want to speak about tonight: the deadly nature of the actual confrontation between resistance movements and increasingly repressive states. Between public power and the agents of Empire.

Whenever civil resistance has shown the slightest signs of evolving from symbolic action into anything remotely threatening, the crackdown is merciless. We've seen what happened in the demonstrations in Seattle, in Miami, in Gothenburg, in Genoa.[24]

In the United States, you have the USA PATRIOT Act, which has become a blueprint for anti-terrorism laws passed by governments around the world. Freedoms are being curbed in the name of protecting freedom. And once we surrender our freedoms, to win them back will take a revolution.

Some governments have vast experience in the business of curbing freedoms and still smelling sweet. The government of India, an old hand at the game, lights the path. Over the years the Indian government has passed a plethora of laws that allow it to call almost anyone a terrorist, an insurgent, a militant. We have the Armed Forces Special Powers Act, the Public Security Act, the Special Areas Security Act, the Gangster Act, the Terrorist and Disruptive Activities Act (which has formally lapsed, but under which people are still facing trial), and, most recently, the Prevention of Terrorism Act (POTA), the broad-spectrum antibiotic for the disease of dissent.[25]

There are other steps that are being taken, such as court judgements that in effect curtail free speech, the right of government workers to go on strike, the right to life and livelihood. Courts have begun to micro-manage our lives in India. And criticizing the courts is a criminal offence.[26]

But coming back to the counter-terrorism initiatives, over the last decade the number of people who have been killed by the police and security forces runs into the tens of thousands. In the state of Andhra Pradesh (the pin-up girl of corporate globalization in India), an average of about 200 'extremists' are killed in what are called 'encounters' every year.[27] The Bombay police boasts of how many 'gangsters' they have killed in 'shoot outs'. In Kashmir, in a situation that almost amounts to war, an estimated 80,000 people have been killed since 1989. Thousands have simply 'disappeared'.[28] In the northeastern provinces, the situation is similar.

In recent years, the Indian police have opened fire on unarmed people at peaceful demonstrations, mostly Dalit and Adivasi. The preferred method is to kill them and then call them terrorists. India is not alone, though. We have seen similar things happen in countries such as Bolivia and Chile.[29] In the era of neoliberalism, poverty is a crime and protesting against it is more and more being defined as terrorism.

In India, POTA is often called the *Production* of Terrorism Act. It's a versatile, hold-all law that could apply to anyone from an Al-Qaeda operative to a disgruntled bus conductor. As with all anti-terrorism laws, the genius of POTA is that it can be whatever the government wants. For example, in Tamil Nadu, it has been used to imprison and silence critics of the state government.[30] In Jharkhand 3200 people, mostly poor Adivasis accused of being Maoists, have been named in criminal complaints under POTA.[31] In Gujarat and Mumbai, the Act is used almost exclusively against Muslims.[32] After the 2002 state-assisted pogrom in Gujarat, in which an estimated 2000 Muslims were savagely killed by Hindu mobs and 150,000 driven from their homes, 287 people have been accused under POTA. Of these, 286 are Muslim and one is a Sikh.[33]

POTA allows confessions extracted in police custody to be admitted as judicial evidence. In effect, torture tends to replace investigation. The South Asia Human Rights Documentation Centre reports that India has the highest number of torture and custodial deaths in the world.[34] Government records show that there were 1307 deaths in judicial custody in 2002 alone.[35]

A few months ago, I was a member of a peoples' tribunal on POTA. Over a period of two days, we listened to harrowing testimonies of what is happening in our wonderful democracy. It's everything—from people being forced to drink urine, being stripped, humiliated, given electric shocks, burned with cigarette butts, having iron rods put up their anuses, to people being beaten and kicked to death.

The new government has promised to repeal POTA.[36] I'd be surprised if that happens before similar legislation under a different name is put in place.

When every avenue of non-violent dissent is closed down, and everyone who protests against the violation of their human rights is called a terrorist, should we really be surprised if vast parts of the country are overrun by those who believe in armed struggle and are more or less beyond the control of the state: in Kashmir, the northeastern provinces, large parts of Madhya Pradesh, Chattisgarh, Jharkhand, and Andhra Pradesh. Ordinary people in these regions are trapped between the violence of the militants and the state.

In Kashmir, the Indian army estimates that 3000 to 4000 militants are operating at any given time. To control them, the Indian government deploys about 500,000 soldiers.[37] Clearly, it isn't just the militants the army seeks to control, but a whole population of humiliated, unhappy people who see the Indian army as an occupation force. The primary purpose of laws like POTA is not to target real terrorists or militants, who are usually simply shot. Anti-terrorism laws are used to intimidate civil society. Inevitably, such repression has the effect of fuelling discontent and anger.

The Armed Forces Special Powers Act allows not just officers, but even junior commissioned officers and non-commissioned officers of the army, to use force and even kill any person on *suspicion* of disturbing public order.[38] It was first imposed on a few districts in the state of Manipur in 1958. Today, it applies to virtually all of the northeast and Kashmir.[39] The documentation of instances of torture, disappearances, custodial deaths, rape, and summary execution by security forces is enough to turn your stomach.

In Andhra Pradesh, in India's heartland, the militant Marxist-Leninist Peoples' War Group—which for years has been engaged in a violent armed struggle and has been the principal target of many of the Andhra police's fake 'encounters'— held its first public meeting in years on 28 July 2004, in the town of Warangal.

The former chief minister of Andhra Pradesh, Chandrababu Naidu, liked to call himself the CEO of the state.[40] In return for his enthusiasm in implementing structural adjustment, Andhra Pradesh received millions of dollars of aid from the World Bank and development agencies such as Britain's Department for International Development.[41] As a result of structural adjustment, Andhra Pradesh is now best known for two things: the hundreds of suicides by farmers who were steeped in debt and the spreading influence and growing militancy of the Peoples' War Group (PWG). During Naidu's term in office, the PWG were not arrested, or captured, they were summarily shot.

In response, the PWG campaigned actively, and let it be said, violently, against Naidu. In May, the Congress won the state elections. The Naidu government didn't just lose, it was humiliated in the polls.[42] When the PWG called a public meeting, it was attended by hundreds of thousands of people. Under POTA, all of them are considered terrorists. Are they all going to be detained in some Indian equivalent of Guantánamo Bay? The whole of the northeast and the Kashmir valley are in ferment. What will the government do with these millions of people?

One does not endorse the violence of these militant groups. Neither morally nor strategically. But to condemn it without first denouncing the much greater violence perpetrated by the state would be to deny the people of these regions not just their basic human rights, but even the right to a fair hearing. People who have lived in situations of conflict are in no doubt that militancy and armed struggle provokes a massive escalation of violence from the state. But living as they do, in situations of unbearable injustice, can they remain silent forever?

There is no discussion taking place in the world today that is more crucial than the debate about strategies of resistance. And the choice of strategy is not entirely in the hands of the public. It is also in the hands of sarkar.

After all, when the United States invades and occupies Iraq in the way it has done, with such overwhelming military force, can the resistance be expected to be a conventional military one?

(Of course, even if it *were* conventional, it would still be called terrorist.) In a strange sense, the US government's arsenal of weapons and unrivalled air and fire power makes terrorism an all-but-inescapable response. What people lack in wealth and power, they will make up for with stealth and strategy.

In the twenty-first century, the connection between corporate globalization, religious fundamentalism, nuclear nationalism, and the pauperization of whole populations is becoming impossible to ignore. The unrest has myriad manifestations: terrorism, armed struggle, non-violent mass resistance, and common crime.

In this restive, despairing time, if governments do not do all they can to honour non-violent resistance, then by default they privilege those who turn to violence. No government's condemnation of terrorism is credible if it cannot show itself to be open to change by non-violent dissent. But instead non-violent resistance movements are being crushed. Any kind of mass political mobilization or organization is being bought off, broken, or simply ignored.

Meanwhile, governments and the corporate media, and let's nor forget the film industry, lavish their time, attention, funds, technology, research, and admiration on war and terrorism. Violence has been deified. The message this sends is disturbing and dangerous: if you seek to air a public grievance, violence is more effective than non-violence.

As the rift between the rich and poor grows, as the need to appropriate and control the world's resources to feed the great capitalist machine becomes more urgent, the unrest will only escalate.

For those of us who are on the wrong side of Empire, the humiliation is becoming unbearable. Each of the Iraqi children killed by the United States was our child. Each of the prisoners tortured in Abu Ghraib was our comrade. Each of their screams was ours. When they were humiliated, we were humiliated.

The US soldiers fighting in Iraq—mostly volunteers in a poverty draft from small towns and poor urban neighbourhoods—are victims, just as much as the Iraqis, of the same horrendous process, which asks them to die for a victory that will never be theirs.

The mandarins of the corporate world, the CEOs,

the bankers, the politicians, the judges and generals look down on us from on high and shake their heads sternly. 'There's no alternative,' they say, and let slip the dogs of war.

Then, from the ruins of Afghanistan, from the rubble of Iraq and Chechnya, from the streets of occupied Palestine and the mountains of Kashmir, from the hills and plains of Colombia, and the forests of Andhra Pradesh and Assam, comes the chilling reply: 'There's no alternative but violence.' Terrorism. Armed struggle. Insurgency. Call it what you want.

Terrorism is vicious, ugly, and dehumanizing for its perpetrators as well as its victims. But so is war. You could say that terrorism is the privatization of war. Terrorists are the free marketeers of war. They are people who don't believe that the state has a monopoly on the legitimate use of violence.

Human society is journeying to a terrible place.

Of course, there is an alternative to terrorism. It's called justice.

It's time to recognize that no amount of nuclear weapons, or full-spectrum dominance, or 'daisy cutters', or spurious governing councils and loya jirgas, can buy peace at the cost of justice.

The urge for hegemony and preponderance by some will be matched with greater intensity by the longing for dignity and justice by others.

Exactly what form that battle takes, whether it's beautiful or bloodthirsty, depends on us.

August 2004

peace and the new corporate
liberation theology

peace and the new corporate liberation theology

It's official now. The Sydney Peace Foundation is neck deep in the business of gambling and calculated risk. Last year, very courageously, it chose Dr Hanan Ashrawi of Palestine for the Sydney Peace Prize. And, as if that were not enough, this year—of all the people in the world—it goes and chooses me.

However, I'd like to make a complaint. My sources inform me that Dr Ashrawi had a picket all to herself. This is discriminatory. I demand equal treatment for all peace prize recipients. May I formally request the Foundation to organize a picket against me after the lecture? From what I've heard, it shouldn't be hard to organize. If this is insufficient notice, then tomorrow will suit me just as well.

When this year's Sydney Peace Prize was announced, I was subjected to some pretty arch remarks from those who know me well: Why did they give a peace prize to the biggest trouble-maker we know? Didn't anybody tell them that you don't have a peaceful bone in your body? And, memorably, Arundhati didi, what's the Sydney Peace Prize? Was there a war in Sydney that you helped to stop?

Speaking for myself, I am utterly delighted to receive the Sydney Peace Prize. But I must accept it as a literary prize that honours a writer for her writing, because contrary to the many virtues that are falsely attributed to me, I'm not an activist, nor the leader of any mass movement, and I'm certainly not the 'voice of the voiceless'. (We know, of course, there's really no such thing as the 'voiceless'. There are only the deliberately silenced, or the preferably unheard.) I am a writer who cannot claim to represent anybody but herself. So even though I would like to, it would be presumptuous of me to say that I accept this prize on *behalf* of those who are involved in the struggle of the powerless and the disenfranchised against the powerful. However, may I say I accept it as the Sydney Peace Foundation's expression of solidarity with a kind of politics, a kind of worldview, that millions of us around the world subscribe to?

It might seem ironic that a person who spends most of her time thinking of strategies of resistance, and plotting to disrupt the putative peace, is given a peace prize. You must remember that I come from an essentially feudal country—and there are few things more disquieting than a feudal peace. Sometimes there's truth in old clichés. There can be no real peace without justice. And without resistance there will be no justice.

Today, it is not merely justice itself, but the *idea* of justice that is under attack. The assault on vulnerable, fragile sections of society is at once so complete, so cruel, and so clever—all encompassing and yet specifically targeted, blatantly brutal and yet unbelievably insidious—that its sheer audacity has eroded our definition of justice. It has forced us to lower our sights, and curtail our expectations. Even among the well-intentioned, the expansive, magnificent concept of justice is gradually being substituted with the reduced, far more fragile discourse of 'human rights.'

If you think about it, this is an alarming shift of paradigm. The difference is that notions of equality, of parity, have been pried loose and eased out of the equation. It's a process of attrition. Almost unconsciously, we begin to think of justice for the rich and human rights for the poor. Justice for the corporate world, human rights for its victims. Justice for Americans, human rights for Afghans and Iraqis. Justice for the Indian upper castes, human rights for Dalits and Adivasis (if that). Justice for white Australians, human rights for Aboriginals and immigrants (most times, not even that).

It is becoming more than clear that violating human rights is an inherent and necessary part of the process of implementing a coercive and unjust political and economic structure in the world. Without the violation of human rights on an enormous scale, the neoliberal project would remain in the dreamy realm of policy. But increasingly human rights violations are being portrayed as the unfortunate, almost accidental fallout of an otherwise acceptable political and economic system. As though they're a small problem that can be mopped up with a little extra attention from some non-governmental organizations (NGOs). This is why in areas of heightened conflict—in Kashmir and in Iraq, for example—human rights professionals are often regarded with a degree of suspicion. Many resistance movements in poor countries that are fighting huge injustices and questioning the underlying principles of what constitutes 'liberation' and 'development' view human rights NGOs as modern-day missionaries who have come to take the ugly edge off imperialism. To defuse political anger and to maintain the status quo.

It has been only a few weeks since a majority of Australians voted to re-elect Prime Minister John Howard, who, among other things, led Australia to participate in the illegal invasion and occupation of Iraq. The invasion of Iraq will surely go down in history as one of the most cowardly wars ever fought. It was a war in which a band of rich nations, armed with enough nuclear weapons to destroy the world several times over, rounded on a poor nation, falsely accused it of having nuclear weapons, used the United Nations to force it to disarm, then invaded it, occupied it, and are now in the process of selling it.

I speak of Iraq not because everybody is talking about it (sadly at the cost of leaving other horrors in other places to unfurl in the dark), but because it is a sign of things to come. Iraq marks the beginning of a new cycle. It offers us an opportunity to watch the corporate–military cabal that has come to be known as Empire at work. In the new Iraq, the gloves are off.

As the battle to control the world's resources intensifies, economic colonialism through formal military aggression is staging a comeback. Iraq is the logical culmination of the process of corporate globalization, in which neocolonialism and neoliberalism have fused. If we can find it in ourselves to peep behind the curtain of blood, we would glimpse the pitiless transactions taking place backstage. But first, briefly, the stage itself.

In 1991, President George Bush Senior mounted Operation Desert Storm. Tens of thousands of Iraqis were killed in the war.[1] Iraq's fields were bombed with more than 300 tonnes of depleted uranium, causing a fourfold increase in cancer among children. [2] For more than thirteen years, 24 million Iraqi people have lived in a war zone and been denied access to medicine and clean water. In the frenzy around the 2004 US presidential elections, let's remember that the levels of cruelty did not fluctuate whether the Democrats or the Republicans were in the White House. Half a million Iraqi children died because of the regime of economic sanctions in the run-up to Operation Shock & Awe.[3] Until recently, while there was a careful record of how many US soldiers had lost their lives, we had no idea of how many Iraqis had been killed. US General Tommy Franks said, 'We don't do body counts' (meaning Iraqi body counts).[4] He could have added, 'We don't do the Geneva Convention, either.' A new detailed study by *The Lancet* medical journal, which was extensively peer reviewed, estimates that there have been as many as 100,000 'excess' Iraqi deaths since the 2003 invasion.[5] That's one hundred halls full of people like this one. That's one hundred halls full of friends, parents, siblings, colleagues, lovers like you. The difference is that there aren't many children here today. Let's not forget Iraq's children.

Technically that bloodbath is called 'precision bombing'. In ordinary language, it's called butchery.

Most of this is common knowledge now. Those who support the invasion and vote for the invaders cannot take refuge in ignorance. They must truly believe that this epic brutality is right and just, or at the very least acceptable, because it's in their interest.

So the 'civilized,' 'modern' world—built painstakingly on a legacy of genocide, slavery, and colonialism—now controls most of the world's oil. And most of the world's weapons, most of the world's money, and most of the world's media. The embedded, corporate media, in which the doctrine of free speech has been substituted by the doctrine of Free (If You Agree) Speech.

The UN's former chief weapons inspectors for Iraq, Hans Blix and Mohamed El Baradei, said they found no evidence of nuclear weapons in Iraq.[6] Every scrap of evidence produced by the US and British governments was found to be false, whether it was 'proof' of Saddam Hussein buying uranium from Niger or the report produced by British intelligence that was discovered to have been plagiarized from an old student dissertation.[7] And yet, in the prelude to the war, day after day, the most 'respectable' newspapers and television channels in the United States headlined the 'evidence' of Iraq's arsenal of weapons, of nuclear weapons. It now turns out that the source for much of the manufactured 'evidence' of Iraq's arsenal of nuclear weapons was Ahmed Chalabi, who—like General Suharto of Indonesia, General Pinochet of Chile, the Shah of Iran, the Taliban, and, of course, Saddam Hussein himself—was bankrolled with millions of dollars from the good old CIA.[8]

And so a country was bombed into oblivion. It's true there have been some murmurs of apology. *Sorry 'bout that folks, but we really have to move on. Fresh rumours are coming in about nuclear weapons in Eye-ran and Syria.* And guess who is reporting on these fresh rumours? The same reporters who ran the bogus 'scoops' on Iraq. The seriously embedded A Team.

The head of Britain's BBC had to step down and one man committed suicide because a BBC reporter accused the Blair administration of 'sexing up' intelligence reports about Iraq's WMD programme.[9] But the head of Britain's government retains his job, even though his government did much more than 'sex up' intelligence reports. It is responsible for the illegal invasion of a country and the mass murder of its people.

Visitors to Australia like myself are expected to answer the following question when they fill in their visa form: 'Have you ever committed or been involved in the commission of war crimes or crimes against humanity or human rights?' Would George W. Bush and Tony Blair get visas to Australia? Under the tenets of international law, they must surely qualify as war criminals.

However, to imagine that the world would change if they were removed from office is naïve. The tragedy is that their political rivals have no real dispute with their policies. The fire and brimstone of the US presidential election campaign was about who would make a better 'Commander-in-Chief' and a more effective manager of the US Empire. Democracy no longer offers voters real choice. Only a specious choice.

Even though no Weapons of Mass Destruction have been found in Iraq, stunning new evidence has revealed that Saddam Hussein was *planning* a weapons programme. (Like I was planning to win an Olympic Gold in synchronized swimming.) Thank goodness for the doctrine of pre-emptive strike. God knows what other evil thoughts he harboured—sending Tampax in the mail to US senators or releasing female rabbits in burqas into the London underground. No doubt all will be revealed in the free and fair trial of Saddam Hussein that's coming up soon in the 'New Iraq'.

All except the chapter in which we would learn of how the United States and Britain plied Hussein with money and material assistance at the time he was carrying out murderous attacks on Iraqi Kurds and Shias.[10] All except the chapter in which we would learn that a 12,000-page report submitted by the Iraqi government to the United Nations was partially censored by the United States because it listed 24 US corporations that participated in Iraq's pre-Gulf War nuclear and conventional weapons programmes. (They included Bechtel, DuPont, Eastman Kodak, Hewlett Packard, and Unisys.)[11]

So, Iraq has been 'liberated'. Its people have been subjugated and its markets have been 'freed'. That's the anthem of neoliberalism. Free the markets. Screw the people.

The US government has privatized and sold off key sectors of Iraq's economy. Economic policies and tax laws have been rewritten. Foreign companies can now buy 100 per cent of Iraqi firms outside of the oil industry, and expatriate the profits.[12] This is an outright violation of international laws that govern an occupying force, and is among the main reasons for the stealthy, hurried charade in which power was 'handed over' to an 'interim Iraqi government'.[13] Once handing over of Iraq to the multinational corporations is complete, a mild dose of genuine democracy won't do any harm. In fact, it might be good PR for the corporate version of liberation theology, otherwise known as 'New Democracy'.

Not surprisingly, the auctioning of Iraq caused a stampede at the feeding trough. Corporations like Bechtel and Halliburton, the company that US vice-president Dick Cheney once headed, have won huge contracts for 'reconstruction' work.[14] A brief cv of any one of these corporations would give us a lay person's grasp of how it all works, not just in Iraq but all over the world. Say we pick Bechtel, only because poor little Halliburton is under investigation on charges of overpricing fuel deliveries to Iraq and for its contracts to 'restore' Iraq's oil industry, which came with a pretty serious price tag: $2.5 billion.[15]

The Bechtel Group and Saddam Hussein are old business acquaintances. Many of their dealings were negotiated by none other than Donald Rumsfeld. In 1988, after Saddam Hussein gassed thousands of Kurds, Bechtel signed contracts with his government to build a dual-use chemical plant in Baghdad.[16]

Historically, the Bechtel Group has had and continues to have inextricably close links to the Republican establishment. You could call Bechtel and the Reagan–Bush administration a team. Former Secretary of Defence Caspar Weinberger was a Bechtel general counsel and director. Former deputy energy secretary W. Kenneth Davis was Bechtel's vice president. Riley P. Bechtel, the company chairman, is on the President's Export Council. Jack Sheehan, a retired marine corps general, is a senior vice president at Bechtel and a member of the US Defence Policy Board. Former Secretary of State George Shultz, who is on the Board of Directors of the Bechtel Group, was the chairman of the advisory board of the Committee for the Liberation of Iraq.[17]

When he was asked by the *New York Times* whether he was concerned about the appearance of a conflict of interest between his two 'jobs', Shultz said, 'I don't know that Bechtel would particularly benefit from it [the invasion of Iraq] . . . But if there's work to be done, Bechtel is the type of company that could do it.'[18] Bechtel has been awarded reconstruction contracts in Iraq worth over $2 billion, which include contracts to re-build power generation plants, electrical grids, water supply, sewage systems, and airport facilities.[19] Never mind revolving doors, this—if it weren't so drenched in blood—would be a bedroom farce.

Between 2001 and 2002, nine out of thirty members of the US Defence Policy Group were connected to companies that were awarded military contracts worth $76 billion.[20] Time was when weapons were manufactured in order to fight wars. Now wars are manufactured in order to sell weapons.

Between 1990 and 2002, the Bechtel Group has contributed $3.3 million to campaign funds, both Republican and Democrat. Since 1990, it has won more than 2000 government contracts worth more than $11 billion.[21] That's an incredible return on investment, wouldn't you say?

And Bechtel has footprints around the world. That's what being a multinational means.

The Bechtel Group attracted international attention when it signed a contract with Hugo Banzer, the former Bolivian dictator, to privatize the water supply in the city of Cochabamba. The first thing Bechtel did was to raise the price of water. Hundreds of thousands of people who simply couldn't afford to pay Bechtel's bills came out onto the streets. A huge strike paralysed the city. Martial law was declared.[22] Although eventually Bechtel was forced to flee its offices, it is currently negotiating an exit payment of millions of dollars from the Bolivian government for the loss of potential profits.[23] Which, as we'll see, is growing into a popular corporate sport.

In India, Bechtel and General Electric are the new owners of the notorious and currently defunct Enron power project. The Enron contract, which legally binds the government of the state of Maharashtra to pay Enron a sum of $30 billion, was the largest contract ever signed in India.[24] Enron was not shy to boast about the millions of dollars it had spent to 'educate' Indian politicians and bureaucrats. The Enron contract in Maharashtra, which was India's first 'fast-track' private power project, has come to be known as the most massive fraud in the country's history. (Enron was another of the Republican Party's major campaign contributors.) The electricity that Enron produced was so exorbitant that the government decided it was cheaper *not* to buy electricity and pay Enron the mandatory fixed charges specified in the contract. This means that the government of one of the poorest countries in the world was paying Enron $220 million a year *not* to produce electricity![25]

Now that Enron has ceased to exist, Bechtel and GE have sued the Maharashtra State Electricity Board for nearly $6 billion.[26] The sum of money that they (or Enron) actually invested in the project is not even a fraction of this. Once more, it's a projection of profit they *would* have made had the project materialized. To give you an idea of scale, $6 billion is roughly half the amount that the government of India would need annually for a rural employment guarantee scheme that would provide a subsistence wage to millions of people currently living in abject poverty, crushed by debt, displacement, and chronic malnutrition.[27] This in a country where farmers steeped in debt are being driven to suicide, not in their hundreds, but in their thousands.[28] The proposal for a Rural Employment Guarantee Scheme is being mocked by India's corporate class as an unreasonable, utopian demand being floated by the 'lunatic' and newly powerful left. Where will the money come from? they ask derisively. And yet, any talk of reneging on a bad contract with a notoriously corrupt corporation like Enron has the same cynics hyperventilating about capital flight and the terrible risks of 'creating a bad investment climate'. The arbitration between Bechtel, GE, and the government of India is taking place right now in London. Bechtel and GE have reason for hope. The Indian finance secretary who was instrumental in approving the disastrous Enron contract has come home after a few years with the International Monetary Fund. Not just home, home with a promotion. He is now Deputy Chairman of the Planning Commission.[29]

Think about it: The *notional* profits of a single corporate project would be enough to provide a hundred days of employment a year at minimum wages (calculated at a weighted average across different states) for *25 million* people. That's five million more than the population of Australia. That is the scale of the horror of neoliberalism.

The Bechtel story gets worse. In what can only be called unconscionable, Naomi Klein writes that Bechtel successfully sued Iraq for 'war reparations' and 'lost profits' after the 1991 Gulf War. It was awarded $7 million.[30]

So, all you young management graduates, don't bother with Harvard and Wharton. Here's the Lazy Manager's Guide to Corporate Success: First, stock your board with senior government servants. Next, stock the government with members of your board. Add oil and stir. When no one can tell where the government ends and your company begins, collude with your government to equip and arm a cold-blooded dictator in an oil-rich country. Look away while he kills his own people. Simmer gently. Use the time to collect a few billion dollars in government contracts. Then collude with your government once again while it topples the dictator and bombs his subjects, taking time to specifically target essential infrastructure, killing 100,000 people on the side. Pick up another billion dollar or so worth of contracts to 'reconstruct' the infrastructure. To cover travel and incidentals, sue for reparations for lost profits from the devastated country. Finally, diversify. Buy a TV station, so that next war around you can showcase your hardware and weapons technology masquerading as coverage of the war. And finally, institute a Human Rights Prize in your company's name. You could give the first one posthumously to Mother Teresa. She won't be able to turn it down or argue back.

Invaded and occupied Iraq has been made to pay out $18.8 billion in 'reparations' since the invasion of Kuwait, including to corporations like Halliburton, Shell, Mobil, Nestlé, Pepsi, Kentucky Fried Chicken, and Toys 'R' Us.[31] That's *in addition to* its $125 billion dollar sovereign debt, forcing it to turn to the IMF, waiting in the wings like the angel of death, with its Structural Adjustment Programme.[32] (Though in Iraq there don't seem to be many structures left to adjust. Except the shadowy Al-Qaeda.)

In New Iraq, privatization has broken new ground. The US army is increasingly recruiting private mercenaries to help in the occupation.[33] The advantage with mercenaries is that when they're killed, they're not included in the US soldiers' body count.[34] It helps to manage public opinion, which is particularly important in an election year. Prison interrogations have been privatized. Torture has been privatized.[35] We have seen what that leads to. Other attractions in New Iraq include newspapers being shut down. Television stations bombed. Reporters killed.[36] US soldiers have opened fire on crowds of unarmed protestors, killing scores of people.[37] Is it a surprise, then, that the resistance that has managed to survive has taken up arms? Is there space for a secular, democratic, feminist, non-violent resistance in Iraq? There isn't really.

That is why it falls to those of us living outside Iraq to create that mass-based, secular, and non-violent resistance to the US occupation. If we fail to do that, then we run the risk of allowing the idea of resistance to be hijacked and conflated with terrorism. And that will be a pity, because they are not the same thing.

So what does 'peace' mean in this savage, corporatized, militarized world? What does it mean in a world where an entrenched system of appropriation has created a situation in which poor countries that have been plundered by colonizing regimes for centuries are steeped in debt to the very same countries that plundered them, and have to repay that debt at the rate of $382 billion a year?[38] What does peace mean in a world in which the combined wealth of the world's 587 billionaires exceeds the combined gross domestic product of the world's 135 poorest countries?[39] Or when rich countries that pay farm subsidies of $1 billion dollars a day try and force poor countries to drop their subsidies?[40] What does peace mean to people in occupied Iraq, Palestine, Kashmir, Tibet, and Chechnya? Or to the aboriginal people of Australia? Or the Ogoni of Nigeria? Or the Kurds in Turkey? Or the Dalits and Adivasis of India? What does peace mean to non-Muslims in Islamic countries, or to women in Iran, Saudi Arabia, and Afghanistan? What does it mean to the millions who are being uprooted from their lands by dams and development projects? What does peace mean to the poor who are being actively robbed of their resources and for whom everyday life is a grim battle for water, shelter, survival, and, above all, some semblance of dignity? For them, peace is war.

We know very well who benefits from war in the age of Empire. But we must also ask ourselves honestly: who benefits from peace in the age of Empire? War-mongering is criminal. But talking of peace without talking of justice could easily become advocacy for a kind of capitulation. And talking of justice without unmasking the institutions and the systems that perpetrate injustice is beyond hypocritical.

It's easy to blame the poor for being poor. It's easy to believe that the world is being caught up in an escalating spiral of terrorism and war. That's what allows the US president to say, 'You are either with us or you are with the terrorists.'[41] But we know that that's a spurious choice. We know that terrorism is only the privatization of war. That terrorists are the free marketers of war. They believe that the legitimate use of violence is not the sole prerogative of the state.

It is mendacious to make a moral distinction between the unspeakable brutality of terrorism and the indiscriminate carnage of war and occupation. Both kinds of violence are unacceptable. We cannot support one and condemn the other.

The real tragedy is that most people in the world are trapped between the horror of a putative peace and the terror of war. Those are the two sheer cliffs we're hemmed in by. The question is: How do we climb out of this crevasse?

For those who are materially well off but morally uncomfortable, the first question you must ask yourself is: do you really want to climb out of it? How far are you prepared to go? Has the crevasse become too comfortable?

If you really want to climb out, there's good news and bad news.

The good news is that the advance party began the climb some time ago. They're already half way up. Thousands of activists across the world have been hard at work preparing footholds and securing the ropes to make it easier for the rest of us. There isn't only one path up. There are hundreds of ways of doing it. There are hundreds of battles being fought around the world that need your skills, your minds, your resources. No battle is irrelevant. No victory is too small.

The bad news is that colourful demonstrations, weekend marches, and annual trips to the World Social Forum are not enough. There have to be targeted acts of real civil disobedience with real consequences. Maybe we can't flip a switch and conjure up a revolution. But there are several things we could do. For example, you could make a list of those corporations that have profited from the invasion of Iraq and have offices here in Australia. You could name them, boycott them, occupy their offices, and force them out of business. If it can happen in Bolivia, it can happen in India. It can happen in Australia. Why not?

That's only a small suggestion. But remember that if the struggle were to resort to violence, it will lose vision, beauty, and imagination. Most dangerous of all, it will marginalize and eventually victimize women. And a political struggle that does not have women at the heart of it, above it, below it, and within it, is no struggle at all.

The point is that the battle must be joined. As the wonderful historian Howard Zinn put it: You can't be neutral on a moving train.[42]

November 2004

Ahimsa

1. The government of India plans to build thirty large, 135 medium, and 3000 small dams on the Narmada river, displacing 400,000 people in the process. See <http://www.narmada.org>.

2. See <http://www.jang.com.pk/thenews/spedition/ pak-india/accord.htm>.

3. The activists ended their fast on 18 June 2002 after an independent committee was set up to look into the issue of resettlement. See <http:// www.narmada.org/nba-press-releases;jun-2002/ fast.ends.html>.

Come September

1. See John Berger, 1990, *Ways of Seeing*, Penguin, New York.

2. See John Pomfret, 'Chinese Working Overtime to Sew US Flags', *Washington Post,* 20 September 2001, p. A14.

3. See Arundhati Roy, 2002, 'Democracy: Who Is She When She's at Home' in *The Algebra of Infinite Justice*, Penguin Books, New Delhi.

4. See David E. Sanger, 'Bin Laden Is Wanted in Attacks, "Dead or Alive", President Says', *New York*

Times, 18 September 2001, p. A1; and John F. Burns, '10-Month Afghan Mystery: Is bin Laden Dead or Alive?' *New York Times,* 30 September 2002, p. A1.

5. See the Associated Press database of those confirmed dead, reported dead or reported missing in the 11 September terrorist attacks <http://attacksvictims. ap.org/totals.asp>.

6. Quoted in Seymour M. Hersh, 1983, *The Price of Power: Kissinger in the Nixon White House*, Summit Books, New York, p. 265.

7. See *Chile: The Other September 11*, 2002, Pilar Aguilera and Ricardo Fredes (eds), Ocean Press, New York; Amnesty International, 'The Case of Augusto Pinochet' <http://www.amnestyusa.org/countries/ chile/pinochet_case.html>.

8. Clifford Krauss, 'Britain Arrests Pinochet to Face Charges by Spain', *New York Times,* 18 October 1998, p. 1:1; National Security Archive, 'Chile: 16,000 Secret US Documents Declassified,' Press Release, 13 November 2000 <http://www.gwu.edu/ ~nsarchiv/news/20001113/>; and selected documents on the National Security Archive website <http://www.gwu.edu/~nsarchiv/news/ 20001113/#docs>.

9. Kissinger said this to Pinochet at a meeting of the Organisation of American States in Santiago, Chile, on 8 June 1976. See Lucy Kosimar, 'Kissinger Covered Up Chile Torture', *The Observer,* 28 February 1999, p. 3.

10. See Eduardo Galeano, 1998, *Open Veins of Latin America: Five Centuries of the Pillage of a Continent,* 2nd edn, trans. Cedric Belfrage, Monthly Review Press, New York; Noam Chomsky, 1985, *Turning the Tide: U.S. Intervention in Central America and the Struggle for Peace,* 2nd edn, South End Press, Boston;

Noam Chomsky, 1983, *The Culture of Terrorism*, South End Press, Boston; and Gabriel Kolko, 1988, *Confronting the Third World: United States Foreign Policy, 1945–1980*, Pantheon, New York.

11. In a public relations move, the SOA renamed itself the Western Hemisphere Institute for Security Cooperation (WHISC) on 17 January 2001. See Jack Nelson-Pallmeyer, 2001, *School of Assassins: Guns, Greed, and Globalization,* 2nd edn, Orbis Books, New York; Michael Gormley, 'Army School Faces Critics Who Call It Training Ground for Assassins', Associated Press, 2 May 1998; and School of the Americas Watch <http://www.soaw.org>.

12. On these interventions, see, among other sources, Noam Chomsky, 2002, *American Power and the New Mandarins*, 2nd edn, New Press, New York; Noam Chomsky, 1970, *At War With Asia*, Vintage Books, New York; and Howard Zinn, 2002, *Vietnam: The Logic of Withdrawal,* 2nd edn, South End Press, Cambridge.

13. See Samih K. Farsoun and Christina E. Zacharia, 1997, *Palestine and the Palestinians*, Westview Press, Boulder, Colorado, p. 10.

14. Quoted in Noam Chomsky, 2000, *Fateful Triangle: The United States, Israel, and the Palestinians*, 2nd edn, South End Press, Cambridge, p. 90.

15. Quoted in Editorial, 'Scurrying Towards Bethlehem', *New Left Review* 10, 2nd series, July/August 2001, p. 9, n. 5.

16. Quoted in Farsoun and Zacharia, *Palestine and the Palestinians,* pp. 10 and 243.

17. Farsoun and Zacharia, *Palestine and the Palestinians,* pp. 111 and 123.

18. Farsoun and Zacharia, *Palestine and the Palestinians,* p. 116.

19. See Chomsky, *Fateful Triangle*, pp. 103–07, 118–32, and 156–60.

20. From 1987 to 2002 alone, more than 2000 Palestinians have been killed. See B'Tselem (The Israeli Information Center for Human Rights in the Occupied Territories), 'Palestinians Killed in the Occupied Territories,' Table <http://www.btselem. org/English/Statistics/Total_Casualties.asp>.

21. See Naseer H. Aruri, forthcoming, *Dishonest Broker: The United States, Israel, and the Palestinians*, South End Press, Cambridge; Noam Chomsky, 1996, *World Orders Old and New*, 2nd edn, Columbia University Press, New York.

22. See Nick Anderson, 'House Panel Increases Aid for Israel, Palestinians', *Los Angeles Times,* 10 May 2002, p. A1; Aruri, *Dishonest Broker,* Appendix 1 and Appendix 2; and Anthony Arnove and Ahmed Shawki, 2002, 'Foreword', *The Struggle for Palestine,* ed. Lance Selfa, Haymarket Books, Chicago, p. xxv.

23. Article 27 of the Charter of the Islamic Resistance Movement (Hamas), quoted in Farsoun and Zacharia, *Palestine and the Palestinians,* Appendix 13, p. 339.

24. George W. Bush, 'Text of Bush's Speech: "It Is Iraq Against the World"', *Los Angeles Times,* 12 September 1990, p. A7.

25. See Glenn Frankel, 'Iraq Long Avoided Censure on Rights', *Washington Post,* 22 September 1990, p. A1.

26. See Christopher Dickey and Evan Thomas, 'How Saddam Happened', *Newsweek,* 23 September 2002, pp. 35–37.

27. See Anthony Arnove (ed), 2002, 'Introduction', *Iraq Under Siege: The Deadly Impact of Sanctions and War*, 2nd edn, South End Press, Cambridge, p. 20.

28. See Arnove, *Iraq Under Siege,* pp. 221–22.

29. See Arnove, *Iraq Under Siege,* pp. 17, 205.

30. See Thomas J. Nagy, 'The Secret Behind the Sanctions: How the US Intentionally Destroyed Iraq's Water Supply', *The Progressive*, 65: 9, September 2001.

31. See Arnove, *Iraq Under Siege,* pp. 121 and 185–203. See also Nicholas D. Kristof, 'The Stones of Baghdad', *New York Times,* 4 October 2002, p. A27.

32. Leslie Stahl, 'Punishing Saddam', produced by Catherine Olian, CBS, *60 Minutes,* 12 May 1996.

33. Elisabeth Bumiller, 'Bush Aides Set Strategy to Sell Policy on Iraq', *New York Times,* 7 September 2002, p. A1.

34. Richard Perle, 'Why the West Must Strike First Against Saddam Hussein', *Daily Telegraph* (London), 9 August 2002, p. 22.

35. See Alan Simpson and Glen Rangwala, 'The Dishonest Case for a War on Iraq', 27 September 2002 <http://www.traprockpeace.org/counter-dossier.html> and Glen Rangwala, 'Notes Further to the Counter-Dossier', 29 September 2002 <http://www.traprockpeace.org/counter-dossier.html#notes>.

36. George Bush, 'Bush's Remarks on US Military Strikes in Afghanistan', *New York Times,* 8 October 2001, p. B6.

37. See Paul Watson, 'Afghanistan Aims to Revive Pipeline Plans', *Los Angeles Times,* 30 May 2002, p. A1; Ilene R. Prusher, Scott Baldauf, and Edward Girardet, 'Afghan Power Brokers', *Christian Science Monitor,* 10 June 2002, p. 1.

38. See Lisa Fingeret et al., 'Markets Worry That Conflict Could Spread in Area That Holds Two-Thirds of World Reserves', *Financial Times* (London), 2 April 2002, p. 1.

39. Thomas L. Friedman, 'Craziness Pays', *New York Times,* 24 February 1998, p. A21.

40. Thomas L. Friedman, 1999, *The Lexus and the Olive Tree: Understanding Globalization*, Farrar, Strauss, and Giroux, New York, p. 373.

41. Statistics from Joseph E. Stiglitz, 2002, *Globalization and Its Discontents*, W.W. Norton, New York, p. 5; Noam Chomsky, 2000, *Rogue States: The Rule of Law in World Affairs*, South End Press, Cambridge, p. 214; and Noreena Hertz, 'Why Consumer Power Is Not Enough', *New Statesman,* 30 April 2001.

42. Surjeet Bhalla, 2003, *Imagine There's No Country: Poverty, Inequality and Growth in the Era of Globalization*, Penguin Books India, New Delhi.

43. Among the many treaties and international agreements the United States has not signed, ignores, violates, or has broken are: UN International Covenant on Economic, Social and Cultural Rights (1966); the UN Convention on the Rights of the Child (CRC); the UN Convention on the Elimination of All Forms of Discrimination Against Women (CEDAW); agreements setting the jurisdiction for the International Criminal Court (ICC); the 1972 Anti-ballistic Missile Treaty with Russia; the Comprehensive Test Ban Treaty (CTBT); and the Kyoto Protocol regulating greenhouse gas emissions.

44. See David Cole and James X. Dempsey, 2002, *Terrorism and the Constitution: Sacrificing Civil Liberties in the Name of National Security*, New Press, New York.

45. Luke Harding, 'Elusive Mullah Omar "Back in Afghanistan"', *Guardian* (London), 30 August 2002, p. 12.

46. See Human Rights Watch, 'Opportunism in the Face of Tragedy: Repression in the Name of Anti-Terrorism' <http://www.hrw.org/campaigns/september11/opportunismwatch.htm>.

47. Donald Rumsfeld, Special Defense Briefing, 'Developments Concerning Attacks on the Pentagon and the World Trade Center Last Week', Federal News Service, 20 September 2001.

The Loneliness of Noam Chomsky

1. R.W. Apple, Jr, 'Bush Appears in Trouble Despite Two Big Advantages', *New York Times,* 4 August 1988, p. A1. Bush made this remark in refusing to apologize for the shooting down of an Iranian passenger plane, killing 290 passengers. See Lewis Lapham, 2002, *Theater of War*, New Press, New York, p. 126.

2. Chomsky would be the first to point out that other pioneering media analysts include his frequent co-author, Edward Herman, Ben Bagdikian (whose 1983 classic *The Media Monopoly* recounts the suppression of Chomsky and Herman's *Counter-Revolutionary Violence*), and Herbert Schiller.

3. Paul Betts, 'Ciampi Calls for Review of Media Laws', *Financial Times* (London), 24 July 2002, p. 8. For an overview of Berlusconi's holdings, see Ketupa.net Media Profiles <http://www.ketupa.net/berlusconi1.htm>.

4. See Sabin Russell, 'US Push for Cheap Cipro Haunts AIDS Drug Dispute', *San Francisco Chronicle,* 8 November 2001, p. A13; Frank Swoboda and Martha McNeil Hamilton, 'Congress Passes $15 Billion Airline Bailout', *Washington Post,* 22 September 2001, p. A1.

5. President George W. Bush Jr, 'President Bush's Address on Terrorism Before a Joint Meeting of Congress', *New York Times,* 21 September 2001, p. B4.

6. Dan Eggen, 'Ashcroft Invokes Religion In US War on Terrorism', *Washington Post,* 20 February 2002, p. A2.

7. President George W. Bush Jr, 'Bush's Remarks on US Military Strikes in Afghanistan', *New York Times,* 8 October 2001, p. B6.

8. President George W. Bush Jr, Remarks at FBI Headquarters, Washington, DC, 10 October 2001, Federal Document Clearinghouse.

9. See Howard Zinn, 2001, *A People's History of the United States: 1492–Present,* 20th anniversary edition, HarperCollins, New York.

10. Bob Marley and N.G. Williams (*aka* King Sporty), 'Buffalo Soldier'.

11. Noam Chomsky, 1987, 'The Manufacture of Consent', in *The Chomsky Reader,* James Peck (ed.) Pantheon, New York, pp. 121–22.

12. See Jim Miller, 'Report from the Inferno', *Newsweek,* 7 September 1981, p. 72; Review of Committee for the Compilation of Materials on Damage Caused by the Atomic Bombs in Hiroshima and Nagasaki, 1981, *Hiroshima and Nagasaki: The Physical, Medical, and Social Effects of the Atomic Bombings,* Basic, New York.

13. David E. Sanger, 'Bush to Formalize a Defense Policy of Hitting First', *New York Times,* 17 June 2002, p. A1; David E. Sanger, 'Bush Renews Pledge to Strike First to Counter Terror Threats', *New York Times,* 20 July 2002, p. A3. See also *The National Security Strategy of the United States of America,* 20 September 2002 <http://www.whitehouse.gov/nsc/nss.html>.

14. See Terence O'Malley, 'The Afghan Memory Holds Little Room for Trust in US', *Irish Times,* 15 October 2001, p. 16.

15. See Anthony Arnove (ed.), 2002, *Iraq Under Siege: The Deadly Impact of Sanctions and War,* 2nd edn, South End Press, Cambridge.

16. See Noam Chomsky, 1995, 'Memories', review of *In Retrospect* by Robert McNamara, Times Books, New York, in *Z* magazine (July–August 1995). Available online at <http://www.zmag.org/>.

17. 'Myth and Reality in Bloody Battle for the Skies', *Guardian* (London), 13 October 1998, p. 15.

18. Bill Keller, 'Moscow Says Afghan Role Was Illegal and Immoral', *New York Times,* 24 October 1989, p. A1.

19. Noam Chomsky, 'Afghanistan and South Vietnam', in *The Chomsky Reader,* Peck (ed.), p. 225.

20. Samuel P. Huntington, 'The Bases of Accommodation', *Foreign Affairs* 46:4 (1968), pp. 642–56 (Quoted in Noam Chomsky, 1970, *At War with Asia*, Vintage Books, New York, p. 87).

21. Ibid.

22. Ibid.

23. T.D. Allman, 'The Blind Bombers', *Far Eastern Economic Review*, 75: 5, 29 January 1972, pp. 18–20 (Quoted in Noam Chomsky, 2003, *For Reasons of State*, New Press, New York, p. 72).

24. Chomsky, *For Reasons of State,* p. 72; Chomsky, *At War with Asia,* p. 87; and Lapham, *Theater of War,* p. 145.

25. T.D. Allman, 'The War in Laos: Plain Facts', *Far Eastern Economic Review*, 75: 2, 8 January 1972, p. 16 (Quoted in Chomsky, *For Reasons of State,* pp. 173–74).

26. Chomsky, *For Reasons of State,* p. 18. See also Noam Chomsky, 'The Pentagon Papers as Propaganda and as History', in Noam Chomsky and Howard Zinn (eds), 1971-72, *The Pentagon Papers: The Defense Department History of United States Decisionmaking on Vietnam: The Senator Gravel Edition: Critical Essays,* Volume 5, Beacon Press, Boston, pp. 79–201.

27. Chomsky, *For Reasons of State,* pp. 67 and 70.

28. William Pfaff, 1971, *Condemned to Freedom: The Breakdown of Liberal Society,* Random House, New York, pp. 75–77 (Quoted in Chomsky, *For Reasons of State,* p. 94).

29. Pfaff, *Condemned to Freedom,* pp. 75–77 (Quoted in Chomsky, *For Reasons of State,* pp. 94–95).

30. *The Pentagon Papers,* Volume 4, p. 43 (Quoted in Chomsky, *For Reasons of State,* p. 67).

31. Philip Jones Griffiths, 2001, *Vietnam Inc.,* 2nd edn, Phaidon, New York (First edition quoted in Chomsky, *For Reasons of State,* pp. 3–4).

32. Noam Chomsky, interview with James Peck, in *The Chomsky Reader,* Peck (ed.), p. 14.

Confronting Empire

1. See Ranjit Devraj, 'Asia's "Outcast" Hurt By Globalization', Inter Press Service, 6 January 2003; Statesman News Service, 'Farm Suicide Heat on Jaya', *The Statesman* (India), 9 January 2003; and 'Government Policies Driving Farmers to Suicide', *The Times of India,* 4 February 2002.

2. See 'Government's Food Policy Gets a Reality Check from States', *Indian Express,* 11 January 2003; and Parul Chandra, 'Victims Speak of Hunger, Starvation Across Country', *The Times of India,* 11 January 2003.

3. See Arundhati Roy, 2002, 'Democracy: Who Is She When She's at Home?', *The Algebra of Infinite Justice*, Penguin Books, New Delhi, p. 265 . See also Pankaj Mishra, 'The Other Face of Fanaticism', *New York Times,* 2 February 2003, p. 6: 42–46; and Concerned Citizens Tribunal, 2002, *Crime Against Humanity: An Inquiry Into the Carnage in Gujarat,* 2 vols, Citizens for Justice and Peace, Mumbai.

4. See Edward Luce, 'Gujarat Win Likely to Embolden Hindu Right', *Financial Times* (London), 16 December 2002, p. 8.

5. See Oscar Olivera, 'The War Over Water in Cochabamba, Bolivia', 'Services for All?' trans. Florencia Belvedere, presented at Municipal Services Project (MSP) Conference, South Africa, 15–18 May 2002 <http://qsilver.queensu.ca/~mspadmin/pages/Conferences/Services/Olivera.htm>.

6. See Tom Lewis, 'Contagion in Latin America', *International Socialist Review*, 24, July–August 2002.

7. See Julian Borger and Alex Bellos, 'US "Gave the Nod" to Venezuelan Coup', *Guardian* (London), 17 April 2002, p. 13.

8. See David Sharrock, 'Thousands Protest in Buenos Aires as Economic Woes Persist', *The Times* (London), 21 December 2002, p. 18.

9. See Mary McGrory, 'A River of Peaceful People', *Washington Post,* 23 January 2003, p. A21.

Peace Is War

1. Mohammed Shehzad, '"Killing Hindus" Better than Dialogue with India: Lashkar-e-Taiba Chief', Agence France-Presse, 3 April 2003.

2. Ben H. Bagdikian, 2004, *The New Media Monopoly*, Beacon Press, Boston.

3. Edward Helmore, 'Who Sets the TV Control?: Battle Is Raging Over a Decision to Allow US Media Giants to Own Even More', *The Observer* (London), 8 June 2003, p. 6.

4. Howard Rheingold, 'From the Screen to the Streets', *In These Times,* 17 November 2003, p. 34; Stephen Labaton, 'Debate/Monopoly on Information: It's a World of Media Plenty: Why Limit Ownership?' *New York Times,* 12 October 2003, p.4:4.

5. See Connie Koch, 2004, *2/15: The Day the World Said No to War*, Hello [NYC], New York.

6. See Edward Luce, 'Battle Over Ayodhya Temple Looms', *Financial Times* (London), 2 February 2002, p. 7.

7. Pankaj Mishra, 'A Mediocre Goddess', *New Statesman*, 9 April 2001; John Ward Andersen, 'The Flame That Lit An Inferno: Hindu Leader Creates Anti-Muslim Frenzy', *Washington Post,* 11 August 1993, p. A14. See also Arundhati Roy, 2002, 'Democracy: Who Is She When She Is at Home?' in *The Algebra of Infinite Justice*, Penguin Books India, New Delhi.

8. See chapter 9, 'In Memory of Shankar Guha Niyogi'.

9. Raja Bose, 'A River Runs Through It', *Times of India,* 25 February 2001.

10. C. Rammanohar Reddy, 'At Loggerheads Over Resources', *The Hindu,* 27 May 2001; Kata Lee, 'India: Unarmed Tribals Killed by Jharkhand Police', Asian Center for the Progress of Peoples (ACPP), Asian Human Rights Commission, 3 March 2003 <http://www.ahrchk.net/news/mainfile.php/ahrnews_200103/1496/?print=yes>.

11. Gurbir Singh, 'Guj[arat] Police Cane Protesters of NATELCO-UNOCAL Port', *The Economic Times,*

12 April 2000; 'Human Rights Defenders Persecuted in India: Amnesty [International]', The Press Trust of India, 26 April 2000. See also Rosa Basanti, 'Villagers Take on Giant Port Project', Inter Press Service, 7 June 2000.

12. Sanjay Kumar, 'The Adivasis of Orissa', *The Hindu,* 6 November 2001; Anu Kumar, 'Orissa: A Continuing Denial of Adivasi Rights', InfoChange News and Features, November 2003, Centre for Communication and Development Studies <http://www.infochangeindia.org/analysis10.jsp>. See also 'When Freedom Is Trampled Upon', *The Hindu,* 24 January 1999.

13. Danielle Knight, 'The Destructive Impact of Fish Farming', Inter Press Service, 13 October 1999.

14. 'Eviction of Tribals by Force in Kerala to be Taken Up with NHRC', *The Hindu,* 26 February 2003.

15. On the Nagarnar attacks, see Kuldip Nayar, 'Pushing the POTO', *The Hindu,* 28 November 2001.

16. People's War Group (PWG), Maoist Communist Centre (MCC), Pakistan's Inter-Services Intelligence (ISI), and the Liberation Tigers of Tamil Eelam (LTTE).

17. 'Mr [Vakkom] Purushothaman said he was of the view that the Adivasis who had "tried to establish a parallel government should have been suppressed or shot."' Quoted in 'Opposition Boycotts Assembly', *The Hindu,* 22 February 2003.

18. See Mari Marcel Thekaekara, 'What Really Happened', *Frontline,* 15–28 March 2003 <http://www.frontlineonnet.com/fl2006/stories/20030328002204600.htm>.

19. Sanjay Nigam, Mangat Verma, Chittaroopa Palit, 'Fifteen Thousand Farmers Gather in Mandleshwar to Protest Against Electricity Tariff Hikes in Madhya

Pradesh', Nimad Malwa Kisan Mazdoor Sangathan press release, 27 February 2003 <http://www.narmada.org/nba-press-releases/february-2003/antitariff. html>.

20. World Commission on Dams, 2000, *Dams and Development: A New Framework for Decision-Making: The Report of the World Commission on Dams*, Earthscan, London, box 4.3, p. 104.

21. Arundhati Roy, 1999, *The Cost of Living*, Modern Library, New York, *Power Politics,* 2nd edn, 2001, South End Press, Cambridge, MA and *The Algebra of Infinite Justice*, 2002, Penguin Books India, New Delhi.

22. L.S. Aravinda, 'Supreme Court Majority Judgement: Mockery of Modern India', Association for India's Development <http://www.aidindia.org/hq/publications/essays/articles.htm>.

23. World Bank Water Resources Management Group, 2004, *The World Bank Water Resources Sector Strategy: Strategic Directions for World Bank Engagement*, International Bank for Reconstruction and Development/World Bank, Washington, DC <http://lnweb18.worldbank.org/ESSD/ardext.nsf/18ByDoc Name/Strategy>; Peter Bosshard, Janneke Bruil, Carol Welch, Korinna Horta, and Shannon Lawrence, 'Gambling with People's Lives: What the World Bank's New "High-Risk/High-Reward" Strategy Means for the Poor and the Environment', 19 September 2003 <http://www.environmentaldefense.org/article.cfm?ContentID=3005>. See also Carrieann Davies, 'From the Editor: Back to the Future', *Water Power & Dam Construction,* 30 April 2003, p. 3.

24. 'Major Rivers to Be Linked by 2016', The Press Trust of India, 17 December 2002. See also Medha

Patkar (ed.), 2004, *River Linking: A Millennium Folly?* National Alliance of People's Movements/Initiative, Pune.

25. See 'Tribals' Promised Land is Kerala Sanctuary', *Indian Express,* 6 February 2003.

26. 'Call to Prosecute Grasim Management for Pollution', *Business Line*, 1 February 1999.

27. R. Krishnakumar, 'Closure of Grasim Industries', *Frontline*, 21 July–3 August 2001 <http://www.frontlineonnet.com/fl1 815/18151320.htm>.

An Ordinary Person's Guide to Empire

1. CNN International, 21 March 2003.

2. Ibid.

3. CNN International, 21 March 2003. See also Dexter Filkins, 'In the Field Marines: Either Take a Shot or Take a Chance,' *New York Times*, 29 March 2003, p. A1. Filkins interviewed Sergeant Eric Schrumpf, aged twenty-eight, of the Fifth Marine Regiment. "'We had a great day," Sergeant Schrumpf said. "We killed a lot of people. . . . "We dropped a few civilians, . . . but what do you do?" . . . He recalled watching one of the women standing near the Iraqi soldier go down. "I'm sorry," the sergeant said. "But the chick was in the way."'

4. Patrick E. Tyler and Janet Elder, 'Threats and Responses: The Poll: Poll Finds Most in U.S. Support Delaying a War', *New York Times*, 14 February 2003, p. A1.

5. Maureen Dowd, 'The Xanax Cowboy', *New York Times*, 9 March 2003, p. 4:13.

6. George W. Bush, joint statement with Tony Blair after the Azores summit. See 'Excerpts From

Remarks by Bush and Blair: "Iraq Will Soon Be Liberated"', *New York Times*, 9 April 2003, p. B7.

7. 'You Cannot Hide, Hoon Tells Saddam', *Birmingham Evening Mail*, 20 March 2003, p. 2; Charles Reiss 'We Had No Option But to Use Force to Disarm Saddam, Says Straw', *The Evening Standard* (London), 20 March 2003, p. 11.

8. General Vince Brooks, deputy director of operations, United States Central Command Daily Press Briefing, Federal News Service, 27 March 2003.

9. CNN International, 25 March 2003.

10. Remarks by President George W. Bush to troops at MacDill Air Force Base, Tampa, Florida, Federal News Service, 26 March 2003.

11. See David Cole, 2003, *Enemy Aliens: Double Standards and Constitutional Freedoms in the War on Terrorism*, The New Press, New York.

12. Charles Lane, 'Justices to Rule on Detainees' Right; Court Access for 660 Prisoners at Issue', *Washington Post*, 11 November 2003, p. 1; David Rohde, 'U.S. Rebuked on Afghans in Detention', *New York Times*, 8 March 2004, p. A6. See also Cole, *Enemy Aliens*, pp. 39–45.

13. Jeremy Armstrong, 'Field of Death: Total Slaughter: Amnesty [International] Demands Probe Be Over Bloody Massacre of Taliban Prisoners', *The Mirror* (London), 29 November 2001, p. 6.

14. 'Injustice in Afghanistan', editorial, *Washington Post*, 21 March 2004, p. B6.

15. Bill O'Reilly, 'Talking Points Memo', *The O'Reilly Factor*, Fox News, 24 March 2003. See also Bill O'Reilly, 'Unresolved Problems: Interview with Kenneth Roth', *The O'Reilly Factor*, Fox News, 27 March 2003.

16. See Rageh Omaar, 2004, *Revolution Day: The Human*

Story of the Battle for Iraq, Viking, London.

17. Martin Bright, Ed Vulliamy, and Peter Beaumont, 'Revealed: US Dirty Tricks to Win Vote on Iraq War', *The Observer* (London), 2 March 2003, p. 1.

18. Marc Santora, 'Aid Workers Fear Dangers of Delay: Basra, Without Power and Water, Is at Risk', *International Herald Tribune*, 25 March 2003, p. 1; John Pilger, 'Gulf War 2: Six Days of Shame', *The Mirror* (London), 26 March 2003, p. 14.

19. Patrick Nicholson, 'The Cans and Buckets Are Empty and People Are Desperate', *The Independent* (London), 5 April 2003, p. 8.

20. Agence France-Presse, 'Iraq's Weekly Oil Production Reaches New Levels', 23 July 2002.

21. Mark Nicholson, 'Troops Prepare to Deliver Supplies', *Financial Times* (London), 27 March 2003, p. 2.

22. Nick Guttmann, 'Humanitarian Aid: Wanted: 32 Galahads a Day', *Independent on Sunday* (London), 30 March 2003, p. 26.

23. Quoted in Noam Chomsky, 2003, *For Reasons of State*, New Press, New York, pp. 67–69.

24. Juan J. Walte, 'Greenpeace: 200,000 Died in Gulf', *USA Today*, 30 May 1991, p. 1A.

25. Kim Cobb, 'Vets Warn of Risks to Soldiers' Health: Critics Fear Repeat of Gulf War Illnesses', *Houston Chronicle*, 9 February 2003, p. 1.

26. James Meikle, '"Health Will Suffer for Years"', *The Guardian* (London), 12 November 2003, p. 17.

27. Joel Brinkley, 'American Companies Rebuilding Iraq Find They Are Having to Start from the Ground Up', *New York Times*, 22 February 2004, p. 1:11; Tucker Carlson, 'Hired Guns', *Esquire*, March 2004, pp. 130–38.

28. Felicity Barringer, 'Security Council Votes to Revive

Oil-for-Food Program in Iraq', *New York Times*, 29 March 2003, p. B7.

29. Dan Morgan and Karen DeYoung, 'Hill Panels Approve War Funds, With Curbs: Most Restrictions Aimed at Pentagon', *Washington Post*, 2 April 2003, p. A26.

30. Lou Dobbs, *Lou Dobb's Moneyline*, CNN, 27 March 2003.

31. Greg Wright, 'French Fries? Mais Non, Congress Calls Em Freedom Fries', Gannett News Service, 12 March 2003 <http://www.gannettonline.com/gns/faceoff2/20030312-18 100.shtml>.

32. Serge Bellanger, 'Of Wal-Marts, BMWs and Brie', *Chicago Tribune*, 27 April 2003, p. 9.

33. George W. Bush, Camp David, Maryland, press briefing, 16 September 2001: '[W]e're going to do it. We will rid the world of the evildoers. We will call together freedom-loving people to fight terrorism. And so on this day of—on the Lord's day, I say to my fellow Americans, thank you for your prayers, thank you for your compassion, thank you for your love for one another and tomorrow when you get back to work, work hard like you always have. But we've been warned. We've been warned there are evil people in this world. We've been warned so vividly and we'll be alert. Your government is alert. The governors and mayors are alert that evil folks still lurk out there.'

Instant-mix Imperial Democracy

1. Molly Moore, 'The USS Vincennes and a Deadly Mistake: Highly Sophisticated Combat Ship at Center of Defense Department Investigation', *Washington Post*, 4 July 1988, p. A23.

2. R.W. Apple, Jr, 'Bush Appears in Trouble Despite Two Big Advantages', *New York Times*, 4 August 1988, p. A1. See Lewis Lapham, 2002, *Theater of War*, New Press, New York, p. 126.

3. Patrick E. Tyler and Janet Elder, 'Threats and Responses: The Poll: Poll Finds Most In U.S. Support Delaying a War', *New York Times*, 14 February 2003, p. A1.

4. Maureen Dowd, 'The Xanax Cowboy', *New York Times*, 9 March 2003, p. 4:13.

5. President George W. Bush, address to the nation, State Floor Cross Hallway, the White House, Federal News Service, 17 March 2003 <http://www.whitehouse.gov/news/releases/2003/03/20030319-17.html>.

6. President George W. Bush, speech at the Cincinnati Museum Center, Cincinnati, Ohio, Federal News Service, 7 October 2002 <http://www.whitehouse.gov/news/releases/2002/10/20021007-8.html>.

7. See Saïd K. Aburish, 2001, *Saddam Hussein: The Politics of Revenge*, Bloomsbury, London. See also the PBS *Frontline* interview with Aburish, 'Secrets of His Life and Leadership', from 'The Survival of Saddam' <http://www.pbs.org/wgbh/pages/frontline/shows/saddam/interviews/aburish.html>.

8. See Anthony Arnove, 'Indonesia: Crisis and Revolt', *International Socialist Review 5*, Fall 1998.

9. Originally stated in a May 1980 interview on the *MacNeil/Lehrer Report* on PBS. Quoted in Philip Geyelin, 'Forget Gunboat Diplomacy', *Washington Post*, 29 September 1980, p. A13.

10. See Anthony Arnove (ed.), 2002, *Iraq Under Siege: The Deadly Impact of Sanctions and War*, 2nd edn, South End Press, Cambridge, MA, especially the chapter by Noam Chomsky, 'US Iraq Policy:

Consequences and Motives', pp. 65–74, and Arnove's Introduction, pp. 11–31.

11. See, among many other of Bush's speeches, his address to the Wings over the Rockies Air and Space Museum, Denver, Colorado, Federal News Service, 28 October 2002, in which he reminded his audience that Hussein 'is a person who has gassed his own people . . . [H]e's anxious to have, once again to develop a nuclear weapon. He's got connections with Al-Qaeda.' Bush also commented: 'We love life, everybody matters as far as we're concerned, everybody is precious. They have no regard for innocent life whatsoever. (Applause.) They hate the fact that we love freedom. We love our freedom of religion, we love our freedom of speech, we love every aspect of freedom. (Applause.) And we're not changing. (Applause.) We're not intimidated. As a matter of fact, the more they hate our freedoms, the more we love our freedoms. (Applause.)' <http:// www.whitehouse.gov/news/releases/2002/10/ 20021028-5.html>.

12. See Arnove, *Iraq Under Siege*, pp. 68–69.

13. 'We are a nation called to defend freedom—a freedom that is not the grant of any government or document, but is our endowment from God.' See Dan Eggen, 'Ashcroft Invokes Religion in U.S. War on Terrorism', *Washington Post*, 20 February 2002, p. A2.

14. Michael R. Gordon, 'Baghdad's Power Vacuum Is Drawing Only Dissent', *New York Times*, 21 April 2003, p. A10.

15. Peter Beaumont, 'Anger Rises as US Fails to Control Anarchy', *The Observer* (London), 13 April 2003, p. 3.

16. Jim Dwyer, 'Troops Endure Blowing Sands and Mud

Rain', *New York Times*, 26 March 2003, p. A1; Neela Banerjee, 'Army Depots in Iraqi Desert Have Names of Oil Giants', *New York Times*, 27 March 2003, p. C14.

17. Secretary of Defence Donald H. Rumsfeld, Defence Department operational update briefing, Pentagon Briefing Room, Arlington, Virginia, Federal News Service, 11 April 2003.

18. Reuters, 'Number Imprisoned Exceeds 2 Million, Justice Dept. Says', *Washington Post*, 7 April 2003, p. A4; The Sentencing Project, 'U.S. Prison Populations: Trends and Implications', May 2003, p. 1 <http://www.sentenceingproject.org/pdfs/1044.pdf>.

19. The Sentencing Project, 'U.S. Prison Populations', p. 1.

20. Fox Butterfield, 'Prison Rates among Blacks Reach a Peak, Report Finds', *New York Times*, 7 April 2003, p. A12.

21. Richard Willing, 'More Seeking President's Pardon', *USA Today*, 24 December 2002, p. 3A.

22. Paul Martin, Ed Vulliamy, and Gaby Hinsliff, 'US Army Was Told to Protect Looted Museum', *The Observer* (London), 20 April 2003, p. 4; Frank Rich, 'And Now: "Operation Iraqi Looting"', *New York Times*, 27 April 2003, p. 2:1.

23. See Scott Peterson, 'Iraq: Saladin to Saddam', *Christian Science Monitor*, 4 March 2003, p. 1.

24. Secretary of Defence Donald H. Rumsfeld, Defence Department operational update briefing, Pentagon Briefing Room, Arlington, Virginia, Federal News Service, 11 April 2003.

25. Martin, Vulliamy, and Hinsliff, 'US Army Was Told to Protect Looted Museum', p. 4.

26. See Robert Fisk, 'Americans Defend Two

Untouchable Ministries from the Hordes of Looters',
The Independent (London), 14 April 2003, p. 7: 'Iraq's
scavengers have thieved and destroyed what they
have been allowed to loot and burn by the
Americans—and a two-hour drive around Baghdad
shows clearly what the US intends to protect. After
days of arson and pillage, here's a short but revealing
scorecard. US troops have sat back and allowed mobs
to wreck and then burn the Ministry of Planning,
the Ministry of Education, the Ministry of
Irrigation, the Ministry of Trade, the Ministry of
Industry, the Ministry of Foreign Affairs, the
Ministry of Culture and the Ministry of
Information. They did nothing to prevent looters
from destroying priceless treasures of Iraq's history
in the Baghdad Archaeological Museum and in the
museum in the northern city of Mosul, or from
looting three hospitals.

'The Americans have, though, put hundreds of
troops inside two Iraqi ministries that remain
untouched—and untouchable—because tanks and
armoured personnel carriers and Humvees have been
placed inside and outside both institutions. And
which ministries proved to be so important for the
Americans? Why, the Ministry of Interior, of
course—with its vast wealth of intelligence
information on Iraq—and the Ministry of Oil.'

27. Carlotta Gall, 'In Afghanistan, Violence Stalls
Renewal Effort', *New York Times*, 26 April 2003,
p. A1. See also David Rohde, 'US Rebuked on
Afghans in Detention', *New York Times*, 8 March
2004, p. A6.

28. Scott Lindlaw, 'Accommodating TV-Friendly
Presidential Visit Caused a Few Changes in Navy
Carrier's Routine', Associated Press, 2 May 2003.

29. Walter V. Robinson, '1-Year Gap in Bush's Guard Duty: No Record of Airman at Drills in 1972–73', *Boston Globe*, 23 May 2000, p. A1.

30. David E. Sanger, 'Bush Declares "One Victory in a War on Terror"', *New York Times*, 2 May 2003, p. A1.

31. James Harding, 'Bush to Hail Triumph but Not Declare a US Victory', *Financial Times* (London), 1 May 2003, p. 8.

32. Quoted in John R. MacArthur, 'In the Psychological Struggle, Nations Wield Their Weapons of Mass Persuasion', *Boston Globe*, 9 March 2003, p. D12.

33. General Tommy Franks, *Sunday Morning*, CBS, 23 March 2003.

34. '"Non" Campaigner Chirac Ready to Address French', *Daily Mail* (London), 20 March 2003, p. 13.

35. Robert J. McCartney, 'Germany Stops Short of Saying "I Told You So": Opposition to War Vindicated, Officials Say', *Washington Post*, 3 April 2003, p. A33: 'Although Germany formally opposes the war, it is supporting the US effort through such steps as overflight rights and special security at US bases in Germany. Officials say Germany is doing more for the war than any country except Britain.' See also Giles Tremlett and John Hooper, 'War in the Gulf: Clampdown on Coverage of Returning Coffins', *The Guardian* (London), 27 March 2003, p. 3.

36. Judy Dempsey and Robert Graham, 'Paris Gives First Signs of Support to Coalition', *Financial Times* (London), 4 April 2003, p. 4.

37. Interfax, 'Putin Wants US Victory', *Hobart Mercury* (Australia), 4 April 2003.

38. Morton Abramowitz, 'Turkey and Iraq, Act II', *Wall*

Street Journal, 16 January 2003, p. A12.

39. Noam Chomsky, 2004, *Hegemony or Survival: America's Quest for Global Dominance*, Metropolitan Books, New York, p. 131.

40. Angelique Chrisafis et al., 'Millions Worldwide Rally for Peace', *The Guardian* (London), 17 February 2003, p. 6 <http://www.guardian.co.uk/antiwar/story/ 0,12809,897098,00.html>.

41. Richard W. Stevenson, 'Antiwar Protests Fail to Sway Bush on Plans for Iraq', *New York Times*, 19 February 2003, p. A1.

42. 'Africa's Engine', *The Economist*, 17 January 2004.

43. Paul Betts, 'Ciampi Calls for Review of Media Laws', *Financial Times* (London), 24 July 2002, p. 8. For an overview of Berlusconi's holdings, see Ketupa.net Media Profiles <http://www.ketupa.net/berlusconi1. htm>.

44. Frank Bruni, 'Berlusconi, in a Rough Week, Says Only He Can Save Italy', *New York Times*, 10 May 2003, p. A1.

45. Tim Burt, 'Mays on a Charm Offensive: The Clear Channel Chief Is Seeking to Answer His Group's Critics', *Financial Times* (London), 27 October 2003, p. 27. See also John Dunbar and Aron Pilhofer, 'Big Radio Rules in Small Markets,' The Center for Public Integrity, 1 October 2003 <http://www. publicintegrity.org/telecom/report.aspx?aid= 63&sid=200>.

46. Douglas Jehl, 'Across Country, Thousands Gather to Back U.S. Troops and Policy', *New York Times*, 24 March 2003, p. B15.

47. Frank Rich, 'Iraq Around The Clock', *New York Times*, 30 March 2003, p. 2:1.

48. Bagdikian, *The New Media Monopoly*.

49. Tom Shales, 'Michael Powell and the FCC: Giving

Away the Marketplace of Ideas', *Washington Post*, 2 June 2003, p. C1; Paul Davidson and David Lieberman, 'FCC Eases Rules for Media Mergers', *USA Today*, 3 June 2003, p. 1A.

50. David Leonhardt, 'Bush's Record on Jobs: Risking Comparison to a Republican Ghost', *New York Times*, 3 July 2003, p. C1.

51. Robert Tanner, 'Report Says State Budget Gaps Jumped by Nearly 50 Percent, with Next Year Looking Worse', Associated Press, 5 February 2003.

52. Dana Milbank and Mike Allen, 'Bush to Ask Congress for $80 Billion: Estimate of War's Cost Comes as Thousands March in Protest', *Washington Post*, 23 March 2003, p. A1.

53. Sheryl Gay Stolberg, 'Senators' Sons in War: An Army of One', *New York Times*, 22 March 2003, p. B10. See also David M. Halbfinger and Steven A. Holmes, 'Military Mirrors a Working-Class America', *New York Times*, 30 March 2003, p. A1.

54. Darryl Fears, 'Draft Bills Stirs Debate Over The Military, Race and Equity', *Washington Post*, 4 February 2003, p. A3.

55. David Cole, 'Denying Felons Vote Hurts Them, Society', *USA Today*, 3 February 2000, p. 17A; 'From Prison to the Polls', editorial, *Christian Science Monitor*, 24 May 2001, p. 10.

56. See Cole, 'Denying Felons' and sidebar 'Not at the Ballot Box'.

57. Kenneth J. Cooper, 'In India's Kerala, Quality of Life Is High but Opportunity Is Limited', *Washington Post*, 3 January 1997, p. A35; Amartya Sen, 1999, *Development As Freedom*, Alfred A. Knopf, New York. See also Fareed Zakaria, 'Beyond Money', *New York Times Book Review*, 28 November 1999, p. 14.

58. Linda Villarosa, 'As Black Men Move Into Middle

Age, Dangers Rise', *New York Times*, 23 September 2002, p. F1.

59. Amy Goldstein and Dana Milbank, 'Bush Joins Admissions Case Fight: U-Mich. Use of Race Is Called "Divisive"', *Washington Post*, 16 January 2003, p. A1; James Harding, 'Bush Scrambles to Bolster Civil Rights Credibility', *Financial Times* (London), 21 January 2003, p. 10.

60. Elizabeth Becker and Richard A. Oppel, Jr, 'Bechtel Top Contender In Bidding Over Iraq', *New York Times*, 29 March 2003, p. B6.

61. André Verlöy and Daniel Politi, with Aron Pilhofer, 'Advisors of Influence: Nine Members of the Defence Policy Board Have Ties to Defence Contractors', Centre for Public Integrity, 28 March 2003 <http://www.publicintegrity.org/report.aspx?aid=91&sid=200>.

62. Laura Peterson, 'Bechtel Group Inc.', Centre for Public Integrity <http://www.publicintegrity.org/wow/bio.aspx?act=pro&ddlC=6>.

63. Peterson, 'Bechtel Group Inc'.

64. Bob Herbert, 'Spoils of War', *New York Times*, 10 April 2003, p. A27.

65. Quoted in Herbert, 'Spoils of War'.

66. Karen DeYoung and Jackie Spinner, 'Contract for Rebuilding of Iraq Awarded to Bechtel: US Firm 1 of 6 Invited to Bid for $680 Million Project', *Washington Post*, 18 April 2003, p. A23. In December 2003, the contract was raised by $350 million, to $1.03 billion. In January 2004, Bechtel won a contract worth another $1.8 billion. See Elizabeth Douglass and John Hendren, 'Bechtel Wins Another Iraq Deal', *Los Angeles Times*, 7 January 2004, p. C2.

67. Stephen J. Glain, 'Bechtel Wins Pact to Help Rebuild Iraq: Closed-Bid Deal Could Total $680M', *Boston*

Globe, 18 April 2003, p. A1.

68. Robin Toner and Neil A. Lewis, 'House Passes Terrorism Bill Much Like Senate's, but with 5-Year Limit', *New York Times*, 13 October 2001, p. B6.

69. See Cole, *Enemy Aliens*, pp. 57–69.

70. Evelyn Nieves, 'Local Officials Rise Up to Defy the Patriot Act', *Washington Post*, 21 April 2003, p. A1.

71. See Cole, *Enemy Aliens*.

72. Amnesty International, 'India: Abuse of the Law in Gujarat: Muslims Detained Illegally in Ahmedabad', 6 November 2003, AI index no. ASA 20/029/2003 < http://web.amnesty.org/library/Index/ENGASA200292003?open&of=ENG-IND>. See also 'People's Tribunal Highlights Misuse of POTA', *The Hindu*, 18 March 2004; and Sanghamitra Chakraborty et al., 'Slaves in Draconia: Ordinary Folks—Minors, Farmers, Minorities—Fall Prey to POTA for No Fault of Theirs', *Outlook India*, 22 March 2004.

73. Greg Myre, 'Shootout in West Bank Kills an Israeli Soldier and a Palestinian', *New York Times*, 13 March 2003, p. A5.

74. Wayne Washington, 'More Opposition to Detentions in Terror Probe', *Boston Globe*, 13 May 2002, p. A1; Tamar Lewin, 'As Authorities Keep Up Immigration Arrests, Detainees Ask Why They Are Targets', *New York Times*, 3 February 2002, p. 1:14.

75. Neil King, Jr, 'Bush Officials Draft Broad Plan For Free-Market Economy in Iraq', *Wall Street Journal*, 1 May 2003, p. A1.

76. Naomi Klein, 'Iraq Is Not America's to Sell', *The Guardian* (London), 7 November 2003, p. 27. See also Jeff Madrick, 'The Economic Plan for Iraq Seems Long on Ideology, Short on Common Sense', *New*

York Times, 2 October 2003, p. C2.

77. David Usborne, 'US Firm Is Hired to Purge Schools of Saddam's Doctrine', *The Independent* (London), 22 April 2003, p. 10; Steve Johnson, 'Scramble to Win the Spoils of War', *Financial Times* (London) 23 April 2003, p. 27; Paul Richter and Edmund Sanders, 'Contracts Go to Allies of Iraq's Chalabi', *Los Angeles Times*, 7 November 2003, p. A1.

78. Heather Stewart, 'Iraq: After the War: Fury at Agriculture Post for US Grain Dealer', *The Guardian* (London), 28 April 2003, p. 11.

79. Alan Cowell, 'British Ask What a War Would Mean for Business', *New York Times*, 18 March 2003, p. W1; 'Spoils of War', editorial, *San Francisco Chronicle*, 29 March 2003, p. A14; Jan Hennop, 'S. African Apartheid Victims File Lawsuit in US Court, Name Companies', Agence France-Presse, 12 November 2002; Nicol Degli Innocenti, 'African Workers Launch Dollars 100bn Lawsuit', *Financial Times* (London), 13 October 2003, p. 9.

80. John Vidal, 'Shell Fights Fires as Strife Flares in Delta', *The Guardian* (London), 15 September 1999, p. 15; Vidal, 'Oil Wealth Buys Health in Country Within a Country', *The Guardian* (London), 16 September 1999, p. 19. See also Ike Okonta and Oronto Douglas, 2003, *Where Vultures Feast: Shell, Human Rights, and Oil*, Verso, New York; and Al Gedicks, 2001, *Resource Rebels: Native Challenges to Mining and Oil Corporations*, South End Press, Cambridge, MA.

81. Tom Brokaw, speaking to Vice Admiral Dennis McGinn, *NBC News Special Report: Target Iraq*, NBC, 19 March 2003.

82. Bryan Bender, 'Roadblocks Seen in Sept. 11 Inquiry', *Boston Globe*, 9 July 2003, p. A2. See also John Meyer, 'Terror Not a Bush Priority Before 9/11, Witness

Says', *Los Angeles Times*, 25 March 2004, p. A1, and Edward Alden, 'Tale of Intelligence Failure Above and Below', *Financial Times* (London), 26 March 2004, p. 2.

83. Howard Zinn, 2000, *A People's History of the United States*, 20th anniversary edn, HarperCollins, New York. See also Anthony Arnove and Howard Zinn, 2004, *Voices of a People's History of the United States*, Seven Stories Press, New York.

When the Saints Go Marching Out

1. See Arundhati Roy, 'Democracy: Who Is She When She Is at Home?' in *War Talk*, pp. 17–44. See Arundhati Roy, 2002, *The Algebra of Infinite Justice*, Revised and Updated Edition, Penguin Books India, New Delhi.

2. 'Cong[ress Party] Ploy Fails, Modi Steals the Show in Pain', *Indian Express*, 16 August 2003.

3. Agence France-Presse, 'Indian Activists Urge Mandela to Snub Gujarat Government Invite', 4 August 2003; 'Guj[arat]–Mandela', The Press Trust of India, 5 August 2003; 'Battle for Gujarat's Image Now on Foreign Soil', *The Times of India*, 7 August 2003.

4. Agence France-Presse, 'Relax, Mandela Isn't Coming, He's Working on a Book', 5 August 2003.

5. Michael Dynes, 'Mbeki Can Seize White Farms under New Law', *The Times* (London), 31 January 2004, p. 26.

6. Dynes, 'Mbeki Can Seize White Farms'.

7. Patrick Laurence, 'South Africa Fights to Put the Past to Rest', *The Irish Times*, 28 December 2000, p. 57.

8. Anthony Stoppard, 'South Africa: Water, Electricity

Cutoffs Affect 10 Million', Inter Press Service, 21 March 2002.

9. Henri E. Cauvin, 'Hunger in Southern Africa Imperils Lives of Millions', *New York Times*, 26 April 2002, p. A8; James Lamont, 'Nobody Says "No" to Mandela', *Financial Times* (London), 10 December 2002, p. 4; Patrick Laurence, 'South Africans Sceptical of Official Data', *The Irish Times*, 6 June 2003, p. 30.

10. See Ashwin Desai, 2002, *We Are The Poors: Community Struggles in Post-Apartheid South Africa*, Monthly Review Press, New York.

11. South African Press Association, 'Gauteng Municipalities to Target Service Defaulters', 4 May 1999; Alison Maitland, 'Combining to Harness the Power of Private Enterprise', *Financial Times* (London), 23 August 2002, Survey: 'Sustainable Business', p. 2.

12. Nicol Degli Innocenti and John Reed, 'SA Govt Opposes Reparations Lawsuit', *Financial Times* (London), 19 May 2003, p. 15.

13. South African Press Association, 'SAfrica Asks US Court to Dismiss Apartheid Reparations Cases', BBC Worldwide Monitoring, 30 July 2003.

14. Martin Luther King, Jr, *A Testament of Hope: The Essential Writings and Speeches of Martin Luther King, Jr*, in James M. Washington (ed.), 1991, HarperCollins, New York, p. 233.

15. King, *A Testament of Hope*, p. 233.

16. 'Men of Vietnam', *New York Times*, 9 April 1967, Week in Review, p. 2E (Quoted in Mike Marqusee, 1999, *Redemption Song: Muhammad Ali and the Spirit of the Sixties*, Verso, New York, p. 217).

17. King, *A Testament of Hope*, p. 245.

18. Halbfinger and Holmes, 'Military Mirrors a

Working-Class America'; Fears, 'Draft Bill Stirs Debate Over The Military, Race and Enquity'.

19. Cole, 'Denying Felons' and sidebar; 'From Prison to the Polls', editorial, *Christian Science Monitor.*

20. King, *A Testament of Hope*, p. 239.

21. Quoted in Marqusee, *Redemption Song*, p. 218.

22. King, *A Testament of Hope*, p. 250.

23. Marqusee, *Redemption Song*, pp. 1–4, 292.

In Memory of Shankar Guha Niyogi

1. Human Rights Watch, 'India: Human Rights Developments', *Human Rights Watch World Report 1993* <http://www.hrw.org/reports/1993/WR93/Asw-06.htm>.

Do Turkeys Enjoy Thanksgiving?

1. See the website of The Project for The New American Century <http://www.newamerican century.org>. See also Verlöy and Politi, with Pilhofer, 'Advisors of Influence'.

2. See 'Peace Is War' in this book (Notes 10–13, pp. 364–65).

3. 'Strike Not Your Right Anymore: SC [Supreme Court] to Govt Staff', *Indian Express*, 7 August 2003; 'Trade Unions Protest Against SC [Supreme Court] Order on Strikes', *The Times of India*, 8 August 2003.

4. See Arundhati Roy, 'On Citizens' Rights to Dissent', in *Power Politics*, pp. 87–104.

5. Michael Jensen, 'Denis Halliday: Iraq Sanctions Are Genocide', *The Daily Star*, Lebanon, 7 July 2000. See also the interview with Halliday and Phyllis

Bennis in Arnove, *Iraq Under Siege*, pp. 53–64.

6. Arnove, *Iraq Under Siege*, pp. 103–04.

7. Joseph E. Stiglitz, 2002, *Globalization and Its Discontents*, W.W. Norton, New York, pp. 7, 61, 253–54.

8. 'World Trade Special Report', *The Independent* (London), 10 September 2003, p. 1; Thompson Ayodele, 'Last Chance for Fair Go on Trade', *Australian Financial Review*, 11 September 2003, p. B63.

9. George Monbiot, 2004, *The Age of Consent*, The New Press, New York, p. 158. See also U.N. General Assembly, *External Debt Crisis and Development: Report to the Secretary-General*, A/57/253, 2003, p. 2 <http://www.un.dk/doc/A570253.pdf>.

10. The Fifth WTO Ministerial Conference was held in Cancún, Mexico, from 10 to 14 September 2003. Sue Kirchhoff and James Cox, 'WTO Talks Break Down, Threatening Future Pact', *USA Today*, 15 September 2003, p. 1B.

How Deep Shall We Dig?

1. Hina Kausar Alam and P. Balu, 'J&K [Jammu and Kashmir] Fudges DNA Samples to Cover Up Killings', *Times of India*, 7 March 2002.

2. See Arundhati Roy, 2002, *The Algebra of Infinite Justice*, Revised and Updated Edition, Penguin Books India, New Delhi.

3. Somit Sen, 'Shooting Turns Spotlight on Encounter Cops', *Times of India*, 23 August 2003.

4. W. Chandrakanth, 'Crackdown on Civil Liberties Activists in the Offing?' *The Hindu*, 4 October 2003: 'several activists have gone underground fearing police reprisals. Their fears are not unfounded, as

the State police have been staging encounters at will. While the police frequently release the statistics on naxalite violence, they avoid mentioning the victims of their own violence. The Andhra Pradesh Civil Liberties Committee (APCLC), which is keeping track of the police killings, has listed more than 4000 deaths, 2000 of them in the last eight years alone.' See also K.T. Sangameswaran, 'Rights Activists Allege Ganglord—Cop Nexus', *The Hindu*, 22 October 2003.

5. David Rohde, 'India and Kashmir Separatists Begin Talks on Ending Strife', *New York Times*, 23 January 2004, p. A8; Deutsche Presse-Agentur, 'Thousands Missing, Unmarked Graves Tell Kashmir Story', 7 October 2003.

6. Unpublished reports from the Association of Parents of Disappeared People (APDP), Srinagar.

7. See also Edward Luce, 'Kashmir's New Leader Promises "Healing Touch"', *Financial Times* (London), 28 October 2002, p. 12.

8. Ray Marcelo, 'Anti-Terrorism Law Backed by India's Supreme Court', *Financial Times* (London), 17 December 2003, p. 2.

9. People's Union for Civil Liberties (PUCL), 'A Preliminary Fact Finding on POTA Cases in Jharkhand', Delhi, India, 2 May 2003 <http://www.pucl.org/Topics/Law/2003/poto-jharkhand.htm>.

10. 'People's Tribunal Highlights Misuse of POTA', *The Hindu*, 18 March 2004.

11. 'People's Tribunal'. See also 'Human Rights Watch Ask Centre to Repeal POTA', The Press Trust of India, 8 September 2002.

12. Leena Misra, '240 POTA Cases, All against Minorities', *Times of India*, 15 September 2003; 'People's Tribunal Highlights Misuse of POTA', 18

March 2004. On Gujarat, see Arundhati Roy, 2002, *The Algebra of Infinite Justice*, Revised and Updated Edition, Penguin Books India, New Delhi.

13. 'A Pro-Police Report', *The Hindu*, 20 March 2004; Amnesty International, 'India: Report of the Malimath Committee on Reforms of the Criminal Justice System: Some Comments', 19 September 2003 (ASA 20/025/2003).

14. 'J&K [Jammu and Kashmir] Panel Wants Draconian Laws Withdrawn', *The Hindu*, 23 March 2003. See also South Asian Human Rights Documentation Centre (SAHRDC), 'Armed Forces Special Powers Act: A Study in National Security Tyranny', November 1995 <http://www.nscnonline.org/webpage/Articles/south_asia_human_rights1.htm>.

15. See 'Growth of a Demon: Genesis of the Armed Forces (Special Powers) Act, 1958' and related documents, in *Manipur Update*, December 1999 <http://www.geocities.com/manipurupdate/december_feature_1.htm>.

16. On the lack of any convictions for the massacres in Gujarat, see Edward Luce, 'Master of Ambiguity', *Financial Times* (London), 3–4 April 2004, p. 16. On the 31 March 1997, murder of Chandrashekhar Prasad, see Andrew Nash, 'An Election at JNU', *Himal*, December 2003 <http://www.himalmag.com/2003/december/perspective.htm>. For more information on the additional crimes listed here, see pp. 87–90 above.

17. N.A. Mujumdar, 'Eliminate Hunger Now, Poverty Later', *Business Line*, 8 January 2003.

18. 'Foodgrain Exports May Slow Down This Fiscal [Year]', *India Business Insight*, 2 June 2003; 'India: Agriculture Sector: Paradox of Plenty', *Business Line*, 26 June 2001; Ranjit Devraj, 'Farmers Protest against

Globalization', Inter Press Service, 25 January 2001.

19. Utsa Patnaik, 'Falling Per Capita Availability of Foodgrains for Human Consumption in the Reform Period in India', *Akhbar* 2, October 2001 <http://66.51.111.239/indowindow/threeessays/contact.php>; P. Sainath, 'Have Tornado, Will Travel', *The Hindu Magazine*, 18 August 2002; See Mike Davis, 2002, *Late Victorian Holocausts: El Niño Famines and the Making of the Third World*, Verso, New York. See also Utsa Patnaik, 'On Measuring "Famine" Deaths: Different Criteria for Socialism and Capitalism?' *Akhbar* 6, November–December 1999 <http://www.indowindow.com/akhbar/article.php?article=74&category=8&issue=9>.

20. Amartya Sen, *Development As Freedom*.

21. 'The Wasted India', *The Statesman* (India), 17 February 2001; 'Child-Blain', *The Statesman* (India) 24 November 2001.

22. Utsa Patnaik, 'The Republic of Hunger', lecture, Jawaharlal Nehru University, New Delhi, India, 10 April 2004 <http://macroscan.com/fet/apr04/fet210404Republic_Hunger.htm>.

23. Praful Bidwai, 'India amidst Serious Agrarian Crisis', *Central Chronicle* (Bhopal), 9 April 2004.

24. Roy, *Power Politics*, 2nd edn, p. 13.

25. Mike Davis, *Late Victorian Holocausts*, Note 19 above.

26. Among other sources, see Edwin Black, 2003, *IBM and the Holocaust: The Strategic Alliance Between Nazi Germany and America's Most Powerful Corporation*, Three Rivers Press, New York.

27. 'For India Inc., Silence Protects the Bottom Line', *The Times of India*, 17 February 2003; 'CII Apologises to Modi', *The Hindu*, 7 March 2003.

28. See 'Peace Is War' in this book (Notes 10–14, pp. 364–65).

29. India was the only country to abstain on 22 December 2003, from UN General Assembly Resolution, 'Protection of Human Rights and Fundamental Freedoms While Countering Terrorism', A/RES/58/ 187. Quoted in Amnesty International India, 'Security Legislation and State Accountability: A Presentation for the POTA People's Hearing, 13–14 March, New Delhi' <http://www.un.org/ Depts/dhl/resguide/r58.htm>.

The Road to Harsud

1. See Arundhati Roy, 2002, *The Algebra of Infinite Justice*, Revised and Updated Edition, Penguin Books India, New Delhi, p. 61.

2. Sanjay Sangvai, 2000, *The River and Life: People's Struggle in the Narmada Valley*, Earth Care Books, Mumbai.

3. *Detailed Project Report of Narmada Sagar Project*, Volume 1, July 1982, Narmada Sagar Project, Bhopal.

4. See Narmada Control Authority website <http:// www.ncaindia.org>.

5. Ibid.

6. *Detailed Project Report of Narmada Sagar Project*, see Note 4 above.

7. Ashish Kothari, 'The Narmada Valley Project: A Critique', 1988 and 'Environmental Aspects of Sardar Sarovar Project', 1994. See also Claude Alvarez and Ramesh Billorey, *Damming the Narmada: India's Greatest Planned Environmental Disaster*, Appen, 1998.

8. K. Sridharan and S. Vedula, 'Groundwater Modelling in Composite Command Area of Narmada Sagar and Omkareshwar Reservoirs', Volume 3, Indian Institute of Science, Bangalore, March 1985.

9. Ministry of Environment and Forests, 'Note for Review Committee', 1993.

10. 'Impact Assessment Studies of Narmada Sagar and Omkareshwar Projects on Flora and Fauna with Attendant Human Aspects', Wildlife Institute of India, Dehradun <http://www.wii.gov.in>.

11. Government of Madhya Pradesh, order dated 2 May 1999.

12. Memorandum of Understanding dated 16 May 2000 between Government of Madhya Pradesh and Government of India.

13. Memorandum of Understanding dated 16 May 2000 between Government of Madhya Pradesh and National Hydroelectric Power Corporation.

14. *Detailed Project Report of Narmada Sagar Project*, see Note 4 above.

15. Ibid.

16. See <http://www.nhpcindia.com> and <http://www.nhpc.co.in>.

17. Ibid.

18. Government of Madhya Pradesh, 'Average Revenue Requirement of MPSEB for FY 04 and FY 05', Madhya Pradesh State Electricity Board, Bhopal, 2004.

19. Ibid.

20. 'Indira Sagar Project Ahead of Schedule', *The Hindu*, 29 March 2004.

21. See <http://www.mp.nic.in/nvda/dispute1.htm>.

22. 'Resettled on Paper', *The Indian Express*, 26 June 2004. Also see 'Without Land or Livelihood—The Indira Sagar Dam: State Accountability and Rehabilitation Issues—Report of the Independent People's Commission, October 2004' <http://www.narmada.org/nvdp.dams/indira-sagar/ISP_report.pdf>.

23. 'Short Takes', *Financial Express*, 28 August 2000 <http://www.financialexpress.com/fe/daily/20000828/fco27035.html>. See also <http://www.ncaindia.org>.

24. Patrick McCully, 1998, *Silenced Rivers: The Ecology and Politics of Large Dams*, Orient Longman, Hyderabad. See also Arundhati Roy, 2002, *The Algebra of Infinite Justice*, Revised and Updated Edition, Penguin Books India, New Delhi, pp. 43–141.

25. See <http://www.nvda.nic.in> accessed on 6 February 2005. See also Patrick McCully, 1998, *Silenced Rivers: The Ecology and Politics of Large Dams*, Orient Longman, Hyderabad.

26. For debates on the judgements see Dilip D'Souza, 'Potato Head Hypothesising' rediff.com, 4 January 2001; Manoj Mitta, 'Verdict That Flummoxes', *Indian Express*, 2 November 2000; <http://www.narmada.org/sardar-sarovar/sc.ruling>; and L.C. Jain, 2001, *Dam vs Drinking Water: Exploring the Narmada Judgement*, Parisar, Pune.

27. See <http://www.mp.nic.in/finance/higheng.pdf>.

28. Letter from Shripad Dharmadhikary, MANTHAN to Secretary, Ministry of Environment and Forests, dated 21 November 2003.

29. *Business Standard*, 19 March 2004.

30. Ibid.

31. See <http://www.nhdcindia.com> accessed on 6 February 2005.

32. See performance highlights of NHDC at <http://www.nhdcindia.com> accessed on 6 February 2005.

33. Memorandum of Understanding dated 16 May 2000 between Government of Madhya Pradesh and National Hydroelectric Power Corporation.

34. *Detailed Project Report of Narmada Sagar Project*, see Note 4 above.

35. Government of Madhya Pradesh order dated 14 May 2004.

36. 'HC Seeks Pictorial Proof of Rehabilitation at Harsud', *Hindustan Times* (Bhopal Edition), 30 June 2004.

37. For press reports see <http://www.narmada.org/nba-press-releases/> and <http://www.narmada.org/pressclippings.html>.

38. On 15 April 1994, the Narmada Bachao Andolan filed a civil writ petition in the Supreme Court on the Sardar Sarovar Project mainly seeking a comprehensive review of the project. The court pronounced its majority judgement (a three judge bench divided 2:1) on 18 October 2000 and disposed off the petition. As per this decision the construction of the dam was permitted up to 90 m-plus and work would continue as per the award of the Tribunal. Any further raising of the dam could only be with the implementation of relief and rehabilitation (R&R) measures, and on the clearance by the R&R Sub-group of the NCA. The Environment Sub-group would also have to give clearance for further construction of the dam at each stage beyond 90 m. The court also directed the NCA to draw up an action plan for the construction of the dam and related R&R measures within four weeks from the date of its judgement. For the full text of the judgement see <http://www.supremecourtonline.com/cases/1189.html>.

39. The river linking project envisages connecting thirty-seven rivers, through thirty-one links and 9000 km of canals, to create irrigation potential for an additional 150 million hectares. A PIL on the clean-up of the River Yamuna filed before the Supreme Court in August 2002, by senior advocate Ranjit Kumar, raised

this issue for the first time in the Supreme Court. A bench headed by the then Chief Justice of India, B.N. Kirpal, passed an order on 31 October 2002. See Sonu Jain, 'The River Sutra', *Indian Express*, 2 March 2003. See also M.V. Kamath, 'The Challenge of Interlinking India's Rivers' <http://www.samachar. com/features/200303-features.html>. See also Medha Patkar (Ed), 2004, *River Linking: A Millennium Folly*, National Alliance of People's Movements & Initiative, Mumbai.

40. 'Kirpal Expresses Concern Over Court Order on Coke', *The Hindu*, 11 March 2004.

41. As per website of the Narmada Control Authority <http://www.nca.nic.in> accessed in February 2002.

42. See 'India: Country Assistance Strategy Report, Volume 1', World Bank, 2004 <http://www-wds. worldbank.org/servlet/WDS_IBank_Servlet?pcont =details&eid= 000160016_20040920102445>. See also, Himanshu Thakkar, 'World Bank Should Stop Funding Large Indian Hydro Projects', One World South Asia, 13 September 2004 < http:// southasia.oneworld.net/article/view/93857/1/5339>.

43. Ibid.

44. See <http://www.nhpcindia.com> accessed on 14 July 2004.

45. 'British Bank Linked to Financing of Omkareshwar Dam', *The Guardian*, 1 October 2004.

Public Power in the Age of Empire

1. Noam Chomsky, 2004, *Hegemony or Survival: America's Quest for Global Dominance*, 2nd edn, Owl/ Henry Holt, New York, p. 9.

2. Chomsky, 2004, p. 109.

3. Chomsky, 2004, p. 190.

4. Ibid.

5. Chomsky, 2004, p. 131.

6. Connie Koch, 2004, *2/15: The Day the World Said No to War*, Hello, New York; AK Press, Oakland.

7. R.W. Apple, Jr, 'Bush Appears in Trouble Despite Two Big Advantages', *New York Times*, 4 August 1988, p. A1. Bush made this remark in refusing to apologize for the shooting down of an Iranian passenger plane, killing 290 passengers. See Lewis Lapham, 2002, *Theater of War*, New Press, New York, p. 126.

8. Rahul Bedi, 'Communists Emerge as Major Political Force in India', *Irish Times,* 17 May 2004, p. 10.

9. Jodi Wilgoren, 'Kerry Says His Vote on Iraq Would Be the Same Today', *New York Times*, 10 August 2004, p. A18.

10. Dan Balz and Robin Wright, 'Kerry Urges Bush to Admit Mistakes: Full Account of Iraq Situation Sought', *Washington Post,* 6 October 2004, p. A1.

11. John Kerry, interviewed by Tim Russert, NBC News, *Meet the Press,* 18 April 2004. Available online at <http://msnbc.msn.com/id/4772030/>.

12. Jim VandeHei, 'Despite Rhetoric, Bush, Kerry Agree on Many Issues', *Washington Post,* 9 May 2004, p. A1.

13. Joshua Chaffin, 'Cheney Pours Scorn on Kerry's "Sensitive War"', *Financial Times* (London), 13 August 2004, p. 8.

14. Michael Hanlon, 'There's No Time Like the Present', *The Spectator* (London), 7 August 2004, p. 12.

15. Editorial, 'Those Illegal Farm Subsidies', *New York Times,* 28 April 2004, p. A20.

16. George Monbiot, 2004, *The Age of Consent*, The New Press, New York, p. 158. See also United Nations General Assembly, *External Debt Crisis and Development: Report to the Secretary-General*, Fifty-seventh Session, 23 July 2002 (A/57/253), p. 2.

Online at <http://www.un.dk/doc/A570253.pdf>.

17. Luisa Kroll and Lea Goldman, 'The Rich Get Richer', Forbes.com, 26 February 2004. Available online at <http://www.forbes.com/maserati/billionaires2004/cz_lk_0226mainintrobill04.html>. See also, 'Special Report: The World's Richest People', Forbes.com, 26 February 2004. Available online at <http://www.forbes.com/2004/02/25/bill04land.html>. Comparison with global GDP based on figures from the World Bank, *World Development Indicators 2004,* and the United Nations, *Human Development Report 2004.* Available online at <http://hdr.undp.org/statistics/data/indic/indic_7_1_1.html>.

18. Comparison of the tables for 2003 and 2004 at <http://www.forbes.com/2003/02/26/billionaireland.html> and <http://www.forbes.com/2004/02/25/bill04land.html>.

19. See, among other reports, Raymond Colitt, 'Workers' Party Seeks Tighter Grip on Brazil at the Polls', *Financial Times* (London), 1 October 2004, p. 10, and Larry Rohter, 'Party Atop Brazil Government Expels 4 Dissident Lawmakers', *New York Times,* 15 December 2003, p. A8.

20. Michael Dynes, 'Mbeki Can Seize White Farms Under New Law', *The Times* (London), 31 January 2004, p. 26. Patrick Laurence, 'South Africa Fights to Put the Past to Rest', *Irish Times*, 28 December 2000, p. 57. Anthony Stoppard, 'South Africa: Water, Electricity Cutoffs Affect 10 Million', Inter Press Service, 21 March 2002. Henri E. Cauvin, 'Hunger in Southern Africa Imperils Lives of Millions', *New York Times*, 26 April 2002, p. A8. James Lamont, 'Nobody Says "No" to Mandela', *Financial Times* (London), 10 December 2002, special section: 'Management', p. 4.

21. Panafrican News Agency (PANA) Daily News Wire, 'Mandela, Mbeki and Other Leaders Mourn Oppenheimer', 25 August 2000.

22. Particularly illustrative of this view is Michael Ignatieff, 2004, *The Lesser Evil: Political Ethics in an Age of Terror*, Princeton UP, Princeton.

23. Farah Stockman and Thanassis Cambanis, 'As Iraq Seeks Its Own Way, Many Involved Have US Links', *Boston Globe,* 10 June 2004, p. A24.

24. See, for example, Naomi Klein, 'America's Enemy Within: Armed Checkpoints, Embedded Reporters in Flak Jackets, Brutal Suppression of Peaceful Demonstrators. Baghdad? No, Miami', *The Guardian* (London), 26 November 2003, p. 25.

25. See Arundhati Roy, 2004, 'How Deep Shall We Dig?' in this book (p. 211).

26. See Arundhati Roy, 2001, 'On Citizens' Rights to Express Dissent', in *Power Politics,* 2nd edn, South End Press, Cambridge, MA, pp. 87–103.

27. W. Chandrakanth, 'Crackdown on Civil Liberties Activists in the Offing?' *The Hindu*, 4 October 2003. K.T. Sangameswaran, 'Rights Activists Allege Ganglord–Cop Nexus', *The Hindu*, 22 October 2003.

28. David Rohde, 'India and Kashmir Separatists Begin Talks on Ending Strife', *New York Times*, 23 January 2004, p. A8. Deutsche Presse-Agentur, 'Thousands Missing, Unmarked Graves Tell Kashmir Story', 7 October 2003.

29. On Bolivia, see Oscar Olivera and Tom Lewis, 2004, *¡Cochabamba! Water War in Bolivia*, South End Press, Cambridge, MA. On Chile, see Larry Rohter, 'Mapuche Indians in Chile Struggle to Take Back Forests', *New York Times,* 11 August 2004, p. A3, and Danna Harman, 'Chile Debates When Crime Is "Terrorism"', *Christian Science Monitor,* 6 December 2004, p. 6.

30. Ray Marcelo, 'Anti-Terrorism Law Backed by India's Supreme Court', *Financial Times* (London), 17 December 2003, p. 2.

31. People's Union for Civil Liberties (PUCL), 'A Preliminary Fact Finding on POTA Cases in Jharkhand', Delhi, India, 2 May 2003, <http://www.pucl.org/Topics/Law/2003/poto-jharkhand.htm>.

32. 'People's Tribunal Highlights Misuse of POTA', *The Hindu*, 18 March 2004; 'Human Rights Watch Ask Centre to Repeal POTA', The Press Trust of India, 8 September 2002.

33. Celia W. Dugger, 'Religious Riots Loom Over Indian Politics', *New York Times*, 27 July 2002, p. A1; Edna Fernandes, 'Gujarat Violence Backed by State Says EU Report', *Financial Times* (London), 30 April 2002, p. 12; 'A Tainted Election', *Indian Express*, 17 April 2002; Leena Misra, '240 POTA Cases, All Against Minorities', *Times of India*, 15 September 2003; 'People's Tribunal Highlights Misuse of POTA', 18 March 2004. On Gujarat, see Arundhati Roy, 2002, 'Democracy: Who Is She When She Is at Home?' *The Algebra of Infinite Justice*, Revised and Updated Edition, Penguin Books India, New Delhi..

34. Reports of the South Asia Human Rights Documentation (New Delhi, India). Available online at <http://www.hrdc.net/sahrdc/>.

35. Rama Lakshmi, 'In India, Torture by Police Is Frequent and Often Deadly', *Washington Post,* 5 August 2004, p. A11.

36. 'Cong[ress Party] under Pressure to Kill POTA', *Times of India,* 18 May 2004. 'New Gov[ernmen]t Promises Repeal of POTA, Reservation for Women', The Press Trust of India, 27 May 2004.

37. 'Your Place or Mine? — Kashmir', *The Economist* (London), 14 February 2004.

38. 'J&K [Jammu and Kashmir] Panel Wants Draconian Laws Withdrawn', *The Hindu*, 23 March 2003. South Asian Human Rights Documentation Centre (SAHRDC), 'Armed Special Power Act: A Study in National Security Tyranny', November 1995, <http://www.nscnonline.org/webpage/Articles/south_asia_human_rights1.htm>.

39. 'Growth of a Demon: Genesis of the Armed Forces (Special Powers) Act, 1958 and related in documents, in *Manipur Update*', December 1999, <http://www.geocities.com/manipurupdate/december_feature_1.htm>.

40. 'Poll-Bound Chandrababu Dumps Reforms', *The Statesman* (India), 11 March 2004.

41. Edward Luce, 'India's Polls Teach World Bank a Lesson', *Financial Times* (London), 27 May 2004, p. 11. Edward Luce, 'Farmers Fail to Reap Poll Rewards in Rural Indian State', *Financial Times* (London), 10 December 2004, p. 10.

42. Amarnath K. Menon, 'Mega Byte Victory', *India Today,* 24 May 2004, p. 44.

Peace and the New Corporate Liberation Theology

1. Juan J. Walte, 'Greenpeace: 200,000 Died in Gulf War', *USA Today,* 30 May 1991, p. 1A; Anthony Arnove (ed.), 2002, *Iraq Under Siege: The Deadly Impact of Sanctions and War*, 2nd edn, South End Press, Cambridge.

2. Morley Safer, 'DU', produced by Peter Klein, CBS, *60 Minutes*, 26 December 1999; Bill Mesler, 'The Pentagon's Radioactive Bullet', *The Nation*, 263: 12, 21 October 1996, p. 13; Jonathan Duffy, 'Iraq's Cancer Children Overlooked in War', BBC News

Online, 29 April 2003 <http://news.bbc.co.uk/1/
hi/world/middle_east/2982609.stm>.

3. United Nation's Children's Fund (Unicef), 1999,
Child and Maternal Mortality Survey 1999, Unicef,
Iraq. See further details in Arnove (ed.), *Iraq Under
Siege*, 2nd edn.

4. Christopher Shea, 'Countless: How Many Civilians
Have Been Killed as a Result of the Iraq War? For
Critics of a New Study, It's as Though They'd
Rather We Never Found Out', *Boston Globe*, 7
November 2004, p. D4.

5. Elisabeth Rosenthal, 'Study Puts Iraqi Deaths of
Civilians at 100,000', *New York Times*, 29 October
2004, p. A8; Les Roberts, Riyadh Lafta, Richard
Garfield, Jamal Khudhairi, and Gilbert Burnham,
'Mortality Before and After the 2003 Invasion of
Iraq: Cluster Sample Survey', *The Lancet* online, 29
October 2004 <http://image.thelancet.com/extras/
04art10342web.pdf>. See also Richard Horton,
'The War in Iraq: Civilian Casualties, Political
Responsibilities', *The Lancet* online, 29 October 2004
<http://image.thelancet.com/extras/04cmt384
web.pdf.>

6. Glenn Kessler and Colum Lynch, 'Blix's Report
Deepens U.N. Rift Over Iraq: Inspection Team's
Assessment Is Cautiously Upbeat', *Washington Post*,
9 March 2003, p. A1.

7. James Risen, 'How Niger Uranium Story Defied
Wide Skepticism', *New York Times*, 14 July 2004,
p. A14. Christopher Adams and James Blitz,
'Discredited Dossier Was "An Embarrassment": Iraq
Investigation', *Financial Times* (London), 25 June
2003, p. 2.

8. Jim Dwyer, 'Defectors' Reports on Iraq Arms Were
Embellished, Exile Asserts', *New York Times*, 9 July

2004, p. A1; Douglas Jehl and David E. Sanger, 'Powell Presses CIA on Faulty Intelligence on Iraq Arms', *New York Times*, 2 June 2004, p. A10; Edward Cody, 'Chalabi, Shunted to Sidelines, Shares his Playbook for Iraq: Party Leader Emphasizes Elections, Shaking Off US Tutelage', *Washington Post*, 30 June 2004, p. A12.

9. Gautam Malkani, 'Ex-BBC Men Say "Sexed-Up" Claim Is Backed', *Financial Times*, 15 July 2004, p. 4; Richard Norton-Taylor and Matt Wells, 'Dossier Findings Support Kelly's Allegations to BBC', *The Guardian* (London), 16 July 2004, p. 5.

10. Arnove (ed.), *Iraq Under Siege*, 2nd edn, pp. 57–58.

11. Andreas Zumach, 'Blühende Geschäfte', *Die Tageszeitung* (Berlin), 19 December 2002, p. 3. Available online at <http://www.taz.de/pt/2002/12/19/a0076.nf/text> (see also sidebar at <http://www.taz.de/pt/2002/12/19/a0080.nf/text>). Amy Goodman, Interview with Andreas Zumach, Pacifica Radio, *Democracy Now!* two parts, 18 and 19 December 2002. Benjamin Pimentel, 'Iraq Got Bay Area Boost in '80s', *San Francisco Chronicle,* 26 January 2003, p. G1.

12. Rania Masri, 'The Corporate Invasion of Iraq', *International Socialist Review* 30, July–August 2003. Available online at <http://www.isreview.org/issues/30/corporateinvasion.shtml>. Yochi J. Dreazen and Christopher Cooper, 'Hand-Picked Proxies, Advisers Will Be Given Key Roles In Interim Government', *Wall Street Journal,* 13 May 2004, p. 1. See also Jeff Madrick, 'The Economic Plan for Iraq Seems Long on Ideology, Short on Common Sense', *New York Times,* 2 October 2003, p. C2.

13. Thomas Catan, 'Iraq Business Deals May Be Invalid, Law Experts Warn', *Financial Times* (London),

29 October 2003, p. 14. See also Antonia Juhasz, 'The Hand-Over That Wasn't', *Los Angeles Times,* 5 August 2004, p. B15.

14. Antonia Juhasz, 'A Nice Little War to Fill the Coffers', *Los Angeles Times,* 14 October 2004, p. B13.

15. Richard A. Oppel, Jr, 'Pentagon Opens Criminal Inquiry of Halliburton Pricing', *New York Times,* 24 February 2004, p. 10; Robert O'Harrow, Jr, 'Army to Pay Halliburton, For Now', *Washington Post,* 18 August 2004, p. E1.

16. Richard A. Oppel, Jr, and Diana B. Henriques, 'Company Has Ties in Washington, and to Iraq', *New York Times,* 18 April 2003, p. B7; Michael Smith, 'Young Saddam "A Man We Could Do Business With"', *Daily Telegraph* (London), 20 December 2003, p. 11; Jim Vallette, 'Rumsfeld's Old Flame', TomPaine.com, 10 April 2003. Available online at <http://www.tompaine.com/feature.cfm/ID/7577>. Jeremy Scahill, 'The Saddam in Rummy's Closet', CounterPunch.org, 2 August 2002. Available online at <http://www.counterpunch.org/scahill0802.html>.

17. See CorpWatch, Global Exchange, and Public Citizen, 'Bechtel: Profiting from Destruction', 5 June 2003. Available online at <http://www.corpwatch.org/article.php?id=6975>.

18. Bob Herbert, 'Spoils of War', *New York Times,* 10 April 2003, p. A27.

19. Michael Janofsky, 'Bechtel Wins Its Second Big Contract for Iraq', *New York Times,* 7 January 2004, p. A8; David R. Baker, 'Bechtel Nowhere Near Done', *San Francisco Chronicle,* 17 April 2004, p. C1.

20. Herbert, 'Spoils of War', p. A27.

21. Amy Goodman and David Goodman, 2004, *The Exception to the Rulers: Exposing Oily Politicians, War*

Profiteers, and the Media That Love Them, Hyperion, New York, p. 62.

22. For a powerful account of the struggle in Cochabamba, see Oscar Olivera and Tom Lewis, 2004, *¡Cochabamba! Water War in Bolivia*, South End Press, Cambridge, MA. See also William Finnegan, 'Leasing the Rain', *New Yorker*, 8 April 2002, p. 43.

23. Editorial, 'Bechtel's Bolivian Debacle', *San Francisco Chronicle*, 29 April 2002, p. B6.

24. Arundhati Roy, 2002, *The Algebra of Infinite Justice*, Revised and Updated Edition, Penguin Books India, New Delhi.

25. Roy, *Power Politics*, p. 56.

26. The suit is for Rs 26,000 crore, or $5.99 billion at December 2004 exchange rates (one crore equals ten million). PTI/UNI, 'GE, Bechtel Serve Notice on MSEB', *The Hindu*, 2 July 2004.

27. The scheme is estimated to cost Rs 44,000 to 50,000 crore annually, including administrative fees. See 'Singh's Song', *India Business Insight*, 24 October 2004.

28. Luke Harding and John Vidal, 'Clare Short in Indian GM Crops Row', *The Guardian* (London), 7 July 2001, p. 1; Ruchir Sharma, 'India Isn't Shining', *Newsweek* (Pacific Edition), 24 May 2004, p. 31.

29. Montek Singh Ahluwalia, 'The Critical Issue Now Is Implementation of Schemes', *Business Line*, 16 August 2004.

30. Naomi Klein, 'Reparations in Reverse', *Globe and Mail* (Toronto), 15 October 2004, p. A23.

31. Klein, 'Reparations in Reverse', p. A23.

32. Paul Richter, 'Nations Slow to Deliver Iraq Aid', *Los Angeles Times*, 12 July 2004, p. A1; Klein, 'Reparations in Reverse', p. A23.

33. Thomas Catan and Stephen Fidler, 'With Post-War

Instability Still a Pressing Concern, Western Companies and Government Agencies are Awarding Big Contracts to Ex-Military Personnel with Expertise in Providing Security', *Financial Times* (London), 30 September 2003, p. 21.

34. 'In Iraq and Afghanistan, more than 70 American companies and private individuals have won up to $8 billion in contracts in the last two years, according to the Centre for Public Integrity in Washington. Much of their work is shielded from the public, critics say, noting that their deaths are not even added to the American body count.' In Juan Forero, 'Private U.S. Operatives on Risky Missions in Colombia', *New York Times,* 14 February 2004, p. A3.

35. Edward Epstein and David R. Baker, 'Abuse Raises Questions About Role of U.S. Contractors', *San Francisco Chronicle,* 4 May 2004, p. A11. See also Fox Butterfield, 'Justice Dept. Report Shows Trouble in Private U.S. Jails Preceded Job Fixing Iraq's', *New York Times,* 6 June 2004, p. 22.

36. 'Media: Caught in the Line of Fire', *The Independent* (London), 13 July 2004, pp. 10–11; Jeffrey Gettleman, 'G.I.'s Padlock Baghdad Paper Accused of Lies', *New York Times,* 29 March 2004, p. A1; Gary Dimmock and Norma Greenaway, 'Three Journalists Killed in Allied Shell Strikes on Hotel, Al Jazeera headquarters', *Ottawa Citizen,* 9 April 2003 p. A3; Ben Rooney, 'TV Stations Bombed to Silence Saddam', *Daily Telegraph* (London), 27 March 2003, p. 11; Nik Gowing, 'Media: "Don't Get in Our Way"', *The Guardian* (London), 8 April 2002, p. 10.

37. For one early example, see Ian Fisher, 'U.S. Force Said to Kill 15 Iraqis During an Anti-American Rally', *New York Times,* 30 April 2003, p. A1; and David Rohde, 'Rights Group Says U.S. Soldiers

Twice Used Excessive Force', *New York Times,* 18 June 2003 p. 12.

38. George Monbiot, 2004, *The Age of Consent*, The New Press, New York, p. 158. See also United Nations General Assembly, *External Debt Crisis and Development: Report to the Secretary-General*, 57th Session, 23 July 2002 (A/57/253), p. 2. Online at <http://www.un.dk/doc/A570253.pdf>.

39. Luisa Kroll and Lea Goldman, 'The Rich Get Richer', Forbes.com, 26 February 2004. Available online at <http://www.forbes.com/maserati/billionaires2004/cz_lk_0226mainintrobill04.html>. See also, 'Special Report: The World's Richest People', Forbes.com, 26 February 2004. Available online at <http://www.forbes.com/2004/02/25/bill04land.html>. Comparison with global GDP based on figures from the World Bank, *World Development Indicators 2004,* and the United Nations, *Human Development Report 2004*. Available online at <http://hdr.undp.org/statistics/data/indic/indic_7_1_1.html>.

40. Barry Bearak, 'Why People Still Starve',' *New York Times Magazine,* 13 July 2003, p. 6: 33.

41. President George W. Bush, Address to Joint Session of Congress, Federal News Service, 20 September 2001.

42. Howard Zinn, 2002, *You Can't Be Neutral on a Moving Train: A Personal History of Our Times,* 2nd edn, Beacon Press, Boston.

publisher's note

'Ahimsa' was first published in the *Hindustan Times*, 12 June 2002.

'Come September' was first presented as a lecture sponsored by the Lannan Foundation in Santa Fe, New Mexico on 18 September 2002, and first published in the *Guardian*, 26 September 2002.

'The Loneliness of Noam Chomsky' was written as an introduction for the new edition of Noam Chomsky's *For Reasons of State* (New York: New Press, published January 2003).

'Confronting Empire' was an address given to the World Social Forum, Porto Allegre, Brazil, 27 January 2003. First published in the *Frankfurter Allgemeine Zeitung*, 5 February 2003.

'Peace Is War' was a speech delivered at the Centre for the Study of Developing Societies (CSDS), New Delhi on 7 March 2003 at a workshop organized by Sarai: The New Media Initiatives, CSDS and the Waag Society in Delhi. First published in the *Sarai Reader 4: Crisis Media*, Sarai, New Delhi, 2004.

'An Ordinary Person's Guide to Empire' was first published in the *Guardian* on 2 April 2003.

'Instant-Mix Imperial Democracy (Buy One, Get One Free)' was first presented as a lecture at the Riverside Church in Harlem, New York on 13 May 2003, in an event sponsored by the Center for Economic and Social Rights (www.cesr.org) and the Lannan Foundation (www.lannan.org), which awarded Arundhati Roy the 2002 Lannan Prize for Cultural Freedom. First published in *Outlook* magazine on 17 May 2003.

'When the Saints Go Marching Out' was broadcast by the BBC on 25 August 2003 on Radio 4. First published in the Swedish language by *Aftonbladet* newspaper, Stockholm on 31 August 2003.

'In Memory of Shankar Guha Niyogi' was a talk delivered in Raipur on 28 September 2003. First published in Hindi in *Hindustan* on 13 October 2003.

'Do Turkeys Enjoy Thanksgiving' was a speech delivered at the World Social Forum in Bombay on 14 January 2004, and published in *The Hindu* on 18 January 2004.

'How Deep Shall We Dig' was delivered as the first I.G. Khan Memorial Lecture, at Aligarh Muslim Univeristy on 6 April 2004. First published in Hindi in *Hindustan*, 23-24 April 2004 and in English in *The Hindu*, 25 April 2004.

'The Road to Harsud' was first published in *Outlook* magazine on 26 July 2004.

'Public Power in the Age of Empire' was delivered as a public address at the American Sociological Association's Ninety-ninth Annual Meeting in San Francisco, California on 16 August 2004. The talk was also aired on C-SPAN Book TV, Democracy Now! and Alternative Radio.

'Peace and the New Corporate Liberation Theology' was a speech first delivered on 3 November 2004, in Sydney, Australia on the occasion of Arundhati Roy winning the 2004 Sydney Peace Prize.